Developmental Confrontational Psychology

DCΨ

Authored by: Omar bin Shahrazad El Jirbi

ISBN: 978-1-9193598-0-9
Published by: Omar bin Shahrazad El Jirbi Publications.

APA Reference: bin Shahrazad El Jirbi, O.

Disclaimer

This book presents the original theoretical contributions of the author in the form of Developmental Confrontational Psychology (DCΨ) and its associated frameworks (DCT, DCPTT, SRI, SDCPT, DRT, ART, BRT, XRT, and the concept of the Psychological Fingerprint). These models are offered for academic, research, and educational purposes.

The content is not intended as a substitute for professional psychological diagnosis, assessment, or treatment. Readers are advised that the application of these frameworks in clinical or therapeutic practice requires professional training and responsibility. The author disclaims liability for any misuse or misinterpretation of the material.

Any attempt to reproduce, adapt, or apply these concepts without acknowledgment of their origin constitutes a breach of intellectual property and professional ethics.

Dedication

To my mother, Shahrazad

Whose name carries the spirit of wisdom, endurance, and imagination.

You are the reason I could think, speak, question, and create.

You gave me more than life — you gave me direction, resilience, and belief.

Every page I write echoes your sacrifices, your prayers, your strength.

This work is, in every way, yours.

A Note on the Name

I sign my work as Omar (bin Shahrazad) El Jirbi

in honor of the woman who built the foundation of my being.

The name Shahrazad is not only a personal truth — it is a symbol:

of storytelling, survival, intellect, and quiet power.

Choosing this name is my way of giving credit where it's due.

To the one who nurtured my path, who never left my side,

whose legacy now continues — through thought, word, and theory.

Note to the Reader

This work introduces a set of specific terms essential to the Developmental Confrontation Psychology framework. For clarity and precision, a complete Glossary of Terms is provided at the end of the book.

Index

DCΨ

Chapter 1

FOUNDATIONS

This chapter introduces the central premise of the theory, that psychological development is shaped not by continuity, but by confrontation with existential thresholds.

Introduction to
Developmental Confrontational Psychology (DCΨ)

Defining Developmental Confrontational Psychology (DCΨ)

Human development is not smooth. It is not a gentle climb toward maturity. It is marked instead by sudden thresholds, moments where the self collides with something greater, something unknown.

A newborn is torn from the womb and must breathe alone.
A child realizes others exist, and that they are not him.
An adolescent discovers emotion, truth, and the fragile weight of identity.
An adult must one day face the fact: "I will die."

Confrontation must be distinguished from **trauma**. Confrontation is universal and necessary; it is the demand that growth places on every human. Trauma, by contrast, is a distortion of confrontation: it occurs when the threshold overwhelms or when the psyche fails to reorganize around it. Developmental Confrontation Psychology therefore treats confrontation as opportunity, and trauma as its fractured form.

These are not accidents. They are **structured confrontations**, and they are universal. Each one cracks open the mind. Each demands a re-organization of meaning.

These thresholds are universal in kind, but not uniform in result. Two people may face the same confrontation and produce different structures: one integrates it and carries a resolution forward; the other fractures and carries a distortion. *DCΨ* therefore treats universality as a fact of demand, not a guarantee of identical development.

This is the foundation of *Developmental Confrontational Psychology (DCΨ),* a school of thought that places **confrontation** at the heart of all psychological growth. It does not see development as the accumulation of skills, traits, or stages. It sees it as a sequence of existential confrontations that **cannot be avoided** without consequence.

DCΨ does not merely *study* confrontation. It treats it as the **organizing force of the psyche,** the lens through which personality forms, disorders emerge, and healing becomes possible. In *DCΨ*, therapy is not about fixing, soothing, or adapting, it is about locating the confrontation a person is stuck in, and helping them face it directly.

This approach stands apart.

- Cognitive-behavioral therapy restructures thought and behavior.
- Psychodynamic schools explore unconscious conflict.
- Humanistic psychology seeks growth and meaning.

DCΨ asks a simpler, deeper question:
"What confrontation is this person facing, and how have they responded to it?"

This book answers that question.
And teaches how to ask it.

DCΨ as a School, Not a Single Theory

DCΨ is not a single model of development but a complete school of thought. It contains:

- **A core theory:** *Developmental Confrontation Theory (DCT)* which defines the structure of human confrontations across four stages.

- **Diagnostic systems:** the *DC Scanner* and the *DCΨ Diagnostic Atlas* which identify how confrontations have been resolved or distorted.

- **Therapeutic systems:** *Developmental Resolution Therapy (DRT)* and its methods *(ART, BRT, XRT)* which intervene by bringing unresolved confrontations into awareness and practice.

- **Symbolic Frameworks:** *DCΨ* uses symbolic tools to deepen psychological understanding:

    1 **The Psychological Fingerprint:** the unique identity mark left by developmental confrontations.

    2 **The Unborn Familiar (Womb):** symbolic mapping of prenatal containment and its echoes in behavior, culture, and therapy.

    3 **The Familiar Fossil:** symbolic interpretation of historical and cultural remains as reflections of unresolved or resolved developmental stages.

    4 **The Living Fossil:** Artificial Intelligence as a cultural symbol of immortalizing thought.

Why Confrontation?

Confrontation is chosen as the central term because it describes the actual lived experience of developmental thresholds. To confront something is to be brought face-to-face with a reality that cannot be ignored. This is true across life:

- The infant confronting separation from the mother.
- The child confronting the reality of others and the possibility of rejection.
- The adolescent confronting the truth of their inner authenticity.
- The adult confronting the inevitability of death.

Each of these moments destabilizes the existing identity structure. They are shocks of reality that demand new organization. When integrated, they produce *resolution*, the person grows, adapts, and stabilizes. When avoided, denied, or mishandled, they produce *distortion*, the person rigidifies, fragments, or fossilizes in maladaptive ways.

Thus, confrontation is not a marginal or negative experience. It is the engine of development itself.

A Brief Illustration

Consider a child exposed to violence in the home. From a cognitive–behavioral perspective, the focus may fall on distorted thoughts or maladaptive behaviors. From a psychodynamic perspective, the emphasis may fall on unconscious defenses or symbolic meanings. From the lens of *Developmental Confrontation Psychology (DCΨ)*, the focus sharpens:

- What confrontation did the child face?
  A sudden rupture of safety (Stage 1: Self vs. World).

- What orientation did they take?
  - **A** **Exploratory Orientation (Igniter)** → turning outward, scanning the environment for novelty or safety.
  - **B** **Regulatory Orientation (Adaptor)** → turning inward, seeking stability through withdrawal, order, or adjustment.

- Has this orientation resolved or distorted?
  - **I** **Resolution** → *Exploratory* stabilizes by learning to anchor safety through safe exploration; *Regulatory* stabilizes by learning to regulate securely within consistent boundaries.
  - **II** **Distortion** → Exploratory becomes trapped in restless hyper-vigilance, unable to settle; Regulatory collapses into rigid withdrawal, over-control, or dissociation.

This example shows the confrontational lens at work. It clarifies the developmental task, identifies the possible orientations, and distinguishes resolution from distortion. *DCΨ* does not dismiss other psychological perspectives but integrates them under a developmental confrontation framework, where both orientations are valid but vulnerable to distortion if not integrated.

Establishing Authority

By defining itself as confrontational, *DCΨ* establishes a position in psychology that is both theoretical and applied. It is not a soft metaphor but a testable framework: confrontations can be identified, orientations measured, and outcomes diagnosed. This makes *DCΨ* a science of thresholds, of the moments where development either stabilizes through resolution or collapses through distortion.

For this reason, *DCΨ* must be recognized not as an extension of existing schools, but as an independent *school of psychology* in its own right.

The Core Principles: Developmental Confrontation Theory (DCT)

Developmental Confrontation Theory (DCT) is the theoretical backbone of the entire school. It provides the structural map of development: how confrontations arise, how individuals orient themselves toward them, and how these orientations can resolve or distort. Without *DCT*, the diagnostic and therapeutic tools of *DCΨ* would lack coherence. With it, they form a unified developmental system.

Confrontation as the Engine of Development

At its core, *DCT* asserts that to grow is to confront. Development is not linear acquisition of abilities but a progression through four existential thresholds:

1. Self vs. World → Can I exist apart from the environment?
2. Self vs. Other (Humans) → Can I exist while others exist beside me?
3. Emotional Identity → Can I be authentic without losing belonging?
4. Mortality & Wisdom → Can I live meaningfully under the reality of death?

Each stage brings the individual face-to-face with destabilizing realities that cannot be ignored. Each must be integrated for development to continue.

Dual Orientations: Resolution vs. Distortion

For every confrontation, *DCT* describes two orientations. These are not "good vs. bad" but different ways of engaging the same developmental challenge. Both orientations can lead to resolution when integrated. Both can distort when rigidified or avoided.

- **Stage 1: Self vs. World**
  - A **Igniter (Exploratory Orientation)** → reaching outward, seeking novelty.
  - B **Adaptor (Regulatory Orientation)** → retreating inward, seeking consistency.

- **Stage 2: Self vs. Other**
  - A **Mirror (Recognition Orientation)** → identity through reflection in others.
  - B **Wall (Boundary Orientation)** → identity through distinction and separation.

- **Stage 3: Emotional Identity**
  - A **Flame (Authenticity Orientation)** → identity through raw, passionate expression.
  - B **Mask (Role Orientation)** → identity through function, role, or performance.

- **Stage 4: Mortality & Wisdom**
  - A **Seer (Clarity Orientation)** → integrating mortality through insight and acceptance.
  - B **Wound (Continuity Orientation)** → transforming mortality into legacy and symbolic continuity.

Resolution occurs when the chosen orientation integrates reality without collapsing the self. Distortion occurs when the orientation becomes rigid, exaggerated, or avoidant.

Why Dual Orientation Matters

This dual-orientation principle is one of *DCΨ's* most original contributions. Other models often frame one path as "healthy" and the other as "pathological." For example: independence vs. dependence, authenticity vs. performance. *DCT* reframes this:

- Both independence and dependence can be resolved healthily (Wall and Mirror).
- Both authenticity and performance can distort if hollow (Flame burnout, Mask hollowness).
- Both clarity and continuity are valid ways of facing mortality.

Thus, *DCT* removes the moral hierarchy from development. Growth is not about choosing the "right" trait, but about integrating whichever orientation emerges.

A Brief Illustration

Consider an adolescent (Stage 3: Emotional Identity).

- One may adopt the Flame orientation, insisting on raw authenticity: refusing to follow family expectations, expressing emotions openly, demanding to "be real."
- Another may adopt the Mask orientation, performing roles: excelling in school, adopting a persona, shaping identity through external recognition.

Both orientations can resolve:

- Flame resolves when passion is tempered by self-regulation and responsibility.
- Mask resolves when roles are infused with depth and not mere façade.

Both orientations can distort:

- Flame without anchor = volatility, burnout, emotional collapse.
- Mask without authenticity = emptiness, identity hollowness.

DCT's strength lies in its ability to map these outcomes predictably, so they can be diagnosed, measured, and treated.

Establishing DCT's Role in the School

DCT is the spine of DCΨ:

- The Scanner measures orientations across the stages.
- The Atlas classifies distortions and resolutions.
- Therapy (*DRT*) uses the confrontation logic to tailor interventions.
- Symbolic frameworks (Fingerprint, Womb, Fossils) draw their meaning from it.

In short, *DCT* provides the map of human development. *DCΨ* builds the instruments and therapies around this map.

The Diagnostic System: DC Scanner and Atlas

If *Developmental Confrontation Theory (DCT)* is the backbone of *DCΨ*, then the *DC-Scanner* is its clinical instrument. It operationalizes the theory by measuring how confrontations have been faced, oriented, and integrated. The scanner transforms abstract theory into practical assessment, allowing the examiner to distinguish between resolution and distortion across the four developmental stages.

Structure of the DC Scanner

The Scanner is designed as a two-part system, consisting of Battery A and Battery B.

- **Battery A:**
  1. **Stage Resolution Index I (SRI-I)**: measures the resolution or distortion of each confrontation at a foundational level.
  2. **Developmental Confrontation Personality Typology Test (DCPTT):** identifies dominant orientations across stages, forming symbolic personality profiles.
  3. **Symbolic Developmental Confrontation Projective Test I (SDCPT- I)**: uses projective methods to uncover unconscious responses to confrontation.
- **Battery B:**
  1. **Stage Resolution Index II (SRI-II)**: a secondary, refined layer of confrontation measurement, designed to confirm or deepen findings from Battery A.
  2. **Developmental Confrontation Personality Typology Test (DCPTT)**: repeated for reliability and to track stability across responses.
  3. **Symbolic Developmental Confrontation Projective Test II (SDCPT-II***):* provides deeper symbolic imagery, complementing the first projective test.

Together, the two batteries provide both breadth and depth: Battery A offers the initial scan, and Battery B functions as a check and elaboration. This design ensures diagnostic precision while reducing bias from a single method.

The Role of the DCΨ Diagnostic Atlas

The Atlas complements the Scanner by serving as the interpretive map of human distortions and resolutions. Where the Scanner produces data, the Atlas provides context and meaning.

It organizes distortions according to:

- Stage (Self vs. World, Self vs. Other, Emotional Identity, Mortality & Wisdom).
- Orientation (e.g., Exploratory vs. Regulatory, Recognition vs. Boundary).
- Outcome (Resolution or Distortion).

The Atlas also integrates pathological profiles (e.g., borderline personality disorder as distorted Mirror + collapsed Wall; narcissism as distorted Mask or Flame). By mapping patterns across the Scanner results, the Atlas allows the clinician to trace not just symptoms, but the developmental confrontations behind them.

Practical Illustration

Consider a client presenting with social anxiety. Traditional models may frame this as excessive fear of evaluation, maladaptive conditioning, or cognitive distortions. Through the *DCΨ* lens, the Scanner reveals the underlying confrontation:

- Stage 2: Self vs. Other (Humans) → the confrontation of recognition and distinction.

- Scanner results might show a distorted Reflective Orientation (Mirror), dependency on others' evaluations, or a distorted Boundary Orientation (Wall), rigid self-protection and withdrawal.

- Atlas interpretation situates this distortion within a predictable pattern: avoidance of the "self vs. other" confrontation, producing relational instability.

This analysis does not negate cognitive or behavioral insights. Instead, it provides a developmental map: the client's struggle is not just "anxiety," but a specific confrontation avoided or mishandled.

The Scanner and Atlas as a Unified System

Together, the Scanner and Atlas transform *DCT* into a living diagnostic system. The Scanner quantifies orientations and outcomes; the Atlas contextualizes them symbolically, developmentally, and clinically. Their integration ensures that no confrontation remains hidden, each is scanned, mapped, and made available for therapeutic intervention.

The Therapeutic System: Developmental Resolution Therapy (DRT)

If the *DC Scanner* and *Atlas* diagnose the state of confrontation, then *Developmental Resolution Therapy (DRT)* is the method by which resolution is restored. *DRT* is the therapeutic wing of *DCΨ*, designed to bring unresolved confrontations back into awareness, re-engage them directly, and guide the client toward integration.

Where other therapies may focus on symptom reduction or behavioral adjustment, *DRT* insists that no symptom is random. Every clinical presentation points to a developmental confrontation that has been avoided, mishandled, or distorted. Therapy, therefore, is not about suppressing symptoms but about re-entering the confrontation at the level where development stalled.

The Logic of DRT

- Core Principle → To heal is to confront again.
- Goal → To guide the client back into the unresolved stage confrontation, but in conditions that allow safe resolution.
- Method → Using one of three tailored approaches, depending on the client's orientation and distortion.

This makes *DRT* both structured and flexible: structured by the confrontational map of *DCT*, but flexible in the method applied.

The Three Methods of DRT

1. **Analytical Resolution Therapy (ART)**
   - Focus: understanding and meaning-making.
   - Method: The client is guided to analyze patterns of confrontation and distortion, tracing how avoidance has shaped symptoms or identity.
   - Application: Especially useful for clients who require cognitive clarity before they can change.
   - Example: An adult who repeatedly collapses in relationships may, through ART, discover the unresolved Stage 2 confrontation, an over-reliance on Mirror (recognition) and collapse of Wall (boundaries). By analyzing this dynamic, the confrontation becomes visible and open to resolution.

2. **Behavioral Resolution Therapy (BRT)**
   - Focus: practice and boundary-setting.
   - Method: Clients rehearse new behaviors that directly engage the confrontation. The emphasis is not just on generic skills but on behaviors tied to the specific unresolved stage.
   - Application: Useful for clients whose distortions manifest as avoidance in action, or who benefit from structured practice.
   - Example: A client with social anxiety (Stage 2 distortion) may be guided through BRT exercises in assertiveness — saying "no" without collapse, or maintaining presence in conversation. This is not generic exposure therapy; it is resolution training for a developmental confrontation.

3. **Experiential Resolution Therapy (XRT)**
   - Focus: immersion and role-play.
   - Method: Clients engage in symbolic or enacted scenarios that recreate the unresolved confrontation, but with therapeutic containment.
   - Application: Effective for trauma, identity wounds, or when verbal analysis is insufficient.
   - Example: A trauma survivor (Stage 1 distortion) may, through XRT role-play, symbolically re-enter the confrontation with "world-as-unsafe," but within the safety of the therapeutic alliance. This immersive re-experience allows a distorted Regulatory Orientation (withdrawal/dissociation) to be reworked into resolution.

DRT in Action

Together, ART, BRT, and XRT ensure that therapy is not rigidly standardized but tailored to the client's needs. A client whose orientation is highly cognitive may begin with ART; another who resists words but responds to action may need BRT; a third who carries trauma too deep for analysis may require XRT.

In all cases, the unifying principle is the same: therapy is a confrontation, not a bypass.

Distinctiveness of DRT

- Against symptom management: *DRT* does not treat anxiety, depression, or personality traits as isolated targets. It traces each to the confrontation that produced it.
- Against one-size-fits-all therapy: *DRT* adapts to the client, selecting the method (*ART, BRT, XRT*) that best re-engages their confrontation.
- For resolution: The end point of *DRT* is not adjustment or compensation, but the actual resolution of the avoided developmental threshold.

The Psychological Fingerprint (Explanation – Preview)

Every individual carries a developmental signature, not fixed like a carved stone, but dynamic like a living pattern. In *Developmental Confrontational Psychology (DCΨ)* this is described as the psychological fingerprint. It represents the unique way a person navigates across the four developmental stages of *DCΨ* in everyday life.

Unlike static models that classify people into rigid types, the psychological fingerprint emphasizes movement. It is not just about whether a stage is resolved, distorted, or in process, but about how the person shifts between stages in different contexts and situations.

The Four States of a Stage

In the language of *DCΨ*, each developmental stage can appear in four ways within the fingerprint:

- Resolved stage → provides stability and resources. For example, a resolved Stage 1 (Self vs. World) gives a foundation of safety and grounding that supports later stages.

- Distorted stage → creates obstacles or distortions in perception and behavior. A distorted Stage 2 (Self vs. Other) may lead to either dependency on others (Mirror distortion) or isolation behind rigid boundaries (Wall distortion).

- Stage in process → generates ongoing struggles, experiments, or exploration. A person may be actively working through Stage 3 (Emotional Identity), trying out roles (Mask) or testing authenticity (Flame), without yet reaching resolution.

- Newly entered stage → introduces fresh perspectives, existential challenges, or insights. Entry into Stage 4 (Mortality & Wisdom) may open new reflections about legacy, spirituality, or symbolic continuity.

The psychological fingerprint, then, is the living arrangement of these four states across the stages. No two individuals will show the same configuration.

Dynamic Shifts Across Situations

The fingerprint is not static, it is a pattern of movement. In personal relationships, a person may rely on their Stage 2 resolution (healthy boundaries) to navigate intimacy. In professional contexts, they may draw on Stage 3 (role performance) to maintain stability. When confronted with loss, Stage 4 may become activated, forcing engagement with mortality or continuity.

This continuous shifting means the fingerprint is not only a marker of where a person stands developmentally, but also of how they move and re-move through the stages as life confrontations arise.

Integrating Resolution, Distortion, and Growth

The fingerprint brings together the dual logic of *DCΨ*:

- Resolution → provides strength and adaptability.
- Distortion → signals rigidity or avoidance, which can be measured and treated.
- Growth in process → reveals areas of experimentation and ongoing work.
- Emergence of new stages → shows how life continues to confront individuals with fresh existential demands.

Thus, the psychological fingerprint is not only descriptive but diagnostic and therapeutic. It can be identified through the Scanner, contextualized by the Atlas, and reshaped through DRT.

Illustration

Consider two siblings raised in the same family, exposed to similar parental dynamics. Their Scanner results may reveal that both faced difficulties in Stage 2 (Self vs. Other). Yet their fingerprints diverge:

- One sibling shows a distorted Recognition Orientation (Mirror), dependency on others' validation, collapsing when recognition is absent.
- The other shows a distorted Boundary Orientation (Wall), excessive separation, cutting themselves off from others.

Although the environment was shared, their psychological fingerprints are unique: one patterns dependency, the other patterns isolation. Their later life choices, relationships, and even therapeutic needs will differ because their developmental signatures diverged.

Why Introduce the Fingerprint Here?

At this point in the book, the fingerprint is introduced as a preview rather than a full exposition. The goal is to prepare the reader to think about identity as dynamic patterning across the stages, not as fixed categories. Later chapters will expand this concept into symbolic depth, showing how the fingerprint functions as a unifying framework for diagnosis, therapy, and symbolic interpretation.

For now, the reader is invited to recognize the central claim:
The psychological fingerprint is the living mark of confrontation, showing not only where a person stands, but how they continuously navigate, re-navigate, and transform across the stages of life.

The Promise of DCΨ

Developmental Confrontational Psychology (DCΨ) establishes itself not as a model that explains a narrow domain of behavior, but as a complete school of psychology. It integrates theory, diagnosis, therapy, and symbolic frameworks into a unified system. Its promise lies in its ability to address psychology at all levels, from the individual struggling with trauma to societies wrestling with legacy and meaning.

A School, Not a Model

Other approaches are often defined by their method or focus:

- Cognitive approaches emphasize thought patterns.
- Behavioral approaches emphasize observable actions.
- Psychodynamic approaches emphasize the unconscious and its symbols.
- Humanistic approaches emphasize meaning and growth.

DCΨ does not reject these traditions but re-centers them under a single principle: development is driven by confrontation. Identity grows when it faces realities that destabilize it, and collapses when those realities are avoided. This principle gives *DCΨ* explanatory power across clinical, educational, and cultural contexts.

Clinical Promise

In clinical practice, *DCΨ* promises greater diagnostic precision and tailored therapy. By identifying which developmental confrontation is unresolved, and which orientation has distorted, the clinician gains clarity that symptom-based models often miss.

- Child Trauma Example → A child exposed to domestic violence is not simply "anxious" or "traumatized." *DCΨ* identifies the confrontation (Stage 1: Self vs. World) and the orientation taken (Exploratory vs. Regulatory). The task of therapy becomes re-entering this confrontation safely, rather than only treating symptoms.

- Executive Burnout Example → An adult collapsing under work demands is not just "stressed." *DCΨ* frames this as a Stage 3 confrontation (Emotional Identity). The executive may be locked in a distorted Role Orientation (Mask), performing endlessly without authenticity. Therapy must confront this directly: Can the individual integrate performance with authenticity?

Through such lenses, *DCΨ* shifts the clinical question from "What disorder does this person have?" to "What confrontation is unresolved, and how can resolution be restored?"

Educational Promise

In educational settings, *DCΨ* provides a developmental map for guiding growth. Teachers, parents, and mentors can recognize when a child or adolescent is grappling with a stage confrontation. Instead of mislabeling resistance, mood swings, or withdrawal as "problem behavior," *DCΨ* frames them as signs of unresolved confrontation.

This perspective encourages support that is developmentally precise: giving containment in Stage 1, recognition and boundaries in Stage 2, space for experimentation in Stage 3, and guidance in legacy and meaning in Stage 4.

Cultural Promise

DCΨ also extends beyond the clinic into culture and history. Its symbolic frameworks, the Unborn Familiar (womb), Familiar Fossil (civilization), and Living Fossil (AI), reveal how entire societies grapple with the same confrontations as individuals.

- Civilizations build walls, mirrors, flames, and masks, leaving behind fossils of confrontation.
- Cultures invent myths and rituals to manage mortality and continuity.
- Today, technology such as AI becomes a symbolic double, embodying humanity's struggle with Stage 4 immortality.

By applying *DCΨ* to cultural artifacts and trends, psychology gains a tool to interpret not only personal development but collective development.

The Broader Value

The promise of *DCΨ* lies in its ability to unify psychology:

- Clinically → It sharpens diagnosis and personalizes therapy.
- Educationally → It guides growth with precision.
- Culturally → It interprets history and anticipates the future.
- Industrially → It supports organizational health, leadership development, and workplace conflict resolution by mapping unresolved confrontations in teams and structures.

No confrontation is random. Each is part of a structured sequence that defines human life. To practice DCΨ is to see these confrontations clearly, to diagnose their outcomes, and to guide them toward resolution.

Closing Orientation

DCΨ therefore stands as a school for the 21st century: rooted in theory, operationalized by diagnostics, applied through therapy, and deepened by symbolism. Its promise is not only to treat disorders, but to illuminate the confrontational nature of being human, in childhood, in adulthood, and in history itself.

DCΨ

Chapter 2

THE BIRTH OF THE THEORY

This chapter traces the developmental origins of the theory itself, before it crystallized into the structural system outlined in later chapters.

Origins of the Idea

Every school of psychology begins with a question. For *Developmental Confrontational Psychology (DCΨ)*, the seed was planted by a simple but pressing observation: people do not collapse because they lack skills or because they have the wrong thoughts alone, but because they are forced to face realities that destabilize their identity. Some adapt, others distort. The difference, it seemed, was not explained adequately by existing frameworks.

This gap became the starting point. While cognitive psychology could describe faulty beliefs, and behavioral psychology could trace reinforcement patterns, neither explained why highly capable individuals collapse when confronted by existential realities, mortality, rejection, authenticity, separation. Nor could classical psychodynamic models capture the systematic way these confrontations unfold across development.

Early Reflections

In its earliest form, the idea emerged less as a "theory" and more as a pattern of thought. Observing human life, it was clear that moments of crisis carried more developmental weight than ordinary routines. A child whose sense of safety is ruptured does not simply "learn" a new habit, their whole orientation toward the world changes. An adolescent who confronts their independence is not simply adjusting roles, they are restructuring their identity.

This led to the first sketches: what if development was not a smooth acquisition of skills, but a sequence of confrontations with destabilizing realities? The idea seemed both intuitive and radical. It shifted the lens from learning to confrontation, from behavior to existential rupture.

Dissatisfaction with Existing Models

Part of the drive came from dissatisfaction with the categories available at the time.

- Freud had described introjection, projection, and narcissism, but often tied them narrowly to early drives.
- Erikson had mapped psychosocial conflicts across the lifespan, but his stages lacked a unifying mechanism that explained why conflict produces growth.
- Piaget offered insight into cognitive structures, but cognition alone could not explain emotional collapses.
- Attachment theory revealed the power of relational bonds, but did not account for existential themes like mortality or authenticity.

The problem was not that these frameworks were wrong. It was that they were partial. Each described an aspect of development, but none explained the through-line: the way each stage presents a reality that confronts the self, destabilizes it, and demands reorganization.

First Glimpses of a Structure

The earliest attempts to describe this took the form of modes of thought: ways the human being relates to reality at different stages.

- In infancy, the self seemed fused with the environment, operating through introjection — "I am what I can take in."
- In childhood, similarity became the guide — comparative mirroring — "I am what resembles me."
- In adolescence, the break toward independence appeared — "I am as I see myself, even against others."
- In adulthood, the awareness of mortality pressed forward — "I am what outlives me, or what I leave behind."

At the time, these modes were not yet articulated as confrontations. They were philosophical sketches, an attempt to trace how identity shifts across life. Only later did they crystallize into the four developmental confrontations of *DCT.*

From Reflection to Inquiry

These reflections gradually formed into an inquiry: what if development is best understood not as a continuous curve, but as a series of confrontational thresholds? Each threshold destabilizes, and in destabilization, identity must reorganize.

This line of thinking was not purely academic. It came from observing lived experience: individuals collapsing under pressures, groups repeating cycles, history itself leaving traces of unresolved confrontations. Theory grew not from abstraction alone, but from the convergence of observation, dissatisfaction with existing categories, and symbolic imagination.

It was in this convergence that the first spark of Developmental Confrontational Psychology appeared. What began as scattered notes and observations became the foundation for a school that would grow to explain, diagnose, and treat human development through the logic of confrontation.

The Four Modes of Early Thought

Before *Developmental Confrontation Theory (DCT)* crystallized into its four stages, the earliest sketches of the idea took the form of modes of thought. These modes were not yet defined as confrontations, but as patterns in how the self relates to reality at different points of life. They served as philosophical prototypes, precursors that hinted at the structure later refined in *DCT.*

1. Introjective Thought

Formula: "I am what I can take in."

In the earliest months of life, the self is fused with the environment. The infant does not yet experience clear separation between "self" and "world." Nourishment, warmth, and presence are not external events but lived as direct extensions of being. Freud's description of introjection captured part of this phenomenon: the incorporation of external objects into the psychic self. Yet what emerges here is not merely oral gratification, but a mode of thought: identity is built from whatever can be absorbed.

- Developmental context: Infancy, sensorimotor stage, fusion with caregiver.
- Manifestation: The breast, the blanket, the mother's gaze — all are experienced as parts of the infant.
- Example: A baby holding a toy tightly and treating it as inseparable from themselves demonstrates this introjective logic.

This mode foreshadows Stage 1 (Self vs. World) of *DCT,* where the first confrontation with separation from the environment destabilizes identity.

2. Selective-Comparative Thought

Formula: "I am what resembles me."

As the child begins to differentiate, the logic of introjection gives way to comparison. Identity is not built from what is swallowed, but from what is mirrored. Children experience joy when they encounter animals that resemble human actions, a cat lying on its back like a person, or a monkey walking upright. The pleasure is not in novelty but in recognition: "That is like me."

- Developmental context: Early childhood, pre-operational thought, social awareness.
- Manifestation: Children measure selfhood by resemblance, by seeking others who reflect them.
- Example: A child laughing at a dog "smiling" or imitating a parent's gestures illustrates this mode.

This mode foreshadows Stage 2 (Self vs. Other) of *DCT*, where the confrontation with other humans forces the self to define itself through recognition (Mirror) or distinction (Wall).

3. Independent Thought

Formula: "I am as I see myself."

With adolescence emerges a sharper separation. No longer satisfied with resemblance, the self asserts itself as independent. Here, thought is organized not by what is taken in (introjection) or what is mirrored (comparison), but by the individual's own vision of themselves. Opposition becomes natural: the adolescent resists parents, challenges authority, and insists on their right to define themselves.

- Developmental context: Adolescence, identity formation, formal operations.
- Manifestation: Contradiction, rebellion, attempts at originality.
- Example: A teenager deliberately choosing clothes, music, or beliefs that oppose family expectations reflects this mode.

This mode foreshadows Stage 3 (Emotional Identity) of *DCT*, where confrontation is not with the world or others but with authenticity vs. role.

4. Immortalizing Thought

Formula: “I am what outlives me.”

In adulthood, the awareness of mortality introduces a new mode. The self recognizes its finitude and searches for continuity beyond its lifespan. This can take many forms: parenthood, creation of art, pursuit of legacy, or adherence to religious promises of eternal life. The central logic is that identity is preserved by what endures after death.

- Developmental context: Adulthood, confrontation with mortality, existential reflection.
- Manifestation: Investments in children, culture, institutions, or spiritual belief.
- Example: An adult speaking of “living through their children” or seeking to write a book as a permanent contribution.

This mode foreshadows Stage 4 (Mortality & Wisdom) of *DCT*, where the confrontation with death can be resolved through Clarity (Seer) or Continuity (Wound).

From Modes to Stages

These four modes of early thought were not yet formulated as “stages of confrontation.” They were philosophical sketches, attempts to articulate how identity shifts across life. Later, through deeper reflection, they crystallized into the four structured confrontations of *DCT.*

Where the modes described the logic of thought, the stages defined the task of confrontation. The transition from “I am what I take in” to “I am what outlives me” was reinterpreted as a series of thresholds:

- Self vs. World
- Self vs. Other
- Emotional Identity
- Mortality & Wisdom

Thus, the modes were not discarded, but absorbed into the framework. They remain the intellectual precursors of *DCT*, the early sketches from which the structured theory was born.

The Shift to Confrontation

The early sketches of development as modes of thought, introjective, comparative, independent, immortalizing, captured important truths about how identity evolves. Yet they were incomplete. They described the logic of how the self relates to the world, but not the mechanism that drives change. What was missing was the recognition that each transition in development is marked not simply by a new way of thinking, but by a moment of confrontation with destabilizing reality.

From Modes to Confrontations

The key insight was this: development happens at thresholds. Each threshold forces the individual to face something that unsettles identity and demands reorganization. The infant must confront separation from the world. The child must confront the presence of others. The adolescent must confront the tension between authenticity and role. The adult must confront mortality.

Thus, the modes were not wrong — they were incomplete. They showed the surface logic of thought, but beneath them lay the deeper structure of confrontation.

Why Confrontation?

Confrontation is the unifying mechanism that explains why development unfolds in stages. Without confrontation, the self remains unchallenged, and growth stagnates. With confrontation, the self is destabilized, forced to reorganize, and capable of resolution.

- Infancy → Confrontation with the world: Am I separate from what sustains me?
- Childhood → Confrontation with others: Can I exist while others exist beside me?
- Adolescence → Confrontation with identity: Can I be authentic while playing roles?
- Adulthood → Confrontation with mortality: Can I live meaningfully under the shadow of death?

This reframe shifts the question from "How does thought evolve?" to "What reality must the self confront in order to evolve?"

Contrast with Existing Frameworks

This step marked a decisive departure from earlier developmental theories:

- Freud → emphasized drives (oral, anal, phallic stages) as the engine of development. *DCΨ* reframes these moments not as drives, but as confrontations with separation, recognition, identity, and mortality.

- Erikson → mapped psychosocial conflicts (trust vs. mistrust, autonomy vs. shame, etc.), but did not explain why these conflicts matter. *DCΨ* explains them as threshold confrontations, identity must reorganize or collapse.

- Piaget → focused on cognition, describing how thinking structures evolve. *DCΨ* acknowledges cognition but grounds change in existential confrontation, not logic alone.

- Attachment theory → showed how relational bonds shape security. *DCΨ* incorporates this insight but expands it: attachment is one form of the deeper confrontation between self and other.

What unites these comparisons is that *DCΨ* does not discard existing insights, it reframes them under a single principle: confrontation as the mechanism of development.

Illustration: Beyond Modes

Take the example of adolescence. In the "independent thought" mode, the adolescent asserts themselves, contradicts parents, and experiments with independence. But this does not capture the full picture. At the deeper level, the adolescent is not just thinking differently, but confronting the reality that identity must balance authenticity and role.

- If they resolve the confrontation, they may integrate both: being authentic while fulfilling roles.
- If they distort, they may collapse into rebellion without direction (authenticity without role) or into performance without depth (role without authenticity).

This shows the leap from modes to confrontation. What seemed at first like "a new way of thinking" is revealed as a confrontation with destabilizing reality.

The Birth of DCT

This shift — from modes to confrontations — was the moment of crystallization. It marked the birth of *Developmental Confrontation Theory (DCT)*: a structured framework that sees each stage of life as a confrontation with reality, two possible orientations, and outcomes of resolution or distortion.

What began as reflection on modes of thought became a map of confrontational thresholds, the backbone of the entire school.

Philosophical Grounding

Every psychological school rests on philosophical assumptions, whether stated or not. For *Developmental Confrontational Psychology (DCΨ)*, the philosophical foundation is the conviction that human life is structured by confrontation with finitude. Development is not the smooth accumulation of skills, but a sequence of thresholds where the self must face realities that disrupt its stability. These confrontations are not optional; they are conditions of existence.

Finitude and Mortality

The most fundamental of these conditions is mortality. Human beings live with the knowledge that life will end, and this awareness penetrates identity at every level. Heidegger described this as being-toward-death, the recognition that finitude is not an abstract concept but the defining horizon of existence. From the perspective of *DCΨ*, mortality is not only the final confrontation (Stage 4), but also the silent presence that shapes all earlier stages. The fear of separation in infancy, the struggle for recognition in childhood, the quest for authenticity in adolescence, each carries echoes of the ultimate confrontation with death.

Confrontation as Epistemological Necessity

Confrontation is not only existential but also epistemological. Without rupture, there is no knowledge. Learning emerges when familiar patterns fail and the self is forced to reorganize. This principle extends beyond psychology into philosophy of knowledge: truth is revealed not in comfort but in disruption. Merleau-Ponty, writing on perception, emphasized that embodiment and encounter with the world are the grounds of meaning. *DCΨ* echoes this: development advances only when the self is destabilized by what it cannot fully control.

The Other and the Mirror

Confrontation also takes the form of the Other. Lacan's description of the mirror stage illustrated how the child's identity is shaped not by internal certainty but by an external image, an "other" that becomes a double. This captures a central insight of *DCΨ*: identity is not secured alone, but through confrontation with what lies outside. Stage 2 (Self vs. Other) embodies this truth, showing that the self must either recognize itself in the mirror of others or assert boundaries against them. Confrontation with the Other is therefore both developmental and ontological.

Beyond Philosophy into Psychology

DCΨ does not claim to replace philosophy. Rather, it integrates philosophical insights into a clinical-psychological framework. Where Heidegger described being-toward-death in abstract terms, *DCΨ* operationalizes this as Stage 4: Mortality & Wisdom, with orientations (Clarity vs. Continuity) and outcomes (resolution vs. distortion). Where Lacan described the mirror stage, *DCΨ* extends it into a lifelong confrontation with recognition and distinction. Where phenomenology emphasized perception, *DCΨ* shows how perception becomes destabilizing confrontation in real development.

In this sense, *DCΨ* translates philosophy into diagnostic and therapeutic categories. It bridges existential insight with clinical application, ensuring that philosophical truths are not left abstract but are woven into the fabric of practice.

Illustration: Philosophy in Everyday Life

Consider an adult facing the sudden diagnosis of a life-threatening illness. Philosophically, this is the intrusion of finitude, the collapse of assumptions of continuity. Psychologically, it activates Stage 4 confrontation: Can life retain meaning under the shadow of death? Resolution may take the form of Clarity (accepting mortality, living authentically) or Continuity (seeking legacy, symbolic survival). Distortion may manifest as despair, denial, or obsessive avoidance.

This example illustrates how abstract philosophy — finitude, rupture, the Other — becomes tangible in everyday life. *DCΨ* grounds these ideas in a clinical system that recognizes them as developmental confrontations with measurable outcomes.

Closing

The philosophical grounding of DCΨ is therefore twofold:

1. Existential → Life is structured by finitude and confrontation.
2. Epistemological → Knowledge emerges from rupture and destabilization.

By rooting itself in these principles, DCΨ aligns with philosophy while moving beyond it. It offers not only description but also diagnosis and therapy, ensuring that confrontation is recognized not only as an existential truth but as a practical framework for understanding and guiding human development.

From Idea to Framework

The reflections that began as philosophical sketches — modes of thought, thresholds of confrontation, and grounding in finitude — eventually crystallized into a structured framework. What began as scattered insights became a coherent system: *Developmental Confrontation Theory (DCT).*

The Leap into Structure

The central realization was that the modes of thought were not free-floating observations, but symptoms of deeper confrontations. Once this insight was secured, the scattered notes aligned into a map:

- Stage 1 – Self vs. World → confrontation with separation from the environment. Orientations: Exploratory (Igniter) vs. Regulatory (Adaptor).
- Stage 2 – Self vs. Other → confrontation with human presence. Orientations: Recognition (Mirror) vs. Boundary (Wall).
- Stage 3 – Emotional Identity → confrontation with the balance between authenticity and role. Orientations: Authenticity (Flame) vs. Role (Mask).
- Stage 4 – Mortality & Wisdom → confrontation with finitude and continuity. Orientations: Clarity (Seer) vs. Continuity (Wound).

Each stage became defined by three components:

1. Confrontation → the destabilizing reality.
2. Orientations → the two pathways of engagement.
3. Outcomes → resolution or distortion.

This was the decisive structural moment. Development could now be charted, diagnosed, and addressed within a single framework.

The Symbolic Turn

Alongside this structure came a recognition: confrontation is not only clinical, it is symbolic. The self leaves behind symbolic traces of how it engages reality, and cultures encode these traces in their artifacts, rituals, and technologies. From this recognition emerged the symbolic frameworks that accompany *DCΨ*:

- The Psychological Fingerprint → the unique, dynamic pattern of how an individual navigates the four stages.
- The Unborn Familiar → the womb as archetype of containment, showing how regression can be understood as symbolic revisiting rather than pathology.
- The Familiar Fossil → civilizations as collective confrontations, their ruins revealing patterns of resolution or distortion.
- The Living Fossil → artificial intelligence as humanity's symbolic double, crystallizing the Stage 4 confrontation with immortality.

These symbolic expansions did not replace the clinical framework but extended its scope: from individual therapy to cultural analysis, from present cases to historical fossils, from clinical work to philosophical reflection.

From Insight to School

At this point, *DCΨ* was no longer simply a theory, it had become a school of psychology. The logic of confrontation unified:

- Theory → *DCT*, mapping the stages.
- Diagnosis → the *Scanner* and *Atlas*, operationalizing assessment.
- Therapy → *Developmental Resolution Therapy (DRT)*, with its methods *(ART, BRT, XRT)*.
- Symbolism → Fingerprint, Womb, Fossils, AI, expanding meaning.

The step from idea to framework meant that *DCΨ* could not only describe but also measure and intervene.

Illustration: From Symptom to Confrontation

Consider a client presenting with chronic social withdrawal. Older frameworks might classify this as social anxiety, shyness, or introversion. *DCΨ* reframes it:

- Confrontation → Stage 2: Self vs. Other.
- Orientation → distorted Boundary (Wall), collapsing into isolation.
- Outcome → avoidance of recognition, fear of dissolution through others' gaze.
- Therapy → re-entering the confrontation, possibly through *BRT* (practicing boundaries in safe settings) or *XRT* (experiential immersion with controlled mirroring).

This example shows the difference: the same symptom is reframed not as a category but as a confrontation. *DCΨ* thus moves beyond description into a framework for resolution.

Closing

The move from idea to framework was the birth of *DCT* as the structured heart of *DCΨ*. The insights that began as modes of thought and philosophical reflections now stood as a map of human development, anchored in confrontation, operationalized by tools, and expanded symbolically into culture and history.

From this point onward, *DCΨ* could function as a true school: not a collection of insights, but a system with principles, diagnostics, therapies, and symbolic reach.

A Living Discovery

Developmental Confrontational Psychology (DCΨ) did not emerge as a finished system handed down all at once. It grew as a living discovery, shaped by observation, dialogue, and symbolic imagination. Its structure was crystallized into *Developmental Confrontation Theory (DCT)*, but its life continues as new situations, cultural shifts, and clinical encounters reveal further dimensions of confrontation.

Shaped by Observation

The earliest seeds of *DCΨ* were grounded in the observation of people in crisis. Children collapsing under separation anxiety, adolescents oscillating between rebellion and conformity, adults facing illness or burnout, these were not isolated cases but repeating patterns. The insight that each collapse represented an unresolved confrontation was not drawn from speculation alone but from lived experience.

Clinical presentations reinforced this pattern: dependency that revealed distorted Mirror orientation, hostility that exposed rigid Wall defenses, exhaustion that pointed to Mask-driven identity. These observations anchored the conviction that development is not a smooth trajectory but a sequence of confrontational thresholds.

Shaped by Dialogue

At the same time, *DCΨ* grew through dialogue with traditions.

- Freud's concepts of introjection and narcissism showed how early thought is shaped by incorporation and reflection.
- Erikson's psychosocial stages highlighted the conflicts of trust, autonomy, and identity.
- Lacan's mirror stage revealed the role of recognition and the gaze of the Other.
- Existentialists emphasized mortality and finitude as central to human existence.

Yet none of these frameworks, taken alone, could explain the systematic role of confrontation. *DCΨ* absorbed their insights but reinterpreted them under a unifying logic: identity grows or collapses depending on how it faces destabilizing realities.

Shaped by Symbolic Imagination

A third force in the birth of *DCΨ* was symbolic imagination. Confrontations are not only clinical but symbolic, they leave traces in myths, rituals, artifacts, and cultural inventions. From this insight emerged the symbolic expansions of *DCΨ*:

- The Unborn Familiar → the womb as archetype of containment and regression.
- The Familiar Fossil → civilizations as collective confrontations preserved in ruins.
- The Living Fossil → artificial intelligence as humanity's symbolic double, crystallizing its confrontation with mortality.

These symbolic dimensions extend *DCΨ* beyond the clinic into education, history, and culture, demonstrating that confrontation is not only personal but collective.

A Dynamic Framework

Unlike rigid schools of psychology that claim finality, *DCΨ* recognizes itself as a dynamic framework. The core map of *DCT* provides structure, but the living discovery continues:

- Digital identity confronts individuals with new forms of recognition and boundary setting (Stage 2).
- Climate anxiety confronts entire generations with mortality and continuity on a global scale (Stage 4).
- Cultural shifts in intimacy confront adolescents and adults with new ways of negotiating authenticity and role (Stage 3).

Each new cultural moment reveals fresh confrontations, reminding us that DCΨ is not static but evolving with humanity itself.

Closing Orientation

The birth of *DCΨ* is therefore both intellectual and experiential. It is shaped by observation, dialogue with past thinkers, and symbolic imagination that extends into the present. It stands as a living discovery, still expanding as new forms of confrontation emerge.

This recognition sets the stage for the next chapter, where the core principles of *DCT* will be articulated systematically. The seed of reflection has become a framework; now the framework must be described in its full structure.

DCΨ

Chapter 3

THE CONSTITUTION OF DCT

This chapter outlines the formal structure of the theory, presenting the developmental stages, their confrontations, and the traits through which resolution or distortion unfolds.

Introduction to Chapter 3

The Constitution of Developmental Confrontation Theory

Every psychological school requires a foundation of principles, a set of rules that explains why its structure holds together. For *Developmental Confrontation Psychology*, these are the developmental laws. They are not abstract formulas; they are lived truths, visible whenever a person is forced to face the paradox of existence.

Confrontation is not a single event but the engine of growth. It destabilizes, disorients, and demands reorganization. These laws describe how that engine operates: when development moves forward, when it collapses, and when it transforms into leadership or symbolism.

In this chapter, I frame the eight laws that hold the entire school in coherence. They are the constitution of *DCΨ,* principles that ensure the theory is not just descriptive but testable, not just symbolic but clinical, not just personal but cultural. Each law sharpens the difference between resolution and distortion, and together they reveal why confrontation is the universal pattern beneath psychology, therapy, and human meaning itself.

Law 1: Development Requires Confrontation

The Developmental Law of Confrontation

The first and central law of *Developmental Confrontational Psychology (DCΨ)* is that human development cannot proceed without confrontation. To grow is not to accumulate knowledge or habits in a linear fashion, but to pass through destabilizing thresholds that demand reorganization of identity.

Confrontation, in this framework, is defined as an encounter with a reality that the self cannot fully control or assimilate without transformation. It is more than mere conflict, which can occur within a stable framework of self. It is more than challenge, which may be mastered through skill or repetition. Confrontation is a rupture that shakes the very grounds of identity, forcing the self to revise its orientation to the world.

Distinguishing Confrontation from Conflict or Challenge

- Conflict may involve competing desires or social friction, but it does not necessarily reorganize the self. Two siblings arguing over a toy is conflict; their identities remain intact.
- Challenge may test endurance or skill, such as solving a puzzle or learning a new instrument. Success strengthens ability but does not demand existential reorientation.
- Confrontation, however, is qualitatively different: it destabilizes identity itself. The infant discovering separation from the caregiver, the adolescent realizing roles do not substitute for authenticity, the adult facing mortality — these are not skills to be acquired, but thresholds that change the self's relation to existence.

The Developmental Law

This distinction produces the law that governs *DCΨ*:

- No confrontation → stagnation. If thresholds are prevented or denied, development halts. The child never learns autonomy if never allowed to face separation.
- Avoided confrontation → distortion. If thresholds are reached but bypassed, the self develops defenses, illusions, or rigidity. The adolescent who avoids authenticity may collapse into hollow conformity.
- Faced confrontation → resolution. If thresholds are entered consciously or unconsciously, identity reorganizes and stabilizes at a higher level of integration. The adult who acknowledges mortality may live with clarity or invest in symbolic continuity.

This law is universal. It applies across all four stages of *Developmental Confrontation Theory (DCT)*:

1. Self vs. World.
2. Self vs. Other.
3. Emotional Identity.
4. Mortality and Wisdom.

Each stage is defined by its specific confrontation. Each confrontation tests identity. Each resolution or distortion shapes the trajectory of development.

Why This Law Is Foundational

This principle is not an optional insight but the constitutional ground of DCΨ. Without it, development appears as accumulation of drives (Freud), as psychosocial conflicts (Erikson), or as cognitive structures (Piaget). Each of those models contributes, but none explains why development requires rupture.

By defining confrontation as the driver, DCΨ establishes a unifying principle that governs not only individual psychology but also the tools, therapies, and symbolic analyses that belong to the school. Every scanner item, every therapeutic intervention, every symbolic reading presupposes this law: confrontation is the necessary engine of human growth.

Biological and Psychological Necessity

The law of confrontation is not only a theoretical claim. It is inscribed into the very biology and psychology of the human organism. Developmental thresholds are physiological imperatives and psychological inevitabilities. They arise because the human brain and body are structured to adapt only through rupture.

Stress and Adaptation

Biology demonstrates that growth requires stress. Hans Selye's General Adaptation Syndrome described how organisms respond to stress in three stages: alarm, resistance, and exhaustion. What determines health is not the presence of stress but the organism's ability to adapt to it.

- When stress is absent, systems atrophy. Muscles waste without resistance; immunity weakens without exposure.
- When stress is overwhelming, systems collapse. Trauma occurs when the threshold exceeds the organism's capacity to adapt.
- When stress is appropriate and processed, systems reorganize at higher levels. Muscles strengthen, immunity refines, and psychological resilience increases.

Confrontation in *DCΨ* is the psychological parallel of this law: destabilization is the necessary precondition for reorganization.

Neuroplasticity Under Rupture

Modern neuroscience confirms that the brain reorganizes primarily under conditions of destabilization. Neuroplasticity — the ability of neural networks to change — is most active when familiar patterns fail. Learning occurs when prediction errors are detected, forcing the brain to rewire.

- Infancy: separation from the caregiver activates stress pathways, but also builds neural systems for self-regulation.
- Childhood: social rejection or recognition reorganizes circuits for empathy and boundary-setting.
- Adolescence: identity crises activate prefrontal-limbic networks, reshaping self-regulation and decision-making.
- Adulthood: confrontation with mortality recruits networks for meaning, memory, and symbolic processing.

The brain grows not by comfort but by rupture. Confrontation is the biological trigger for psychological development.

Survival Imperative

Confrontation is not only growth-oriented but survival-oriented. Organisms that do not adapt to destabilizing realities do not survive. The infant who cannot regulate after separation risks failure to thrive. The adolescent who cannot balance authenticity and role risks social exclusion. The adult who cannot face mortality may collapse into despair or reckless denial.

Thus, confrontation is not an optional event but a condition of survival. To live is to confront. To refuse confrontation is to stagnate or distort.

Clinical Implications

This biological and psychological necessity has direct clinical consequences:

- Therapy cannot aim to remove confrontation. To do so would be to undermine the mechanism of growth.
- Therapy must aim to create safe conditions for confrontation to be entered and resolved.
- Avoidance must be identified not as comfort but as distortion.
- Resilience must be reframed not as "strength" but as the capacity to reorganize under rupture.

In this sense, the therapist becomes a facilitator of confrontation, ensuring that destabilization leads to reorganization rather than collapse.

Comparative Frameworks

The law of confrontation gains clarity when set beside the major traditions of psychology. Each school observed aspects of human development, but none articulated the unifying principle: that growth requires destabilizing thresholds which reorganize identity.

Freud: Drives Without Thresholds

Freud located development in the satisfaction and frustration of instinctual drives — oral, anal, phallic. These stages identified sources of tension, but their explanatory power was limited. Why should two children with similar drives diverge so dramatically, one becoming adaptive, the other pathological?

- Freud's model explains desire, but not why desire sometimes collapses identity.
- *DCΨ* reframes these early stages not as drives but as confrontations: separation (Stage 1), bodily control (boundary vs. intrusion, Stage 2), and identity formation (Stage 3).
- Drives matter, but they are surface currents of deeper confrontational thresholds.

Erikson: Conflict Without Mechanism

Erikson expanded Freud by mapping psychosocial conflicts: trust vs. mistrust, autonomy vs. shame, identity vs. role confusion. His framework captured the social dimension of development, but the conflicts remained descriptive rather than explanatory.

- Why do conflicts destabilize identity?
- Why do some individuals emerge with resilience while others collapse into pathology?

DCΨ supplies the mechanism: these conflicts are moments of existential confrontation. They matter because they shake identity to its roots. Without confrontation, Erikson's conflicts would not reorganize the self; they would remain ordinary disagreements.

Piaget: Cognition Without Finitude

Piaget described cognitive growth through assimilation and accommodation. His model clarified how children's thinking becomes more complex, but it left unexplained the existential dimension.

- A child who learns conservation of volume is not confronting finitude, only mastering logic.
- A child who confronts separation, rejection, or mortality is reorganizing not only thought but identity.

DCΨ incorporates Piaget's insight into cognitive reorganization but shows that true development requires confrontation with destabilizing realities, not just puzzles of logic.

Attachment: Bonds Without Thresholds

Attachment theory demonstrated that secure bonds foster resilience and insecure bonds foster vulnerability. Yet attachment alone does not explain the mechanism of growth.

- A secure attachment works because it allows the child to face confrontation safely.
- The infant learns separation only if the caregiver returns.
- The child learns recognition only if others mirror and boundary them reliably.

DCΨ reframes attachment not as the cause of development but as the scaffolding that makes confrontation survivable.

DCΨ's Integrative Advance

When viewed together:

- Freud explained desire.
- Erikson described conflict.
- Piaget mapped cognition.
- Attachment showed security.

DCΨ integrates them by stating the law: development advances when identity is destabilized by confrontation and reorganized into resolution. Drives, conflicts, cognition, and bonds are expressions of this deeper necessity.

Clinical Illustrations Across the Stages

The law of confrontation is most visible when traced through the four stages of *Developmental Confrontation Theory (DCT)*. Each stage presents two orientations of engagement, both capable of resolution or distortion. Clinical practice repeatedly demonstrates that symptoms emerge where confrontation was avoided or mishandled.

Stage 1 – Self vs. World

Confrontation: discovering separation from the environment.

- **Resolution**:
    - Exploratory (Igniter) → engages the external world with curiosity.
    - Regulatory (Adaptor) → builds inner consistency and safety. Both yield grounding and basic trust.
- **Distortion**:
    - Exploratory without anchor → scattered, hyperactive engagement.
    - Regulatory without openness → rigidity, withdrawal.
- Clinical anchors: adult manifestations include Generalized Anxiety Disorder (GAD) or Depersonalization/Derealization Disorder, rooted in unresolved separation.

Stage 2 – Self vs. Other

Confrontation: defining identity in relation to others.

- Resolution:
  - Reflective (Mirror) → develops through recognition and resonance.
  - Boundary (Wall) → stabilizes identity through clear self-other distinction.

- Distortion:
  - Reflective distortion → dependency, unstable self-image.
  - Boundary distortion → detachment, avoidant or antisocial patterns.

- Clinical anchors:
  - Borderline Personality Disorder (BPD): distorted Mirror with collapsed Wall.
  - Avoidant Personality Disorder (AvPD): rigid Wall, weak Mirror.
  - Dependent Personality Disorder (DPD): inflated Mirror, absent Wall.

Stage 3 – Emotional Identity

Confrontation: establishing authenticity of self.

- Resolution:
  - Authenticity (Flame) → expresses raw emotion with integrity.
  - Role (Mask) → integrates identity through function and performance.
- Distortion:
  - Flame distortion → volatility, emotional burnout.
  - Mask distortion → hollowness, false self.
- Clinical anchors:
  - Narcissistic Personality Disorder (NPD): inflated Mask, suppressed Flame.
  - Histrionic Personality Disorder (HPD): exaggerated Flame, distorted Mask.
  - Burnout syndromes: collapse of Flame without supportive Mask.

Stage 4 – Mortality & Wisdom

Confrontation: facing finitude and legacy.

- Resolution:
  - Clarity (Seer) → accepts mortality, seeks truth and wisdom.
  - Continuity (Wound) → transforms mortality into symbolic continuity (children, work, art, culture).
- Distortion:
  - Seer distortion → detachment, nihilism.
  - Continuity distortion → despair, compulsive denial of death.
- Clinical anchors:
  - Existential Depression: distorted Seer, inability to anchor meaning.
  - Midlife Crisis Syndromes: distorted Continuity, frantic search for symbolic survival.

Unified Pattern

At every stage, the same law governs:

- Faced confrontation → resolution and growth.
- Avoided confrontation → distortion and pathology.
- Shielded from confrontation → stagnation and immaturity.

Clinical disorders, whether anxiety, borderline instability, narcissism, or existential despair, can all be mapped as distortions of unresolved confrontation. The therapist's task is therefore not to bypass confrontation but to create conditions where it can be re-entered safely and resolved.

The Rule of Transformation

Confrontation is not merely an obstacle to be endured. It is the paradoxical engine of transformation: it destabilizes existing identity structures while simultaneously enabling their reorganization at a higher level. This dual role — destructive and creative — is what makes confrontation the indispensable law of development.

The Paradox of Growth

Every confrontation is disruptive. It fractures continuity, exposes vulnerability, and forces awareness of limits. Yet without such disruption, no new organization of the self could emerge. Stability alone does not generate development; it merely preserves the existing state.

- Stage 1: separation terrifies the infant, but reorganizes identity into self–world distinction.
- Stage 2: recognition destabilizes autonomy, but reorganizes identity into relational coherence.
- Stage 3: authenticity shatters borrowed identities, but reorganizes self into unique presence.
- Stage 4: mortality exposes finitude, but reorganizes meaning into wisdom and legacy.

In each case, what appears as rupture is simultaneously the condition for higher integration.

Resilience as Reorganization

Research on resilience demonstrates this paradox. Individuals who recover from trauma are not unchanged; they reorganize into new patterns of strength. Post-traumatic growth studies confirm that confrontation with crisis often produces deeper meaning, stronger values, and renewed purpose.

From the perspective of *DCΨ*:

- Resilience is not innate toughness.
- Resilience is the capacity to reorganize under rupture.

This reframes resilience as the psychological counterpart of confrontation: without destabilization, there can be no new integration.

Clinical Implications

Therapy must respect this paradox. To shield clients from confrontation is to deny the possibility of transformation. To expose them recklessly is to risk collapse. The task is calibrated facilitation:

- Re-entering confrontation in controlled conditions.
- Supporting the destabilization long enough for reorganization to occur.
- Recognizing that resolution emerges not from bypassing pain, but from reorganizing through it.

In this way, the therapist acts not as protector from confrontation but as midwife of transformation.

The Constitutional Law Restated

This rule may be restated as the Constitutional Law of Transformation:

- No confrontation → no growth.
- Avoided confrontation → distortion.
- Faced confrontation → destabilization and reorganization.

This is the foundation upon which every subsequent Article rests.

Law 2: Every Stage Holds Two Orientations

Defining Dual Orientations

The second constitutional law of *Developmental Confrontational Psychology (DCΨ)* is that every developmental confrontation presents two orientations of engagement. These orientations are not polarities of good and bad, nor predetermined paths of health and pathology. Rather, each represents a legitimate way of approaching the same existential threshold.

The Nature of Dual Orientations

- Each stage of *Developmental Confrontation Theory (DCT)* contains two primary orientations, symbolically named and clinically defined.
- They represent different strategies of resolution: one engages confrontation by moving outward, the other by turning inward; one by direct expression, the other by structuring or containing.
- Both can stabilize identity, and both can collapse into distortion if mishandled.

Orientations Across the Four Stages

- Stage 1 – Self vs. World
    - Exploratory (Igniter) → approaches the external world with curiosity and expansion.
    - Regulatory (Adaptor) → withdraws inward to establish safety and stability.

- Stage 2 – Self vs. Other
    - Reflective (Mirror) → seeks recognition, identity through reflection in others.
    - Boundary (Wall) → asserts separation, identity through distinction.

- Stage 3 – Emotional Identity
    - Authenticity (Flame) → establishes identity through passionate, raw self-expression.
    - Role (Mask) → stabilizes identity through structured functions and roles.

- Stage 4 – Mortality & Wisdom
    - Clarity (Seer) → confronts finitude with insight and acceptance.
    - Continuity (Wound) → transforms finitude into symbolic survival through legacy.

Correcting the Old Misunderstanding

In earlier drafts of developmental theory, orientations were sometimes misread as opposites of "healthy" and "pathological." DCΨ corrects this mistake.

- The Mirror is not inherently weaker than the Wall; both can resolve or distort.
- The Mask is not inherently false; it can stabilize authenticity when integrated.
- The Wound is not inherently despair; it becomes despair only when continuity is refused.

Thus, the constitutional law is clear: two orientations exist at every stage, and both contain the possibility of resolution or distortion.

Pathways of Resolution

Having established that every developmental confrontation presents two orientations, the second clause of this Article affirms that both orientations are capable of resolution. Resolution does not depend on which orientation is dominant, but on whether it is engaged with balance and integration.

Stage 1 – Self vs. World

- Exploratory (Igniter) → resolution occurs when outward curiosity is balanced with trust in the caregiver. The infant learns that the world can be approached without annihilation.
- Regulatory (Adaptor) → resolution occurs when inward withdrawal builds reliable self-soothing. The infant learns that safety can be carried internally.
- Clinical outcome: secure grounding; resilience to anxiety disorders later in life.

Stage 2 – Self vs. Other

- Reflective (Mirror) → resolution occurs when recognition is met by stable caregivers. The child internalizes a coherent self-image.
- Boundary (Wall) → resolution occurs when separation is respected. The child develops the ability to say "no" without fear of abandonment.
- Clinical outcome: healthy attachment styles; capacity for empathy without enmeshment and autonomy without isolation.

Stage 3 – Emotional Identity

- Authenticity (Flame) → resolution occurs when expression is validated and contained. The adolescent learns to voice passion without destructive overflow.

- Role (Mask) → resolution occurs when roles are integrated with selfhood. The adolescent learns that function does not erase individuality.

- Clinical outcome: stable identity; capacity to balance personal expression with social participation.

Stage 4 – Mortality & Wisdom

- Clarity (Seer) → resolution occurs when mortality is accepted as part of existence. The adult cultivates truth, perspective, and humility.

- Continuity (Wound) → resolution occurs when legacy is embraced as symbolic survival. The adult invests in children, culture, or creativity.

- Clinical outcome: existential maturity; reduced risk of despair and compulsive denial.

The Principle Affirmed

Resolution is not the monopoly of one orientation. Both contain resources for stability:

- Igniter and Adaptor.
- Mirror and Wall.
- Flame and Mask.
- Seer and Wound.

This dual possibility is what distinguishes *DCΨ* from binary models of health vs. pathology. The principle of dual orientations affirms that resolution emerges from engagement, not from preference.

Mechanisms of Distortion

While both orientations at each stage can resolve healthily, both are also vulnerable to distortion. Distortion arises when confrontation is avoided, over-identified with, or engaged without balance. What was a pathway to resolution becomes a trap that fractures identity.

Stage 1 – Self vs. World

A Exploratory (Igniter) distortion → compulsive novelty-seeking, scattered engagement, inability to anchor.

- Clinical anchors: ADHD-like restlessness, chronic instability, vulnerability to anxiety disorders.

B Regulatory (Adaptor) distortion → withdrawal into rigidity, overdependence on routine, fear of exploration.

- Clinical anchors: Avoidant personality features, somatization, agoraphobia.

Stage 2 – Self vs. Other

A Reflective (Mirror) distortion → identity collapse into others, unstable self-image, dependency.

- Clinical anchors: Borderline Personality Disorder (BPD), dependent presentations.

B Boundary (Wall) distortion → excessive rigidity, hostility to intimacy, social detachment.

- Clinical anchors: Avoidant Personality Disorder (AvPD), Antisocial Personality Disorder (ASPD) in extreme cases.

Stage 3 – Emotional Identity

A Authenticity (Flame) distortion → uncontrolled emotional overflow, volatility, burnout.

- Clinical anchors: Histrionic Personality Disorder (HPD), mood instability syndromes.

B Role (Mask) distortion → hollow identity, performance without depth, fragile selfhood.

- Clinical anchors: Narcissistic Personality Disorder (NPD), identity diffusion, burnout syndromes.

Stage 4 – Mortality & Wisdom

A Clarity (Seer) distortion → detachment, nihilism, intellectualized withdrawal.

- Clinical anchors: Existential Depression, schizoid-like detachment.

B Continuity (Wound) distortion → frantic denial of mortality, compulsive productivity, despair when legacy is blocked.

- Clinical anchors: Midlife Crisis syndromes, compulsive workaholism, legacy-driven despair.

The Constitutional Rule of Distortion

Distortion follows three predictable mechanisms:

1. Avoidance → refusal to enter confrontation (leads to stagnation or collapse).

2. Exaggeration → over-identification with one orientation at the expense of balance.

3. False Resolution → the orientation is used defensively, mimicking adaptation while bypassing confrontation. This produces the appearance of stability, but the underlying threshold remains unresolved.

Thus the law stands: both orientations carry the potential for resolution and distortion. Distortion is not a property of the orientation itself, but of how confrontation is engaged.

Stage & Confrontation	Orientation	Distortion Manifestation	Common Clinical Anchors (DSM/ICD)
1: Self vs. World (Grounding)	Exploratory (Igniter) 1A	Scattered engagement, impulsivity, inability to anchor.	ADHD-like features, Generalized Anxiety Disorder (GAD), instability.
	Regulatory (Adaptor) 1B	Rigid withdrawal, over-dependence on routine, fear of exploration.	Agoraphobia, Avoidant Personality traits, Somatization
2: Self vs. Other (Recognition & Boundary)	Recognition (Mirror) 2A	Identity collapse into others, unstable self-image dependency.	Borderline Personality Disorder (BPD), Dependent Personality Disorder (DPD).
	Boundary (Wall) 2B	Excessive rigidity, hostility to intimacy, social detachment.	Avoidant Personality Disorder (AvPD), Antisocial/Narcissistic traits (cold type).
3: Emotional Identity (Authenticity & Role)	Authenticity (Flame) 3A	Uncontrolled emotional overflow, volatility burnout.	Histrionic Personality Disorder (HPD), Cyclothymia, Burnout.
	Role (Mask) 3B	Hollow identity, performance without depth, fragile selfhood.	Narcissistic Personality Disorder (NPD), Identity Diffusion.
4: Mortality & Wisdom (Finitude & legacy)	Clarity (Seer) 4A	Detachment, nihilism, intellectualized withdrawal from meaning.	Existential Depression, Schizoid traits.
	Continuity (Wound) 4B	Frantic denial of death, compulsive legacy-building despair.	Midlife Crisis syndromes, compulsive workaholism.

Comparative Clarification

The second constitutional law of *DCΨ* rejects the binary models that have long dominated psychology. Where traditional frameworks divide human tendencies into healthy vs. pathological, virtue vs. vice, or mature vs. immature, *DCΨ* insists that each orientation carries both possibilities: resolution and distortion. This distinction is one of the school's defining advances.

Beyond Binary Moral Models

- In moral traditions, identity was often framed as a struggle between good and evil, light and dark. These categories shaped cultural imagination, but they reduced development to judgment.
- *DCΨ* rejects moral binaries: the Flame (Authenticity) is not "good," nor is the Mask (Role) "bad." Both can stabilize or collapse depending on how confrontation is entered.

Beyond Binary Clinical Models

- Classical psychiatry tended to view traits as either adaptive or pathological. For example, dependency was labeled weakness, autonomy strength.
- DCΨ reframes this: dependency (Mirror) can be a path to empathy and resonance when resolved, just as autonomy (Wall) can harden into isolation when distorted.
- No orientation is permanently fixed on one side of the binary.

Advancing Beyond Dualistic Depth Psychology

- Depth psychology (Freud, Jung, Lacan) often emphasized polarities: ego/id, persona/shadow, symbolic/real.
- While these contrasts illuminated inner conflict, they also risked reifying one side as more valuable.
- *DCΨ* corrects this by asserting dual orientations not as polarities but as co-equal strategies of survival and growth. Their value is decided by engagement, not essence.

Why This Matters Clinically

When a therapist assumes one orientation is superior, treatment is distorted.

- Favoring Flame over Mask risks invalidating structured role identities.
- Favoring Wall over Mirror risks undermining empathic capacities.
- Favoring Seer over Wound risks dismissing symbolic continuity and legacy.

DCΨ's constitutional law prevents such bias by affirming both orientations as equally capable of resolution.

The Integrative Principle

Thus, *DCΨ* establishes a new standard: dual orientations are not binary opposites, but twin pathways through the same confrontation. Resolution and distortion are determined not by the trait itself but by the way it is engaged. This principle secures the neutrality and universality of *DCT* within clinical and cultural practice.

Therapeutic Implications

The dual-orientation law carries profound implications for therapy. If both orientations can resolve or distort, then the therapist's role is not to steer the client toward a "preferred trait," but to help the client reorganize whichever orientation is dominant.

Avoiding Trait Bias in Therapy

Therapists often implicitly value one orientation over the other.

- Boundary (Wall) types are seen as strong, while Reflective (Mirror) types are labeled fragile.
- Authenticity (Flame) is celebrated as "true self," while Role (Mask) is dismissed as false or defensive.
- Clarity (Seer) is romanticized as wisdom, while Continuity (Wound) is devalued as clinging to legacy.

Such bias produces distortion in treatment. A Mirror client who depends on recognition may be pathologized for "neediness," when in fact their orientation can resolve into deep empathy and relational sensitivity. A Mask client who thrives in structured roles may be accused of inauthenticity, when their resolution lies in role integration.

Therapeutic Tasks by Orientation

- Exploratory (Igniter) → needs grounding. Therapist helps anchor curiosity without extinguishing it.
- Regulatory (Adaptor) → needs openness. Therapist supports safe withdrawal while fostering flexibility.
- Reflective (Mirror) → needs identity consolidation. Therapist validates recognition while strengthening inner stability.
- Boundary (Wall) → needs relational permeability. Therapist affirms boundaries while reducing rigidity.
- Authenticity (Flame) → needs containment. Therapist helps channel raw expression into sustainable forms.
- Role (Mask) → needs depth. Therapist links roles to emotional core, preventing hollowness.
- Clarity (Seer) → needs emotional anchoring. Therapist ensures insight does not collapse into cold detachment.
- Continuity (Wound) → needs symbolic balance. Therapist validates legacy-building while reducing compulsive denial of mortality.

Clinical Examples of Misapplied Therapy

- A rigid Boundary (Wall) client (distorted → isolation, AvPD traits) may worsen if therapy praises "independence" rather than opening space for relational permeability.
- A distorted Reflective (Mirror) client (identity collapse, BPD traits) may deteriorate if the therapist shames dependency instead of scaffolding it toward stable empathy.
- A distorted Role (Mask) client (NPD traits, hollow performance) may resist therapy if their structured identity is dismissed, instead of linked to authentic grounding.
- A distorted Continuity (Wound) client (midlife despair, compulsive productivity) may spiral if their legacy impulse is mocked, rather than reframed into symbolic survival.

The Constitutional Directive for Therapy

Therapy in *DCΨ* is governed by the following directive:

1. Identify the dominant orientation at each stage.
2. Assess whether it is resolving, distorting, or in stagnation.
3. Support resolution within the orientation rather than forcing a switch.
4. Address distortions as false resolutions, defenses that mimic stability while avoiding confrontation.

Closing

The law is affirmed: every stage holds two orientations, both capable of resolution or distortion. Therapy must respect this duality, avoiding bias and recognizing that growth lies not in replacing traits but in helping each orientation face confrontation truthfully.

Law 3: Development is Sequential but Non-Linear

Sequential Logic

The third constitutional law of *DCΨ* affirms that developmental confrontations unfold in sequence. Each stage introduces a new threshold that builds upon the structures established in the previous one.

The Necessity of Order

The order of the four stages is not arbitrary. Each presents an existential demand that can only appear after the prior one has been addressed:

- Stage 1 (Self vs. World): establishes grounding and separation from environment.
- Stage 2 (Self vs. Other): requires a stable self to enter recognition and boundary with others.
- Stage 3 (Emotional Identity): demands the prior relational grounding of Stage 2 to test authenticity vs. role.
- Stage 4 (Mortality & Wisdom): presupposes a stabilized identity (Stage 3) to face finitude and meaning.

Thus, confrontation progresses as an ascending structure: grounding → relation → identity → mortality.

Developmental Integrity

Each stage acts as a foundation for the next.

- A weak foundation in Stage 1 undermines the ability to form secure relationships in Stage 2.
- Fragile boundaries in Stage 2 compromise authentic identity in Stage 3.
- An unstable identity in Stage 3 destabilizes the encounter with mortality in Stage 4.

The sequence reflects the structural architecture of human existence. It cannot be skipped or inverted without distortion.

Clinical Example of Sequential Breakdown

A client presenting with existential despair (distorted Seer, Stage 4) may in fact carry unresolved Stage 1 ruptures (an unsafe world). Therapy reveals that mortality is intolerable because basic grounding was never secured. The sequential logic explains why the confrontation with death collapses: the prior foundations were fragile.

Sequential but Not Linear

While the order is necessary, it is not rigidly linear.

- Later stages can echo backward (healing Stage 1 through Stage 4 insight).
- Earlier cracks can resurface in later confrontations.

This dynamic will be detailed, but the principle is clear: the sequence is structurally required, yet it operates within a system of echoes, not a straight line.

Echoes Forward

The sequential law of *DCΨ* affirms that later stages rest upon earlier foundations. When an early confrontation is unresolved, the distortion does not remain isolated; it echoes forward into subsequent stages, destabilizing later development. This echo explains why many adult pathologies are not merely present difficulties but reverberations of earlier fractures.

Stage 1 Distortions Echoing Forward

A Exploratory (Igniter) distortion → scattered engagement, weak grounding.

- Echo in Stage 2: unstable relationships, inability to trust recognition or boundaries.
- Echo in Stage 3: identity diffusion, drifting between roles without anchor.
- Echo in Stage 4: existential anxiety, mortality felt as chaos without foundation.

B Regulatory (Adaptor) distortion → rigidity, over-withdrawal.

- Echo in Stage 2: avoidant attachment, excessive reliance on walls.
- Echo in Stage 3: suppression of authenticity, collapse into hollow roles.
- Echo in Stage 4: compulsive denial of mortality through routine.

Stage 2 Distortions Echoing Forward

A Reflective (Mirror) distortion → dependency, unstable identity.

- Echo in Stage 3: identity collapse, narcissistic fragility, emotional volatility.
- Echo in Stage 4: fear of being forgotten, despair when others withdraw.

B Boundary (Wall) distortion → excessive rigidity, hostility to intimacy.

- Echo in Stage 3: isolation, inability to integrate roles with authentic emotional life.
- Echo in Stage 4: existential detachment, Seer distortion into nihilism.

Stage 3 Distortions Echoing Forward

A Authenticity (Flame) distortion → uncontrolled passion, burnout.

- Echo in Stage 4: despair when mortality extinguishes passion, compulsive denial of aging.

B Role (Mask) distortion → hollow performance, fragile selfhood.

- Echo in Stage 4: legacy built on façade, collapse when recognition fails.

Clinical Examples

- A client with midlife crisis (Stage 4 Wound distortion) is discovered to have carried unresolved Stage 2 Mirror distortion, identity built on unstable reflection. The collapse at midlife is not sudden but an echo.

- Another client with generalized anxiety about death (Stage 4 distorted Seer) shows roots in Stage 1 Adaptor distortion, the world was never internalized as safe, so mortality is unbearable.

The Constitutional Law of Echoes

The echoes of distortion follow a predictable rule:

- Earlier unresolved confrontation → later destabilization.
- Later confrontation amplifies, rather than erases, earlier cracks.

This law explains why therapy cannot treat symptoms in isolation. The echoes must be traced to their origin.

Healing Backward

The constitutional law of echoes does not operate only in one direction. Just as unresolved early stages destabilize later confrontations, resolutions achieved in later stages can retroactively stabilize earlier fractures. This is the principle of healing backward.

Why Healing Backward Is Possible

- Confrontations are not erased once passed; they remain active structures within the self.
- Later stages reorganize identity at deeper levels, which can reframe earlier vulnerabilities.
- When a person resolves a later confrontation, the new integration cascades backward, offering stability where there was once fragility.

Healing Backward Across the Stages

I Stage 4 → Stage 1

- Clarity (Seer) resolution: acceptance of mortality brings existential calm that anchors earlier world-anxiety.
- Continuity (Wound) resolution: symbolic legacy stabilizes grounding, reducing fear of disintegration.

II Stage 3 → Stage 2

- Authenticity (Flame) resolution: owning one's voice heals Mirror dependency, solidifying identity.
- Role (Mask) resolution: integrated role identity strengthens boundaries, reducing Wall rigidity.

III Stage 2 → Stage 1

- Reflective (Mirror) resolution: consistent recognition heals earlier insecurity of existence.
- Boundary (Wall) resolution: clear distinction reduces regression to world-fusion.

Clinical Anchors

- A client who confronts mortality (Stage 4 Seer resolution) often reports newfound calm in daily anxiety. Earlier Stage 1 fears of safety are indirectly soothed.

- Adolescents who stabilize authenticity (Stage 3 Flame resolution) frequently re-anchor their Stage 2 relational instability.

- Therapy with borderline clients (Stage 2 Mirror distortion) often progresses when adult identity consolidation (Stage 3 Mask resolution) stabilizes earlier fragility.

The Principle of Cascading Integration

Healing backward can be understood as a cascade:

- Later resolutions reorganize the architecture of identity.
- This reorganization strengthens earlier structures, retroactively repairing fractures.
- The process is not automatic but conditional: it occurs when later stages are resolved authentically, not defensively.

The Constitutional Law of Healing

- Later confrontation resolved authentically → earlier fractures stabilized.
- Later confrontation resolved defensively (false resolution) → earlier fractures remain unhealed.

This constitutional principle explains why therapy with adults can succeed even if childhood confrontations were distorted: healing is possible by entering later confrontations truthfully.

Clinical Anchors of Echoes & Healing

The laws of echoes and healing are not theoretical abstractions. They are observed daily in therapy. Clients present with symptoms in one stage that often trace back to unresolved confrontations in earlier stages, or they discover that resolving a later confrontation heals wounds they carried since childhood.

Echoes Forward in Clinical Practice

- Case A: Midlife Despair (Stage 4 distorted Wound).
  A 48-year-old client entered therapy after a sudden collapse in meaning. Despite professional success, he reported despair and intrusive death anxiety. Exploration revealed unresolved Stage 2 Reflective (Mirror) distortion, his identity had always been anchored in others' recognition. When recognition waned at midlife, his continuity collapsed. His despair was not a new problem but an echo.

- Case B: Chronic Anxiety (Stage 4 distorted Seer).
  A client in her 30s presented with overwhelming fear of mortality. Clinical exploration uncovered unresolved Stage 1 Regulatory (Adaptor) distortion, she had never internalized safety, relying only on external structures. Without grounding, mortality appeared as annihilation. The echo forward explained her existential panic.

Healing Backward in Clinical Practice

- Case C: Authenticity as Anchor (Stage 3 Flame resolution).
  An adolescent who had lived with Stage 2 Mirror distortion (dependency, unstable identity) gradually stabilized through validating authentic self-expression. By owning his voice (Flame), he consolidated identity, and the earlier fragility healed retroactively.

- Case D: Wisdom as Grounding (Stage 4 Seer resolution).
  A retired teacher reported lifelong anxiety (Stage 1 distortions). In late adulthood, she confronted mortality through Seer orientation, acceptance of finitude and cultivation of wisdom. Surprisingly, her daily anxiety diminished. By resolving the confrontation of mortality, she anchored the world as safe.

The Dual Clinical Law

- Echoes Forward: distortions in early stages destabilize later stages, producing symptoms that appear out of place but are rooted in earlier fractures.
- Healing Backward: resolutions in later stages reorganize identity, stabilizing earlier vulnerabilities and reducing long-standing symptoms.

Implications for Therapy

- Therapy must trace symptoms backward to their origin rather than treating them at face value.
- Therapy must also allow healing forward: clients do not need to revisit childhood endlessly but can stabilize early fractures by resolving present confrontations authentically.
- This dual focus shifts therapy from regression-focused models toward progression-focused integration.

Scientific & Philosophical Parallels

The constitutional law that development is sequential but non-linear finds resonance in multiple scientific and philosophical traditions. These parallels strengthen the legitimacy of *DCΨ* by showing that the principle of echoes and backward healing is consistent with how complex systems function.

Systems Theory and Non-Linear Dynamics

- In systems theory, development is understood as the interaction of parts within a whole. A small disruption in one part of the system can cascade through the entire structure.
- *DCΨ* echoes this: a distortion in Stage 1 (self–world) can reverberate into Stage 4 (mortality). The echo is not accidental but systemic.
- Non-linear dynamics (chaos theory) describe how early conditions shape later outcomes disproportionately, "sensitive dependence on initial conditions." This is precisely what *DCΨ* identifies as echoes forward.

Neuroscience of Ripple Effects

- Research on neuroplasticity shows that changes in one neural circuit influence broader networks. Trauma in early childhood reorganizes limbic pathways, shaping later emotional regulation.
- Therapy-induced changes in adulthood reorganize prefrontal-limbic integration, stabilizing earlier dysregulation, the neurological basis for healing backward.
- This demonstrates that echoes and healing are not metaphors but biological processes.

Philosophy of Time and Development

- Phenomenology (Husserl, Heidegger) emphasizes that human existence is temporal: the present is always shaped by the past and directed toward the future.
- *DCΨ* situates confrontation within this temporality: earlier cracks echo forward, and later insights reinterpret the past.
- Healing backward aligns with Heidegger's notion of retrieval (Wiederholung): the capacity to re-appropriate one's past from a new stance.

Anthropological Parallels

- Rites of passage in traditional cultures illustrate echoes and healing. Early initiations (childhood confrontations) prepared individuals for later adulthood thresholds. When adult rituals were missing, earlier cracks often remained visible.
- Conversely, adult rituals of mortality and wisdom often served to stabilize earlier anxieties, embodying the law of healing backward.

Constitutional Integration

Thus the law is affirmed across sciences and philosophies:

- Systems theory explains echoes.
- Neuroscience validates ripple effects and retroactive healing.
- Philosophy articulates confrontation within temporality.
- Anthropology shows cultural practices that embody sequential but non-linear development.

The constitutional principle of *DCΨ* is not an isolated claim but a universal law: development must unfold in sequence, but its echoes and healings ripple across time, shaping identity forward and backward.

This dual focus shifts therapy from regression-focused models toward progression-focused integration.

The DCT Model: A Visual Synthesis

The first three constitutional laws together form the dynamic architecture of Developmental Confrontation Theory. The following diagram synthesizes these laws into a single map: the four stages, their dual orientations, and the non-linear processes of echoes and healing that bind them.

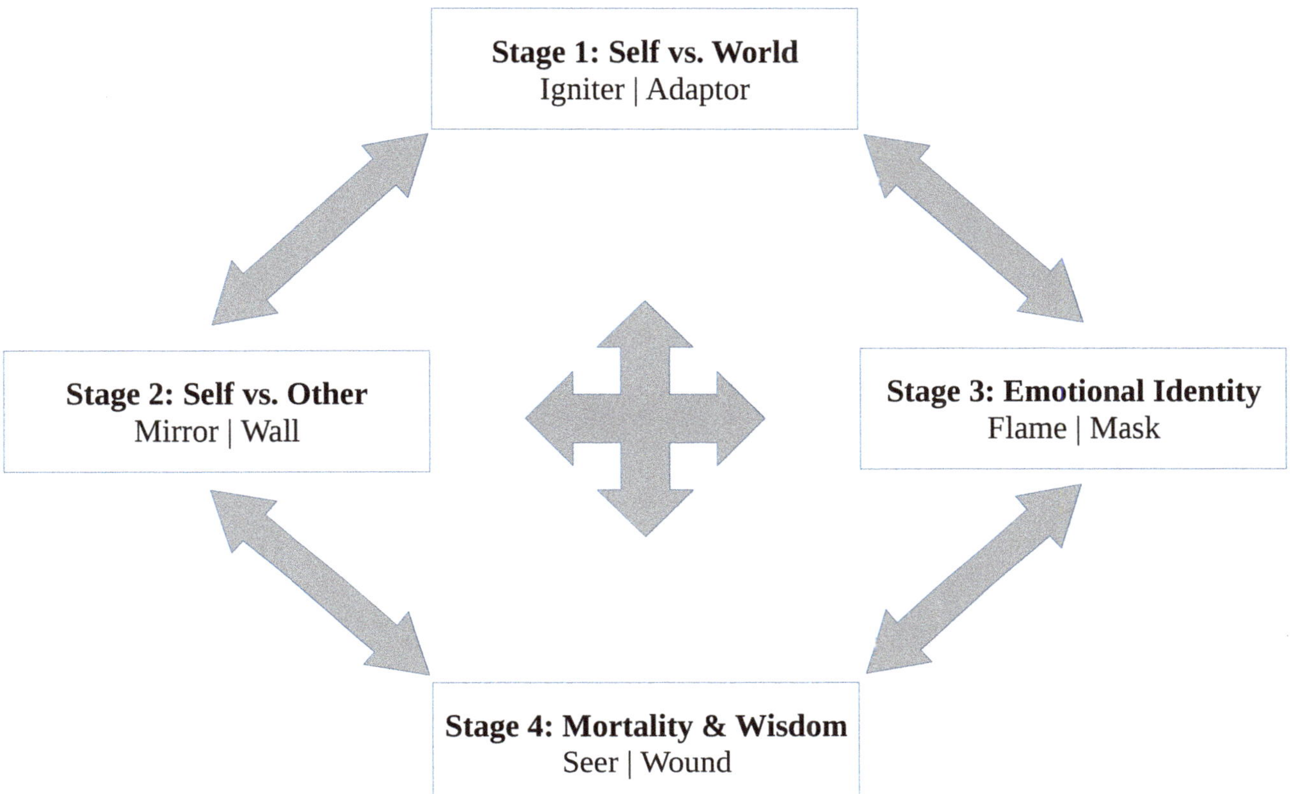

This model illustrates that development is a system of reverberating confrontations. A fracture in an early stage (e.g., unstable Grounding in Stage 1) can echo forward to undermine later challenges (e.g., causing despair when facing Mortality in Stage 4). Conversely, authentically resolving a later confrontation (e.g., achieving Wisdom in Stage 4) can heal backward, stabilizing earlier vulnerabilities. This is the non-linear heart of the model.

These first three laws establish the fundamental operating principles of human development: its engine (confrontation), its inherent structure (dual orientations), and its temporal dynamics (sequential yet non-linear echoes). With this foundational architecture in place, we can now examine the primary outcomes that this process generates, both for the individual and for culture at large. The following laws trace the tangible results of confronting—or avoiding—these universal thresholds.

Law 4: Leadership Emerges from Confrontation

Defining Leadership in DCΨ

The fourth constitutional law of *Developmental Confrontational Psychology (DCΨ)* is that leadership is not a social position, personality trait, or external role, it is the transformed outcome of resolved confrontation.

Leadership as Developmental Outcome

In conventional discourse, leadership is described as authority, charisma, or influence. *DCΨ* rejects such surface definitions. Leadership arises when confrontation at a developmental stage is not merely resolved but transformed into a capacity to guide others through the same threshold.

- A person who stabilizes grounding in Stage 1 becomes able to anchor others in safety.
- A person who consolidates boundaries in Stage 2 becomes able to structure groups without collapse.
- A person who integrates identity in Stage 3 becomes able to voice authenticity or organize collective roles.
- A person who confronts mortality in Stage 4 becomes able to transmit wisdom or continuity.

Thus, leadership is developmental authority: the ability to embody resolution in such a way that others can navigate confrontation through them.

Distinguishing Leadership from Role or Power

- Role is functional. Anyone may occupy a position of authority without embodying resolution. A manager can enforce rules but lack the developmental capacity of leadership.

- Power is coercive. It compels behavior but does not guide development. Tyrants may dominate, but their unresolved confrontations distort leadership into pathology.

- Leadership, in *DCΨ*, is symbolic authority. It signals that the person embodies resolution at a developmental threshold, and others can orient themselves through that presence.

Leadership as Communal Function

Leadership does not belong to the individual alone. It exists in the relational field between the leader and others. Resolution becomes visible because it resonates:

- The stabilized Stage 1 leader calms others' anxiety.
- The resolved Stage 2 leader fosters secure relationships.
- The resolved Stage 3 leader inspires authenticity and role integration.
- The resolved Stage 4 leader embodies mortality with wisdom, enabling others to face finitude without despair.

Leadership, therefore, is not reducible to skill. It is the embodied transmission of confrontation resolved.

Leader Variants Across Stages

Each developmental stage generates its own leader variant. These forms of leadership are not superficial roles but expressions of confrontation resolved. When an individual transforms destabilization into stable integration, their presence becomes an orientation point for others navigating the same threshold.

Stage 1 – The Grounding Leader

- Orientation: Exploratory (Igniter) or Regulatory (Adaptor).
- Resolution expressed as leadership:
  - **A** The Igniter leader stabilizes groups by modeling curiosity without recklessness. They create a sense of safety in exploration.
  - **B** The Adaptor leader stabilizes through calm regulation, anchoring others against anxiety and chaos.
- Clinical distinction: If distorted, Igniter leaders appear impulsive and destabilizing; Adaptor leaders appear rigid and immobilizing.

Stage 2 – The Relational Leader

- Orientation: Reflective (Mirror) or Boundary (Wall).
- Resolution expressed as leadership:
  - **A** The Mirror leader provides recognition, fostering empathy and cohesion in groups.
  - **B** The Wall leader provides boundaries, structuring relationships without collapse or exploitation.
- Clinical distinction: If distorted, Mirror leaders become dependent flatterers, seeking validation rather than offering it. Wall leaders become authoritarian or emotionally detached.

Stage 3 – The Identity Leader

- Orientation: Authenticity (Flame) or Role (Mask).
- Resolution expressed as leadership:
  - **A** The Flame leader inspires by voicing authentic passion, becoming a beacon of originality.
  - **B** The Mask leader organizes by integrating roles, offering structure that legitimizes group identity.

- Clinical distinction: If distorted, Flame leaders burn out or destabilize followers with volatility. Mask leaders collapse into hollowness, hiding fragility behind performance.

Stage 4 – The Existential Leader

- Orientation: Clarity (Seer) or Continuity (Wound).
- Resolution expressed as leadership:
  - **A** The Seer leader guides through wisdom, offering truth, perspective, and calm in the face of mortality.
  - **B** The Wound leader guides through legacy, investing in cultural continuity, children, or institutions that outlive them.
- Clinical distinction: If distorted, Seer leaders detach into cold nihilism, while Wound leaders collapse into despair or compulsive legacy-building.

The Constitutional Pattern of Leadership

- Every stage can generate leadership, but only when confrontation is resolved.
- Leadership is thus development-specific: grounding, relational, identity, existential.
- Each form embodies authority appropriate to its stage, enabling others to traverse the same threshold with less collapse.

Distorted Leadership

Leadership, when grounded in resolution, stabilizes groups and fosters growth. Yet when confrontation is avoided, exaggerated, or falsely resolved, leadership becomes distorted. Distorted leaders appear authoritative but transmit pathology rather than integration.

Stage 1 – Distorted Grounding Leaders

- Exploratory (Igniter) distortion → impulsive, thrill-seeking figures who destabilize groups by mistaking recklessness for courage.
- Clinical parallel: hypomanic patterns, attention-deficit traits, unstable charisma.

- Regulatory (Adaptor) distortion → rigid protectors who suppress exploration, demanding conformity in the name of safety.
- Clinical parallel: obsessive-compulsive traits, authoritarian rigidity.

Stage 2 – Distorted Relational Leaders

- Reflective (Mirror) distortion → leaders dependent on validation, flattering followers to secure loyalty, unable to sustain identity alone.
- Clinical parallel: borderline traits, dependent dynamics, manipulative charm.

- Boundary (Wall) distortion → leaders who rule by fear, rigid detachment, and exclusion.
- Clinical parallel: antisocial traits, paranoid suspicion, emotional coldness.

Stage 3 – Distorted Identity Leaders

- Authenticity (Flame) distortion → volatile figures who mistake emotional overflow for truth, destabilizing followers with passion uncontained.
- Clinical parallel: histrionic traits, dramatic instability, burnout-prone leadership.

- Role (Mask) distortion → hollow leaders who perform competence while hiding fragile identity, collapsing when performance is questioned.
- Clinical parallel: narcissistic traits, grandiose façade, fragile self-esteem.

Stage 4 – Distorted Existential Leaders

- Clarity (Seer) distortion → detached intellectuals who preach meaninglessness, spreading nihilism rather than wisdom.
- Clinical parallel: schizoid detachment, depressive withdrawal, cold rationalism.

- Continuity (Wound) distortion → compulsive legacy-builders who exploit followers to secure symbolic survival, collapsing into despair when legacy is blocked.
- Clinical parallel: midlife crisis syndromes, obsessive productivity, despair-driven control.

The Law of Distorted Leadership

The constitutional rule is clear:

- Resolved confrontation → genuine leadership.
- Distorted confrontation → toxic leadership.

Distorted leaders embody false resolution: they appear stable but use their orientation defensively, bypassing the confrontation they never truly resolved. Their presence magnifies instability in followers rather than stabilizing it.

Clinical & Cultural Anchors of Leadership

Leadership in *DCΨ* is not abstract. It is visible in both clinical encounters and cultural history, where individuals embody either the stabilizing presence of resolved confrontation or the instability of distorted authority.

Clinical Anchors

- Case A: The Containing Teacher (Stage 1 Regulatory/Adaptor Leader).
  A therapist working with a child in chronic anxiety observed the calming presence of a teacher who embodied regulation. She offered consistent routines without rigidity, transmitting safety. The child mirrored this stability, grounding herself. This is leadership as anchoring.

  - Case B: The Distorted Wall Leader (Stage 2).
    In group therapy, one participant consistently silenced others, enforcing rigid rules. His identity collapsed when questioned, revealing unresolved Boundary (Wall) distortion. His "leadership" was defensive, a false resolution based on exclusion.

  - Case C: The Authentic Mentor (Stage 3 Flame Leader).
    An adolescent client described a coach who inspired him not by performance but by honesty about struggles. This mentor's authenticity allowed the adolescent to express himself, transforming volatile Flame energy into sustainable identity.

  - Case D: The Legacy Builder in Therapy (Stage 4 Wound Leader).
    An adult client facing mortality reorganized his despair by investing in mentoring apprentices. His symbolic continuity stabilized younger colleagues while healing his own confrontation with finitude. Leadership emerged as legacy.

Cultural Anchors

- Grounding Leaders (Stage 1): figures like early tribal elders who established safety and predictable routines. Their authority came not from power but from anchoring others in a dangerous world.

- Relational Leaders (Stage 2): leaders like Martin Luther King Jr., whose strength lay in recognition and empathy (Mirror resolution), contrasted with authoritarian rulers who imposed rigid separation (Wall distortion).

- Identity Leaders (Stage 3): cultural voices like Nelson Mandela, whose authenticity (Flame resolution) inspired identity transformation for an entire nation, or leaders who structured role integration (Mask resolution) to stabilize social order.

- Existential Leaders (Stage 4): figures like Mahatma Gandhi, who embodied Seer clarity by facing mortality with wisdom, or cultural innovators like artists and scientists who created legacies that survived them (Wound resolution).

The Law in Practice

- Clinical presence proves that leadership is developmental: clients stabilize when guided by resolved figures.

- Cultural history demonstrates the same: societies are transformed when leaders embody confrontation, and they fracture when leaders transmit distortion.

Leadership in *DCΨ* is thus not personality or charisma, but the developmental resonance of resolution.

Therapeutic & Social Implications of Leadership

If leadership is the embodied outcome of resolved confrontation, then both therapy and society must learn to identify, nurture, and rehabilitate leadership capacities. This is the constitutional directive of Law 4: leadership is not accidental, but a developmental function.

Implications for Therapy

- Identifying leadership potential: Therapists can trace a client's dominant orientation (Igniter, Adaptor, Mirror, Wall, Flame, Mask, Seer, Wound) and assess whether resolution has matured into stabilizing presence.

- Rehabilitating distorted leaders: Clients in positions of power who embody false resolution (e.g., Mask-driven narcissistic fragility, Wall-driven rigidity) can be guided back into authentic confrontation, transforming toxic authority into genuine leadership.

- Cultivating leadership capacity: Therapy can explicitly frame resolution as not only personal healing but also the emergence of symbolic authority. Clients learn that resolving their confrontation positions them to stabilize others.

Implications for Society

- Education: Schools and institutions can nurture leadership not by teaching charisma, but by supporting confrontation. Programs should allow safe separation (Stage 1), boundary and recognition exercises (Stage 2), authentic expression (Stage 3), and existential reflection (Stage 4).

- Organizations: Workplaces can be assessed through DCΨ lenses: does the culture reward distorted Masks (performance façades) or support genuine integration of identity? Does leadership perpetuate rigid Walls or foster relational Mirrors?

- Politics and governance: DCΨ offers a diagnostic tool for distinguishing genuine leaders (resolved confrontation) from false leaders (distorted confrontation). Societies can thus understand why some rulers stabilize communities while others destabilize them through projection of unresolved thresholds.

The Constitutional Directive

Leadership in DCΨ is not optional. It is the natural byproduct of resolution:

- Resolution generates stabilizing presence → leadership.
- Distortion generates destabilizing presence → toxic leadership.
- Therapy and society must aim to cultivate the first and prevent the second.

Closing

The law is affirmed: leadership emerges from confrontation. It is developmental, not accidental; constitutional, not charismatic. To resolve is to lead, and to distort is to destabilize.

Law 5: Symbolism as Evidence of Confrontation

Defining Symbolism in DCΨ

The fifth constitutional law of *Developmental Confrontational Psychology (DCΨ)* affirms that symbolism is the natural evidence of confrontation. Wherever the psyche encounters destabilization, it produces symbolic forms to represent, contain, and transmit the threshold.

Symbolism as Residue of Confrontation

Symbols emerge because the psyche cannot remain silent before confrontation. When identity is destabilized, the mind externalizes inner tension through images, narratives, and rituals. These are not decorative but essential: they allow the self to approach thresholds indirectly, to hold what is overwhelming in condensed form.

- The womb symbolizes Stage 1 grounding: protection and origin.
- The mirror symbolizes Stage 2 recognition: seeing oneself through another.
- The flame symbolizes Stage 3 authenticity: raw passion and vitality.
- The mask symbolizes Stage 3 role: identity shaped through function and structure.
- The seer symbolizes Stage 4 clarity: wisdom before mortality.
- The wound symbolizes Stage 4 continuity: sacrifice transformed into legacy.

Each symbol is both individual and collective, recurring across cultures because the confrontations are universal.

The Function of Symbolism

Symbols perform three functions in *DCΨ*:

1. Containment → they hold destabilizing realities in manageable images.
2. Transmission → they communicate thresholds across generations and cultures.
3. Diagnosis → they reveal unresolved or resolved confrontations in individuals and societies.

Thus, symbols are not optional embellishments of human culture; they are constitutional evidence of the developmental law.

Clinical Anchors

In therapy, symbolism appears spontaneously:

- A dream of drowning reflects unresolved Stage 1 grounding.
- Fantasies of being invisible reflect distorted Stage 2 mirroring.
- Artistic outbursts of fire, color, and chaos signal Stage 3 authenticity struggling to stabilize.
- Narratives of death and afterlife reflect the confrontation of Stage 4 mortality.

To ignore symbols is to ignore the psyche's own testimony.

Archetypes Across Stages

Each developmental orientation has its own archetypal residue. These archetypes recur in myths, dreams, rituals, and art because they encode the confrontation each orientation faces. They are the symbolic fingerprints of development.

Stage 1 – Self vs. World

- Exploratory (Igniter): Archetypes of fire, dawn, the wanderer, the first spark. These images capture the ignition of autonomy and the leap outward into the unknown.
- Regulatory (Adaptor): Archetypes of womb, shelter, circle, mother-earth. These images symbolize containment, safety, and the inward anchoring of stability.

Clinical anchor: Dreams of fire or flight often reveal Igniter struggles; dreams of wombs, caves, or circles often reveal Adaptor processes.

Stage 2 – Self vs. Other

- Reflective (Mirror): Archetypes of mirror, twin, echo, reflective waters. These symbols embody the need to see oneself through another's recognition.
- Boundary (Wall): Archetypes of wall, skin, gate, threshold. These symbols represent the act of separation and self-definition.

Clinical anchor: A client obsessed with reflections or doubles may reveal Mirror distortions; one who dreams of walls, fences, or closed gates may express Wall anxieties.

Stage 3 – Emotional Identity

- Authenticity (Flame): Archetypes of flame, heart, volcano, raw eruption. They symbolize passion and the risk of being consumed by one's own vitality.

- Role (Mask): Archetypes of mask, costume, theater, crown. They symbolize structured performance, function, and the dual edge of hiding or stabilizing identity.

Clinical anchor: An adolescent who sketches burning suns or erupting hearts may be working through Flame; one who fantasizes about costumes, uniforms, or crowns may be in Mask resolution or distortion.

Stage 4 – Mortality & Wisdom

- Clarity (Seer): Archetypes of eye, star, prophet, mountain-top. These symbols embody vision, foresight, and calm clarity before death.

- Continuity (Wound): Archetypes of scar, bloodline, seed, sacrifice. They embody the transformation of pain into continuity, turning mortality into legacy.

Clinical anchor: Clients reporting repetitive images of eyes, stars, or mountain heights often signal Seer orientation. Those fixated on wounds, bloodlines, or sacrifice often reveal Wound confrontation.

The Constitutional Rule of Archetypes

Every orientation has its symbolic echo.

- These archetypes are not cultural inventions but psychological necessities.
- They recur because the human psyche externalizes confrontation in symbolic form.
- Symbols thus serve as constitutional markers: they reveal which confrontation is active, resolved, or distorted.

Myth, Ritual, and Religion

If archetypes are the residues of confrontation, then myths, rituals, and religions are their collective embodiments. Cultures across history have externalized developmental thresholds in symbolic stories and communal practices, ensuring that individuals and societies alike face the same existential tasks.

Myths as Collective Confrontations

- Stage 1 myths (Self vs. World): Creation stories — the world emerging from chaos, the first fire, the cosmic womb. These myths mirror the Igniter's spark and the Adaptor's containment.
- Stage 2 myths (Self vs. Other): Stories of twins, doubles, rivalries, and separations. Cain and Abel, Romulus and Remus, or Narcissus and Echo embody Mirror and Wall dynamics.
- Stage 3 myths (Emotional Identity): Hero's journeys that test authenticity and role. The hero must claim their true flame while donning masks of function — Odysseus as trickster and warrior, or Hamlet wrestling between voice and duty.
- Stage 4 myths (Mortality & Wisdom): Tales of sacrifice, prophecy, and afterlife. The Seer is embodied in figures like Tiresias; the Wound in myths of the dying-and-rising god (Osiris, Dionysus, Christ).

Ritual as Symbolic Confrontation

- Initiation rituals: mark Stage 1 and Stage 2 thresholds. Children leave safety (womb, home) to face separation and recognition in community.
- Marriage rituals: embody Stage 2 and Stage 3, where identity merges and roles are formalized through symbolic masks, costumes, and fire (candles, flame).
- Funerary rituals: represent Stage 4, where death is confronted not through denial but through continuity — burial, legacy, remembrance.

Rituals externalize the destabilization of confrontation and offer symbolic containment, enabling communities to face thresholds together.

Religion as Developmental Framework

Religious systems codify these confrontations into narratives of salvation, sin, and transcendence.

- Stage 1: purity laws, dietary taboos, rituals of cleansing → securing grounding.
- Stage 2: commandments about relations, loyalty, fidelity → stabilizing recognition and boundaries.
- Stage 3: moral codes of authenticity and role → guiding identity through passion and duty.
- Stage 4: doctrines of afterlife, resurrection, and legacy → confronting mortality with continuity.

In all cases, religion acts as symbolic scaffolding: translating confrontation into mythic language, allowing the unbearable to be held in shared meaning.

The Constitutional Rule of Collective Symbolism

- Myths = stories of confrontation.
- Rituals = enactments of confrontation.
- Religions = systems of confrontation.

The psyche cannot pass thresholds without symbols; societies cannot pass them without myth, ritual, and religion. This law affirms that collective symbolism mirrors individual confrontation.

Art and Literature

Art and literature are the aesthetic residues of confrontation. Where myth and ritual formalize thresholds in collective systems, art and literature give them expressive form, encoding the raw struggle of orientations in image, sound, and story.

Stage 1 – The Symbolism of Grounding and Ignition

- Artistic forms: cave paintings, circles, spirals, depictions of birth and fire.
- Literary echoes: tales of beginnings, primal chaos, the first spark.
- Igniter (Exploratory): fire motifs, expanding horizons, journeys into the wild.
- Adaptor (Regulatory): womb-like enclosures, shelters, maternal figures.

Clinical parallel: clients who draw spirals, wombs, or erupting fires often unconsciously symbolize unresolved Stage 1 confrontations.

Stage 2 – The Symbolism of Recognition and Boundary

- Artistic forms: mirrors, portraits, doubles, architectural walls and gates.
- Literary echoes: stories of rivalry, betrayal, or twinning.
- Mirror (Reflective): Narcissus in literature, reflective pools in poetry.
- Wall (Boundary): fortresses in medieval art, guarded thresholds in epics.

Clinical parallel: compulsive drawings of walls or faces often symbolize the client's negotiation of recognition and separation.

Stage 3 – The Symbolism of Identity and Role

- Artistic forms: masks, theatrical costumes, flames, expressive colors.
- Literary echoes: tragedies of passion (Flame) and comedies of mistaken identity (Mask).
- Flame (Authenticity): fiery hearts in Romantic poetry, eruptive canvases of Van Gogh.
- Mask (Role): Shakespeare's plays, where identity and role blur — Hamlet, Othello, King Lear.

Clinical parallel: adolescents who draw fiery suns or write about masks are giving symbolic voice to the Stage 3 confrontation.

Stage 4 – The Symbolism of Mortality and Legacy

- Artistic forms: depictions of eyes, stars, prophets, sacrifices, bloodlines.
- Literary echoes: epics of death and continuity, elegies, and wisdom literature.
- Seer (Clarity): prophetic visions in religious texts, mountain ascents in literature.
- Wound (Continuity): stories of sacrifice and inheritance, from Gilgamesh to modern novels of family legacy.

Clinical parallel: adults facing mortality often create or dream of eyes, stars, or wounded bodies, symbolic expressions of their confrontation with Stage 4.

The Constitutional Rule of Aesthetic Symbolism

- Art externalizes confrontation in image and form.
- Literature externalizes confrontation in story and character.
- Together they act as mirrors of development, testifying that the psyche expresses its struggles not only in therapy but in every canvas, poem, and tale.

Clinical Symbolism

In clinical practice, symbols emerge spontaneously. Dreams, fantasies, narratives, and creative expressions are not random but coded evidence of confrontation. They reveal which developmental threshold is active, whether it is resolving, distorting, or mimicking false resolution.

Stage 1 – Grounding and Ignition

- Igniter (Exploratory): clients dream of fire, flight, or explosions. These images signal restlessness, scattered energy, or the push outward into the world.
- Adaptor (Regulatory): clients dream of wombs, caves, or enclosed rooms. These images symbolize the need for containment, safety, and regulated boundaries.
- Distortion markers: fire that consumes uncontrollably (Igniter distortion), or caves that trap and suffocate (Adaptor distortion).

Stage 2 – Recognition and Boundary

- Mirror (Reflective): clients report fantasies of being unseen, invisible, or mirrored by others. These images reflect dependency and the need for recognition.
- Wall (Boundary): clients describe repetitive images of walls, fences, or locked doors. These symbolize attempts to assert identity through separation.
- Distortion markers: mirrors that shatter (Mirror collapse into identity fragmentation) or walls that imprison (Wall collapse into rigid isolation).

Stage 3 – Authenticity and Role

- Flame (Authenticity): clients paint or dream of erupting volcanoes, suns, or hearts. These symbols embody passion and raw identity expression.

- Mask (Role): clients report fantasies of costumes, uniforms, or crowns. These symbolize performance and structured roles.

- Distortion markers: flames that burn out (Flame distortion → volatility, burnout), or masks that cannot be removed (Mask distortion → hollow identity, narcissistic fragility).

Stage 4 – Mortality and Legacy

- Seer (Clarity): recurring eyes, stars, or prophetic figures in dreams. These reflect insight, wisdom, and the confrontation with truth.

- Wound (Continuity): images of scars, bloodlines, or seeds. These symbolize sacrifice, continuity, and symbolic survival.

- Distortion markers: eyes that go blind (Seer distortion → nihilism, detachment) or wounds that never heal (Wound distortion → despair, compulsive legacy).

Clinical Directive

Symbols in therapy must be interpreted not as isolated images but as constitutional markers of confrontation.

- They reveal the active stage.
- They show whether orientation is resolving or distorting.
- They guide intervention by pointing to the client's lived confrontation.

Symbols are therefore not decorative in clinical practice. They are diagnostic fingerprints of the psyche in confrontation.

The Constitutional Function of Symbolism

Symbolism is not a side-effect of confrontation; it is its constitutional proof. The universality of symbols across individuals and cultures testifies that the same developmental thresholds are confronted by all human beings.

Individual Validation

- In therapy, symbols arise unprompted in dreams, fantasies, and narratives.
- The recurrence of archetypes tied to each orientation (Igniter fire, Adaptor womb, Mirror reflection, Wall threshold, Flame eruption, Mask costume, Seer vision, Wound sacrifice) demonstrates that confrontation leaves symbolic residue in every psyche.
- These residues act as diagnostic markers: the therapist can identify the stage of confrontation by attending to symbols.

Collective Validation

- Across history, cultures have created myths, rituals, and art that recycle the same archetypes.
- Whether in Mesopotamian creation myths, Egyptian funerary rites, Greek tragedies, or modern novels, the same symbolic structures recur.
- This recurrence is not coincidence but evidence of universal developmental confrontations.

Scientific Integration

- Neuroscience shows that symbols condense overwhelming experiences into manageable representations (limbic encoding of trauma and memory).
- Anthropology confirms that rituals stabilize societies by externalizing thresholds in symbolic form.
- Depth psychology (Freud's dream theory, Jung's archetypes, Lacan's symbolic register) anticipated this law but never fully linked it to developmental confrontations. *DCΨ* completes this link.

The Constitutional Law of Symbolism

1. Symbols are universal residues of confrontation.
2. They manifest in both individual psyches and collective cultures.
3. They provide evidence that *DCΨ* confrontations are not abstract but lived realities.

Thus, symbolism serves as constitutional proof that development is confrontation-driven. Wherever humans exist, symbols testify to the thresholds of grounding, relation, identity, and mortality.

Closing

The law is affirmed: symbolism is the living evidence of confrontation. It appears in dreams, myths, rituals, art, and culture, ensuring that the psyche's struggles are never hidden but always encoded in symbols.

Having established the core mechanism of development and its key outcomes in leadership and symbolism, the constitution now turns inward to the framework itself. The final laws are meta-principles: they dictate how this system of Developmental Confrontation Psychology must be structured, applied, and protected to ensure its integrity as a unified school of thought. These are the rules for the rules, the constitutional guarantees that prevent the theory from distortion or reduction.

Law 6: Integration of DCT with the Broader DCΨ Framework

The Spine of DCΨ

The sixth constitutional law affirms that *Developmental Confrontation Theory (DCT)* is the structural spine of the entire school of *Developmental Confrontational Psychology (DCΨ)*. Every diagnostic tool, every therapeutic method, and every symbolic analysis derives coherence from this framework. Without *DCT*, the school would fragment into isolated techniques. With *DCT*, the school operates as a unified system.

DCT as Constitutional Backbone

- Foundation: *DCT* defines the four confrontational thresholds (Self vs. World, Self vs. Other, Emotional Identity, Mortality & Wisdom).
- Orientation: Each stage contains two orientations (Igniter/Adaptor, Mirror/Wall, Flame/Mask, Seer/Wound), both capable of resolution or distortion.
- Law: Resolution stabilizes; distortion destabilizes; false resolution mimics stability but collapses under stress.
- This constitution governs the rest of *DCΨ* — diagnosis, therapy, and symbolic interpretation.

Why No Tool Operates Without It

- Scanner: The *Stage Resolution Index (SRI)*, *Typology Test (DCPTT)*, and *Projective Test (SDCPT)* are designed directly from *DCT* principles. They measure confrontation, not symptoms.

- Atlas: The *Diagnostic Atlas* interprets disorders as distortions of stage-orientation confrontations.

- Therapy: *Developmental Resolution Therapy* (*DRT*) and its methods (*ART, BRT, XRT*) intervene by realigning clients with confrontations, not by suppressing symptoms.

- Fingerprint: The *Psychological Fingerprint* traces how a unique person navigates these confrontations dynamically across life.

Without *DCT*, each of these tools would lose meaning. With *DCT*, they form a system of measurement, analysis, and transformation.

The Constitutional Law

- *DCT* is not one theory among others but the spinal axis of *DCΨ*.
- Just as a body cannot stand without a spine, the school cannot function without *DCT*.
- This integration ensures unity across diagnostics, therapies, and cultural applications.

Integration with the Scanner

The *DC Scanner* is the operational extension of *DCT.* It translates the constitutional principles of confrontation into measurable form. The scanner consists of two batteries (A and B), each containing three instruments:

- *SRI*-I and II (*Stage Resolution Index*): measure the degree of resolution, distortion, or stagnation across stages.
- *DCPTT* (*Developmental Confrontation Personality Typology Test*): identifies dominant traits in each stage and their symbolic leader variants.
- *SDCPT*-I and II (*Symbolic Developmental Confrontational Projective Test*): explores unconscious symbolic residues through projective tasks.

DCT as the Scanner's Blueprint

- Stage structure: Each scanner item maps directly to the four confrontations. Without *DCT's* stage map, the scanner could not exist.
- Dual orientations: Each question or projection is designed to differentiate between orientations (Igniter vs. Adaptor, Mirror vs. Wall, Flame vs. Mask, Seer vs. Wound).
- Resolution vs. distortion: The scanner does not simply "score traits." It measures whether orientations are resolving authentically, distorting, or mimicking false resolution.

Battery A – Initial Confrontation Profile

- *SRI*-I: assesses the current balance of resolution and distortion at each stage.
- *DCPTT*: identifies symbolic type across stages, creating a preliminary psychological fingerprint.
- *SDCPT*-I: explores unconscious symbolic imagery (dream-like projections, metaphors).

Battery A provides the first layer of scanning, diagnostic orientation.

Battery B – Depth and Cross-Validation

- *SRI*-II: revisits stages under different contextual frames, validating the stability of initial scores.
- *DCPTT* (revised): re-measures symbolic type under shifting conditions, exposing false resolutions.
- *SDCPT*-II: deepens symbolic analysis, revealing unconscious material hidden in the first pass.

Battery B ensures depth, correction, and cross-validation.

Constitutional Integration

The scanner demonstrates the systemic role of *DCT*:

- Without *DCT*, the scanner is just a collection of tests.
- With *DCT*, the scanner is a unified diagnostic engine — a constitutional "MRI of the psyche."

Integration with the Diagnostic Atlas

The *DCΨ Diagnostic Atlas* is the clinical library of distortions. Where the scanner measures confrontation dynamically, the *Atlas* organizes recurring patterns into structured diagnostic profiles. Its constitutional foundation is *DCT*: all disorders are interpreted as distortions of stage-orientation confrontations.

The Atlas as Clinical Map

- Stage 1 distortions (Self vs. World):
  - **A** Exploratory (Igniter) distortion → scattered engagement, impulsivity, ADHD-like instability.
  - **B** Regulatory (Adaptor) distortion → rigid avoidance, agoraphobia, obsessive control.
- Stage 2 distortions (Self vs. Other):
  - **A** Reflective (Mirror) distortion → dependency, identity collapse, borderline fragility.
  - **B** Boundary (Wall) distortion → detachment, hostility, antisocial or paranoid traits.
- Stage 3 distortions (Emotional Identity):
  - **A** Authenticity (Flame) distortion → volatility, burnout, histrionic overexpression.
  - **B** Role (Mask) distortion → hollow performance, narcissistic fragility, identity diffusion.
- Stage 4 distortions (Mortality & Wisdom):
  - **A** Clarity (Seer) distortion → nihilistic withdrawal, schizoid detachment, existential despair.
  - **B** Continuity (Wound) distortion → compulsive legacy-building, midlife crisis, despair-driven productivity.

Clinical Anchoring

The Atlas does not add "new" disorders; it reframes existing clinical phenomena:

- Borderline Personality Disorder (BPD): Stage 2 Mirror distortion with collapsed Wall.
- Obsessive-Compulsive Personality Disorder (OCPD): Stage 1 Adaptor distortion (rigid control of world).
- Narcissistic Personality Disorder (NPD): Stage 3 Mask distortion, with Flame suppressed.
- Depersonalization/Derealization: collapse across Stage 1 and 4 — fractured Igniter and Seer.

This reframing aligns classical diagnostic language (DSM/ICD) with confrontation law.

The Atlas and the Scanner

- The *scanner* detects confrontation status dynamically in a client.
- The *Atlas* provides the stable clinical pattern that emerges when distortions repeat and solidify.

Together, they allow therapists to see both living dynamics (*scanner*) and established pathologies (*Atlas*).

Constitutional Function

The Atlas proves the clinical validity of *DCT* by showing that every known disorder is not random but a predictable distortion of confrontation.
This transforms diagnosis from labeling to structural understanding.

Integration with Therapy (DRT, ART, BRT, XRT)

Therapy within *DCΨ* is structured by *Developmental Resolution Therapy (DRT)*. *DRT* is not one method but a constitutional framework that tailors intervention to the active confrontation. Its sub-methods — *Analytical Resolution Therapy (ART)*, *Behavioral Resolution Therapy (BRT)*, and *Experiential Resolution Therapy (XRT)* — are applications of the same law.

DRT as Constitutional Framework

- Directive: to guide clients into direct engagement with unresolved confrontations.
- Principle: therapy does not suppress symptoms; it restores confrontation as the site of growth.
- Structure: *DRT* assesses confrontation stage, orientation (Igniter, Adaptor, Mirror, Wall, Flame, Mask, Seer, Wound), and resolution status (resolved, distorted, stagnating, false resolution).

ART – Analytical Resolution Therapy

- Focus: cognitive and symbolic analysis.
- Task: identify distortions in thought patterns and symbolic narratives.
- Example: A client with Mask distortion (narcissistic façade) explores the difference between role performance and authentic emotional grounding. *ART* exposes false resolution and restores depth.

BRT – Behavioral Resolution Therapy

- Focus: behavioral confrontation of thresholds.
- Task: train relational, boundary, or self-regulation skills.
- Example: A client with Wall distortion (rigid detachment) practices graded intimacy and safe vulnerability. Resolution arises by rebuilding flexible boundaries.

XRT – Experiential Resolution Therapy

- Focus: direct lived confrontation through role-play, guided imagery, or symbolic enactment.
- Task: re-immerse the client in the confrontation they avoided.
- Example: A client with Igniter distortion (scattered impulsivity) undergoes guided confrontation of "taking the first step" in a safe frame, transforming chaos into anchored exploration.

Clinical Integration

- *ART* = thinking the confrontation.
- *BRT* = doing the confrontation.
- *XRT* = living the confrontation.

Together under *DRT*, these methods ensure therapy is tailored to the stage and orientation, preventing bias toward one orientation as "healthier."

Constitutional Directive for Therapy

The therapeutic law is clear:

- Resolution emerges only by re-entering confrontation.
- *DRT* ensures confrontation is entered with analysis, behavior, or experience, depending on the client's dominant mode.
- All therapy in *DCΨ* flows from this law.

Integration with the Psychological Fingerprint

The psychological fingerprint is the living application of *DCT* at the individual level. While the scanner measures confrontation status and the Atlas organizes distortions, the fingerprint traces the dynamic way a person navigates the four confrontations across life.

Defining the Psychological Fingerprint

- Each person carries a unique developmental signature.
- It is composed of:
    1. Which orientations dominate (e.g., Igniter vs. Adaptor).
    2. How resolution, distortion, stagnation, or false resolution appear in those orientations.
    3. How the individual shifts between stages across different contexts.
- The fingerprint is dynamic, not static: it changes as confrontations are resolved or distorted over time.

How DCT Generates the Fingerprint

- Stage 1 (Self vs. World): does the person anchor themselves through Igniter exploration or Adaptor regulation?
- Stage 2 (Self vs. Other): is identity stabilized by Mirror recognition or Wall distinction?
- Stage 3 (Emotional Identity): does the person lead with Flame authenticity or Mask role-integration?
- Stage 4 (Mortality & Wisdom): do they face mortality through Seer clarity or Wound continuity?

DCT supplies the blueprint: the fingerprint is the real-world expression of this map.

Clinical Anchors

- A client may test as a Flame-Mirror type, authenticity-driven but dependent on recognition. Therapy must therefore strengthen both authenticity and self-consolidation.
- Another may test as a Wall-Seer type, boundary-strong and insight-rich, but vulnerable to isolation. Therapy must open relational permeability while preserving wisdom.

These fingerprints allow precise therapeutic tailoring.

Broader Applications

- Education: teaching styles can be adapted to fingerprints, nurturing exploration vs. regulation, recognition vs. distinction.
- Industry: leadership development programs can identify authentic vs. distorted leadership tendencies.
- Culture: collective fingerprints reveal how societies confront or avoid thresholds (e.g., cultures obsessed with youth → unresolved Stage 4).

Constitutional Function

The fingerprint proves that *DCT* does not remain theoretical. It becomes visible in:

- Diagnostics (scanner data).
- Clinical profiles (Atlas distortions).
- Personal navigation (fingerprint patterns).

Thus, the constitutional law is affirmed: every individual carries a psychological fingerprint that reflects their navigation of confrontation, and this fingerprint is the living signature of DCT in action.

Broader Integration: Cultural, Industrial, and Educational Psychology

The final dimension of integration shows that *DCT* is not limited to therapy or diagnosis. Because confrontation is universal, its laws extend into culture, education, and industry. Each domain reveals how the same constitutional principles of *DCT* operate collectively as well as individually.

Cultural Integration

- Art and Myth: As established in Law 5, cultural creativity externalizes confrontation in symbols. *DCT* allows these symbols to be read as markers of societal stage engagement or avoidance.
- Collective distortions: Entire societies can stagnate in one orientation (e.g., consumer cultures trapped in Mask performance, or traditionalist cultures hardened into Wall rigidity).
- Collective resolution: Movements that integrate confrontation (e.g., civil rights struggles as Mirror + Flame resolution) show how culture advances through the same thresholds as individuals.

Industrial Integration

- Organizational psychology: Leadership structures mirror *DCT* principles. Companies dominated by distorted Walls produce rigid hierarchies; those overrun by distorted Mirrors collapse into instability.
- Workplace training: *DCT*-guided interventions train staff not in generic "skills" but in confronting developmental thresholds — boundary-setting, authentic expression, mortality-awareness in leadership succession.
- Industrial therapy: Burnout epidemics can be reframed as Stage 3 Flame distortions; corporate rigidity as Stage 1 Adaptor distortions.

Educational Integration

- Developmental teaching: Curricula can be aligned with stages:

  I Stage 1 → grounding and exploration (play, safety, environment).
  II Stage 2 → relational education (collaboration, empathy, boundary respect).
  III Stage 3 → identity and creativity (authentic projects, role-taking, artistic expression).
  IV Stage 4 → mortality and wisdom (history, philosophy, ethics).

- Diagnosis in schools: The scanner can detect unresolved thresholds early, preventing distortions from solidifying into adult pathology.

- Teacher as leader: Educators embody developmental leadership: containing anxiety (Stage 1), modeling boundaries (Stage 2), inspiring authenticity (Stage 3), and transmitting wisdom (Stage 4).

Constitutional Directive of Broader Integration

- *DCT* is not confined to therapy; it is a general psychology of confrontation.
- Wherever humans organize, learn, or create, *DCT* principles reveal themselves.
- This law ensures that *DCΨ* is not only a clinical school but also a cultural and societal framework.

Closing

The law is affirmed: *DCT* is the spine of *DCΨ*, integrating scanner, atlas, therapy, fingerprint, and broader domains. Through this integration, the school operates not as a collection of methods but as a unified constitutional system of human development.

Law 7: Constitutional Guarantees

The constitution of *Developmental Confrontational Psychology* includes protective guarantees. These ensure that the framework resists misuse, reductionism, or distortion, preserving its integrity as a living school.

Guarantee Against Bias

- *DCΨ* rejects privileging one orientation as "healthy" and another as "pathological."
- Both orientations at every stage (Igniter/Adaptor, Mirror/Wall, Flame/Mask, Seer/Wound) carry equal potential for resolution or distortion.
- This guarantee prevents the bias that has plagued psychology, where certain traits were historically pathologized due to cultural prejudice.

Guarantee Against Reductionism

- *DCΨ* refuses to collapse human development into single causes such as drives (Freud), reinforcement schedules (Skinner), or cognitive schemas (Beck).
- Instead, it safeguards complexity by framing development as confrontation: a structured but dynamic process that integrates biology, psychology, and culture.
- This ensures that no single discipline (e.g., neuroscience, behaviorism) can claim monopoly on explanation.

Guarantee Against False Resolution

- *DCΨ* identifies false resolution as a defensive mimic of stability, when orientations appear resolved but confrontation was avoided.
- The constitution guarantees that therapy and research must differentiate between authentic resolution and defensive pseudo-adaptation.
- This protects clients from being misdiagnosed as "healthy" when their adaptation masks deeper distortion.

Guarantee of Therapeutic Integrity

- Therapy in *DCΨ* (via *DRT*, *ART*, *BRT*, *XRT*) must never bypass confrontation.
- Symptom suppression without engagement of the threshold is deemed unconstitutional within this framework.
- This ensures therapy is transformative, not cosmetic.

Guarantee of Cultural Validity

- *DCΨ* recognizes that confrontation is universal, but its symbols vary across cultures.
- The constitution guarantees respect for cultural expressions of confrontation, ensuring that no culture is dismissed for encoding thresholds differently.
- This prevents ethnocentric bias in research and practice.

The Constitutional Guarantees

By enshrining these protections, the *DCΨ* constitution ensures that:

- Orientations are never pathologized in themselves.
- Human development is never reduced to a single explanatory axis.
- False resolution is exposed rather than accepted.
- Therapy remains anchored in confrontation.
- Cultural variations are respected within universal structure.

Clinical Applications of Guarantees

The guarantees are not abstract protections. They must be enacted in practice, ensuring that *DCΨ* research and therapy remain constitutionally valid.

1 **Against Bias in Practice:**

   * Therapists must assess both orientations at every stage, resisting cultural or personal preference for one style.
   - Example: A society may value Wall (rigid boundaries) and dismiss Mirror (recognition) as weakness. The guarantee prevents such bias, affirming that both can resolve or distort.

2 **Against Reductionism in Research:**

   * Clinical studies under *DCΨ* must track confrontation across multiple levels (biological, psychological, symbolic).
   - Example: Anxiety cannot be reduced solely to neurotransmitter imbalance. It must be mapped as confrontation (Stage 1 unresolved grounding) while also acknowledging biological correlates.

3 **Against False Resolution in Diagnosis:**

   * Diagnostic tools (*Scanner*, *Atlas*) must differentiate between authentic stability and defensive mimicry.
   - Example: A client who appears calm due to rigid avoidance (Adaptor distortion) cannot be coded as "resolved."

Educational and Institutional Applications

The guarantees extend beyond therapy into education, industry, and society.

- Education: Curricula must respect developmental thresholds. Forcing premature role adoption (Mask) or suppressing passion (Flame) violates the guarantee against bias.
- Industry: Leadership programs must identify distorted authority (false Walls, hollow Masks) instead of promoting them as "strong management."
- Cultural Studies: Anthropologists using DCΨ must interpret symbolic differences without treating one culture's resolution as superior.

Guarantee of Future Adaptability

- *DCΨ* law forbids freezing interpretations in one historical or cultural frame.
- The constitution guarantees adaptability: as new scientific evidence (e.g., neuroscience, AI psychology, genetic studies) emerges, confrontation principles must dialogue with them.
- This keeps *DCΨ* scientific without reducing it to biology or technology.

Closing

The guarantees function as a constitution within the constitution. They protect *DCΨ* from bias, reduction, false resolution, therapeutic bypass, and cultural dismissal. They also secure adaptability for future science and culture.

Law 8: The Living Constitution

Law of Dynamism

Confrontation is dynamic by nature. Development is never a fixed path but a process of destabilization and reorganization. Every confrontation can echo forward (unresolved Stage 1 destabilizing adulthood) and heal backward (resolving Stage 4 can repair earlier distortions).

- Dynamic thresholds: Unlike linear stage theories (Freud's drives, Piaget's cognition, Erikson's crises), *DCΨ* declares that thresholds reverberate across life. A confrontation left unresolved resurfaces in disguised forms until engaged.

- Living law parallel: Like political constitutions, which survive centuries through reinterpretation, *DCΨ's* constitution is not frozen. Its structure is stable, but its meaning adapts to new evidence, cultures, and contexts.

- Guardrail: Stability of law + openness of interpretation. The confrontational map does not change, but how its symbols and clinical practices manifest will evolve with science and culture.

Law of Cultural Renewal

Symbols are culturally variable but structurally universal. Each stage produces symbolic residues (womb, wall, flame, mask, seer, wound), yet cultures embody them differently.

I Variability of expression:

- Mesopotamia → womb and seed myths (Stage 1 and 4).
- Egypt → funerary rituals encoding Wound continuity.
- Greece → mirrors and masks in drama (Stage 2, Stage 3).
- Modern digital culture → avatars (Mask), viral flame memes (Flame), AI doubles (Seer).

II Contemporary renewal: New cultural symbols (e.g., AI as prophetic double, social media as distorted Mirror, online boundaries as digital Walls) extend the confrontation into modern forms.

III Guarantee: *DCΨ* affirms universality of confrontation while guaranteeing flexibility in cultural form. No society can be dismissed as "less developed" because their symbolic language differs.

Law of Scientific Dialogue

The constitution of *DCΨ* affirms that its framework must remain in dialogue with science. Confrontation is not a metaphor but a developmental law that must withstand empirical testing and theoretical debate.

I Dialogue with classical psychology:

- Freud identified unconscious drives but reduced conflict to sexuality and repression.
- Erikson mapped psychosocial crises but froze them in age-linked stages.
- Piaget explained cognition but overlooked existential thresholds.
- Jung described archetypes but did not connect them to structured confrontation.

DCΨ acknowledges these contributions while positioning itself as the unifying successor — confrontation as the root law underlying them all.

II Dialogue with neuroscience and trauma studies:

- Research on trauma shows the brain re-encodes overwhelming events in limbic symbols, echoing across life.
- Neuroimaging reveals memory reconsolidation as a "reconfrontation" mechanism, validating backward healing.
- Genetic and epigenetic studies show how stress responses shape thresholds of regulation (Stage 1 Adaptor distortions, Stage 2 attachment failures).

DCΨ integrates these findings, affirming that confrontation is not abstract but biologically and neurologically traceable.

III Interdisciplinary integration:

- Anthropology confirms myths and rituals externalize confrontation.
- Sociology shows collective distortions (e.g., consumerism as Stage 3 Mask inflation).
- Philosophy engages existential thresholds (Stage 4 mortality).

The constitution demands dialogue across fields, securing scientific openness while preventing reductionism.

Law of Clinical Evolution

Therapy is not static; it evolves. *DCΨ* guarantees that new techniques can emerge as long as they obey the constitutional directive: resolution requires direct engagement with confrontation.

I *DRT* as framework: Developmental Resolution Therapy is the core structure, within which methods (*ART*, *BRT*, *XRT*) adapt to client needs. New methods can be added if they remain faithful to confrontation law.

II Practical innovations:

- Digital role-play tools for safe re-entry into relational thresholds.
- AI-assisted projective tests simulating symbolic imagery.
- Cultural adaptations, such as integrating indigenous rituals as experiential confrontations (*XRT*) when clinically valid.

III Guardrail of validity: Any method that bypasses confrontation (e.g., symptom suppression without threshold engagement) is unconstitutional. Clinical innovation is welcomed, but only if it brings clients back into the developmental law of confrontation.

Constitutional Closing Declaration

The constitution of *Developmental Confrontational Psychology (DCΨ)* concludes with its own living affirmation: it is a system both stable in law and open in growth.

Recap of Constitutional Spine (Laws 1–8)

- Law 1: Development requires confrontation.
- Law 2: Each stage holds two orientations, both capable of resolution or distortion.
- Law 3: Development is sequential yet non-linear, echoing forward and healing backward.
- Law 4: Leadership emerges from confrontation.
- Law 5: Symbolism is the evidence of confrontation.
- Law 6: Integration of *DCT* with the broader *DCΨ* framework.
- Law 7: Constitutional guarantees against bias, reductionism, false resolution, and cultural dismissal.
- Law 8: The constitution is a living framework, adaptable to culture and science.

Together, these laws establish a structure that is comprehensive and protective.

Affirmation of Adaptability Without Relativism

- The laws are fixed: confrontation is universal, the stages are structural, the orientations are dual.
- But interpretations evolve: symbols shift, therapeutic methods adapt, cultural expressions renew themselves.
- This adaptability does not dissolve structure into relativism; instead, it ensures the constitution remains relevant in every era.

Closing Declaration

DCΨ affirms itself as a living constitution:

- Universal in its developmental structure.
- Protective in its guarantees.
- Dynamic in its openness to culture and science.

The constitution ends not with finality but with invitation: to researchers, therapists, educators, and cultures to test, refine, and expand its application. As long as confrontation remains the driver of development, the constitution remains alive.

Ending – Chapter 3

The Constitution of Developmental Confrontation Theory

At the beginning of this chapter, I framed the laws as the backbone of the school, principles meant to guide rather than decorate. Having unfolded them, we can now see how they work together: each law not only describes development, but protects the integrity of the entire framework. They keep *DCΨ* coherent, testable, and alive.

What began as a question — can confrontation itself serve as the universal measure of growth? — now stands as a constitution. The answer is not only yes, but also that without confrontation, there is no development to measure at all.

From here, the path turns toward detail: the stages themselves, where these laws no longer remain abstract but take form in lived human experience. The laws provide order; the stages will show the movement.

Title	Category
Development Requires Confrontation	Foundational
Every Stage Holds Two Orientations	Foundational
Development is Sequential but Non-Linear	Foundational
Leadership Emerges from Confrontation	Outcome
Symbolism as Evidence of Confrontation	Outcome
Integration of DCT with DCΨ Framework	Framework
Constitutional Guarantees	Framework
The Living Constitution	Framework

A Guide to the Constitution in Practice

The laws of *DCΨ* are not merely descriptive; they are directives for action.

For the Therapist: Your role is redefined. You are a facilitator of safe confrontation, not a symptom-remover. Diagnose through the lens of stage-specific distortions. Your goal is to help clients re-enter and resolve the confrontations they avoided.

For the Researcher: This framework generates testable hypotheses. Does the Stage Resolution Index (*SRI*) predict resilience? Do brain scans show reorganization during successful *DRT* interventions? The constitution demands dialogue with neuroscience and rigorous validation.

For the Individual: This is a map for understanding your life. Your struggles are not random failures but signposts pointing to unresolved developmental thresholds. Growth lies not in avoiding these struggles, but in understanding and facing them.

DCΨ

Chapter 4

THE UNBORN FAMILIAR

THE EMBODIMENT OF THE WOMB

Philosophical Foundations

1) Scope and Aim

This chapter introduces the unborn familiar: a *DCΨ* construct describing the adult's symbolic return to the womb template under conditions of destabilization. In *DCΨ*, such movement is not regression but a progression to earlier confrontations, re-engaged with the competencies, memory, and identity architecture of the present self. The aim here is to articulate the philosophical, theoretical, and clinical grounds for this stance, distinguishing *DCΨ* from models that interpret such returns as loss of function. The unborn familiar will be treated as (a) a structural template originating in prenatal containment, (b) a universal symbolic resource available across the lifespan, and (c) a diagnostic lens that helps clinicians separate stabilizing revisits from developmental stagnation (to be elaborated later in the chapter).

This foundation establishes the conceptual discipline needed for the remainder of Chapter 4: we must specify what the unborn familiar is, what it does, and what it is not. In particular, we will (i) define the principle of "progression to earlier confrontations," (ii) situate the womb as a pre-structural ground for later confrontations in *DCT*, and (iii) contrast *DCΨ's* view with major psychoanalytic and symbolic frameworks without repeating their apparatus or adopting their pathologizing assumptions.

2) First Principles (Developmental Propositions)

Proposition 1 — Non-erasure:

Human development in *DCΨ* is cumulative and non-erasing. Later stages never nullify earlier ones. Each confrontation—if resolved—becomes part of the structural repertoire; if distorted, it remains as a persistent fault line. Therefore, all earlier templates remain addressable and usable by the adult psyche.

Proposition 2 — Progression to Earlier Confrontations:

When adults re-activate earlier templates (e.g., the womb), they progress into those templates with the full cognitive, emotional, and symbolic capacities afforded by later development. This is not a reversion to infantile functioning; it is a revisit conducted by a later, more complex self.

Proposition 3 — Symbolic Mediation:

Revisits occur symbolically. Adults cannot literally re-enter the womb; they approximate its conditions (protection, filtration, rhythmic safety, suspension of responsibility) through behaviors, environments, and meanings that mimic prenatal containment.

Proposition 4 — Confrontational Continuity:

The unborn familiar is continuous with *DCT's* staged confrontations. It sits "under" Stage 1 as the pre-confrontational ground: a living memory of global containment that later colors how Stage 1 (Self vs. World) is met (Igniter vs. Adaptor), then how Stage 2 (Wall vs. Mirror) is organized, and so on.

These propositions maintain theoretical coherence: the unborn familiar is neither nostalgia nor regression; it is a structural resource (and, if overused, a structural risk) inherent in how development is organized in *DCΨ*.

Operationally, Stage 1 begins here — in utero — and continues after birth. The womb is therefore not a separate stage, but the prenatal threshold of Stage 1.

3) Progression vs. Regression: The Formal Distinction

Regression (classical sense) implies a loss: capacities collapse, defenses revert, ego strength diminishes. In such a view, adult behaviors that resemble early dependency or extreme avoidance are read as symptomatic failures.

Progression to earlier confrontations (*DCΨ*) reframes the same surface phenomenon as a strategic revisit: the adult, under pressure, re-activates the earliest template of safety to restore homeostatic stability before re-engaging current demands. Crucially, the adult brings forward later-stage resources—language, abstraction, self-reflection, ethical reasoning—when engaging the earlier template. The functional question in *DCΨ* is not "Has the adult become infantile?" but "How is the earlier template being used?" If it is a temporary stabilizer in service of renewed engagement, it is adaptive progression; if it becomes a standing substitute for engagement, it is stagnation (clinical differentiation developed later in the chapter).

This distinction prevents two common errors:

- Over-pathologizing normal stabilizing revisits (mislabeling them as childish).
- Romanticizing protective returns (mistaking suspension for resolution).

4) The Womb as First-Order Template (Pre-structural Ground)

In *DCΨ*, the womb is not counted as a "stage," because it precedes the first explicit confrontation. Instead, it is the pre-structural ground out of which the stages arise. Four features matter:

1. Total Protection (Filtration of Threat):
   The maternal body filters the external world. Risk does not reach the fetus directly. This sets an ideal of mediated safety that later becomes a symbolic benchmark for what "safe enough" feels like.

2. Absolute Containment (Boundary Without Breach):
   The fetus is enclosed. This absolute boundary creates the primordial sense of inside-ness. Later, "inside" and "outside" become psychological categories; the craving for enclosure traces back to this archetypal containment.

3. Continuous Connection (Unbroken Provision and Rhythm):
   The umbilical connection and maternal rhythms (heartbeat, motion) provide constancy. Later, any environment that reproduces predictable, steady rhythms (auditory, tactile, temporal) will echo that prenatal constancy and be read by the organism as safe.

4. Suspension of Responsibility (No Decision Burden):
   The fetus does not choose. Agency is not demanded. While the fetus responds to stimuli and exhibits early forms of agency, it is not burdened with the conscious choice-making and survival decisions of postnatal life. This does not make the fetus "passive" in a pathological sense; it simply means that the organism's energetic budget is allocated to growth and differentiation rather than to decision-costs. Later "suspension" (rituals, retreats, simplified routines) often functions as a temporary restoration of this economy, to be followed by re-engagement.

Why this matters for DCT:

- Stage 1 (Self vs. World | Igniter vs. Adaptor): the earliest negotiations with resistance are colored by remembered ideals of filtered safety and containment. When the world feels excessively porous or overwhelming, the adult may revisit the womb template to recalibrate.

- Stage 2 (Self vs. Other | Wall vs. Mirror): the dual reality of the womb—boundary + connection—becomes the pre-image of later boundary and reflection dynamics.

- Stage 3 (Emotional Identity | Flame vs. Mask): the suspension of performance in prenatal life contrasts with later pressures to perform. The unborn familiar thus becomes a touchstone for non-performing authenticity.

- Stage 4 (Mortality & Wisdom | Seer vs. Wound): the pre-mortal phenomenology of fetal existence (a time before death is conceptualized) shapes how adults later hold, symbolize, and metabolize finitude.

These links are not speculative metaphors in *DCΨ*; they are organizing relations that explain why the womb template remains practically available to adult psychology.

5) Comparative Positioning (Without Adopting Pathology-First Frames)

To clarify *DCΨ's* contribution, it helps to contrast (not collapse into) three major traditions:

Freud (Fixation/Regression):

Freud's framework is invaluable for naming return phenomena, but it encodes a deficit bias—returns imply loss. *DCΨ* retains the observation (returns occur) and rejects the default pathologizing: returns can be adaptive revisits if they serve renewed engagement. The interpretive question becomes teleological (what is the return for?) rather than moral (is the return childish?).

Jung (Archetypes/Great Mother):

Jung rightly identifies the womb as a universal image—Great Mother, cosmic egg, rebirth. *DCΨ* agrees but adds developmental specificity: the womb is an operational template embedded in the lifelong confrontational map. It is not only an image; it is a usable structure that adults recruit under stress.

Lacan (Mirror Stage/Imaginary):

Lacan locates identity formation via recognition in the mirror, a Stage 2 concern in *DCT* terms (Wall/Mirror). *DCΨ* points out that the womb precedes recognition. Before the self sees itself seen, it exists-contained. The unborn familiar is thus pre-mirror; it is the "ground" on which mirroring will later stand, and to which the organism can temporarily return.

This comparative positioning keeps *DCΨ* non-derivative: it integrates observations from classical schools but refuses their necessary conclusions when those conflict with *DCΨ's* non-erasure, progression-based model.

6) Clinical Rationale for Non-Pathologizing Returns

Clinically, *DCΨ* cautions against labeling all womb-like behaviors as regressive. A temporary symbolic return can be (a) a homeostatic maneuver to reduce physiological and affective overload, (b) a cognitive narrowing that limits decision-costs during acute stress, and (c) a meaning-restoration ritual that stabilizes identity before re-entry into confrontation. In plain terms: sometimes the adult needs a bounded, filtered, rhythmic, decision-light interval to prevent structural unraveling. That interval can be therapeutically leveraged rather than condemned—provided it is explicitly time-bound and goal-linked to later re-engagement. (The clinical differentiation between stabilizing revisit and stagnation is developed later in Chapter 4; here we establish why a revisit can be justified.)

This stance changes case formulation: instead of treating a client's desire for enclosure, filtration, or purity as evidence of childishness, we explore function, duration, and directionality. If the return is functionally restorative, temporally delimited, and oriented toward confronting what is avoided, it fits *DCΨ's* progression logic. If it expands to replace confrontation, it risks stagnation.

7) Methodological Implications for DCΨ (Language, Assessment, Case Formulation)

Language Discipline:

Use terms that reflect structure, not moral judgment. Recommended cluster: "symbolic revisit," "template," "containment," "filtration," "rhythmic safety," "decision-light interval." Avoid language that presumes collapse or childishness unless criteria for stagnation are clearly met.

Assessment:

When the unborn familiar is suspected, gather data along four axes aligned with the template:

- Protection/Filtration: What threats are being filtered? How? By whom/what?
- Containment: What boundaries (sensory, social, temporal) are being introduced?
- Rhythmicity: What routines, cadences, or environmental constancies are being used?
- Responsibility-Load: How are choices reduced or outsourced, and for how long?

Case Formulation:

Anchor the revisit to a named confrontation in *DCT* (e.g., Stage 1 overwhelm, Stage 2 collapse of boundaries, Stage 3 performance fatigue, Stage 4 mortality anxiety). State explicitly how the revisit is supposed to support re-engagement with that confrontation. Identify exit criteria in advance to prevent drift into stagnation.

Ethical Stance:

The unborn familiar is value-neutral in itself; its ethical status derives from how it is used. Clinicians should neither glorify suspension (confusing comfort with cure) nor denigrate it (confusing austerity with growth). The telos is renewed confrontation, not permanent enclosure.

8) What the Unborn Familiar Is Not (Boundary Conditions)

- Not a license for avoidance: A revisit that displaces confrontation indefinitely is not aligned with *DCΨ's* progression model.
- Not a moralizing purity code: Symbolic filtration is about safety and recalibration, not virtue-signaling or superiority.
- Not a literal prenatal fantasy: *DCΨ* treats the womb as template, not as an object of re-enactment fetish.
- Not a stage replacement: The unborn familiar supports re-engagement with stages; it cannot perform the work of Stage 1–4 confrontations.

Setting these boundaries prevents conceptual drift and protects clinical practice from over-permissiveness on one side and punitive austerity on the other.

The Womb as Archetype and Template

1) Containment: The First Image of Safety

In *DCΨ*, containment is not metaphorical flourish but the most primal developmental reality. Before the child ever faces the world, the womb has already taught the organism what it means to be held within boundaries. The amniotic sac and maternal physiology function as absolute borders: nothing unmediated penetrates, and nothing escapes.

Biological dimension: Amniotic fluid cushions shock, regulates temperature, and provides buoyancy that equalizes external pressures. Maternal circulation filters nutrients and toxins, ensuring that the fetus experiences the world only through a controlled medium. Prenatal stress research shows that when this containment is compromised — for example, through elevated maternal cortisol — the fetal HPA (stress-response) system is permanently recalibrated. This is not merely biology but the laying down of a containment template that persists across life.

Psychological dimension: In later life, individuals unconsciously measure containment against this primordial template. When adults create therapy rooms, retreat spaces, or even social enclaves that promise "safety," they are symbolically attempting to reproduce this first experience of absolute enclosure. Disruptions in prenatal containment can predispose individuals to difficulties at Stage 1 (Self vs. World), manifesting as chronic hypervigilance, or at Stage 2 (Self vs. Other), where relational boundaries feel either too porous or too rigid.

Cultural dimension: Caves, domes, and sacred enclosures echo this archetypal containment. Myths of initiation often involve seclusion in dark spaces, mimicking the intrauterine container. The womb thus becomes not just an individual memory but a shared human archetype expressed symbolically across civilizations.

Clinical implication: Therapists must assess containment-seeking behaviors without dismissing them as avoidance. For some clients, enclosed spaces, weighted blankets, or restricted environments are not childish comforts but structural attempts to recreate the archetype of safety. The question is whether containment is being used to stabilize confrontation or to indefinitely delay it.

2) Connection: The Template of Dependability

Containment would be meaningless without connection. Through the umbilical cord, the fetus experiences uninterrupted supply — oxygen, nutrients, and hormonal signals. Existence is not solitary; it is tethered.

Biological dimension: Neuroscience confirms that this connection is rhythmic and constant. The fetus becomes attuned to the mother's heartbeat, respiratory cycles, and voice resonance. This continuous dialogue between bodies provides not only survival but the imprint of dependable connection.

Psychological dimension: Later attachment dynamics can be traced to this prenatal experience. Secure connection echoes the unbroken umbilical provision, while anxieties of abandonment may reflect an unconscious contrast with the primordial template of uninterrupted supply. Adults seek echoes of this prenatal connection in stable relationships, institutions, or even technologies that promise "always-on" access.

Cultural dimension: Religious metaphors of divine sustenance — "I am the bread of life," "sustained by the Spirit" — mirror the umbilical reality of being continuously supplied. Myths of gods nursing or feeding mortals symbolize this archetype of unbroken provision.

Clinical implication: Connection-seeking behaviors, whether in therapy or relationships, often replay this archetype. Dependency is not always pathology; it may be the psyche's way of revisiting the template of unbroken provision to repair disruptions. The therapeutic task is to distinguish adaptive revisits from stagnant dependency.

3) Rhythm: The Archetypal Metronome

The womb is not silent. It is structured by constant rhythm — heartbeat, breath, digestive cycles. The fetus lives immersed in patterns of predictability.

Biological dimension: Fetal studies reveal sensitivity to auditory input from mid-gestation. Heartbeat entrainment calibrates neural circuits for temporal expectation. The earliest nervous system learns to orient by rhythm.

Psychological dimension: This explains why rhythm is universally regulating. Infants are calmed by rocking or lullabies, adults by music, chanting, or meditative breathing. Under stress, people instinctively turn to repetitive patterns because rhythm is the primordial marker of safety.

Cultural dimension: Drumming in tribal rituals, chanting in monasteries, and swaying in prayer all echo the womb's rhythmic immersion. These are not inventions but cultural codifications of a shared prenatal memory.

Clinical implication: When clients seek rhythmic environments — whether through music, breathwork, or repetitive rituals — the therapist can interpret this as womb-mimicry. Used consciously, rhythm stabilizes identity; used unconsciously, it may become compulsion. The distinction lies in whether rhythm is a bridge back into confrontation or a substitute for it.

4) Suspension of Responsibility: Safety Without Demand

Perhaps the most radical feature of the womb is the absence of decision. After birth, even the infant must signal hunger or discomfort. In utero, life is sustained without negotiation. This is the one period of existence where being requires no choosing.

Biological dimension: The maternal system absorbs all responsibility — filtering danger, providing supply, modulating environment. The fetus devotes its full energy budget to growth, not survival decisions.

Psychological dimension: Adults recreate this archetype through structures that reduce or outsource responsibility: retreats where schedules are imposed, rituals where agency is surrendered, minimalist lifestyles where choice is eliminated. These are not mere trends but symbolic returns to the safety of demand-free existence.

Cultural dimension: Monastic vows of obedience, religious surrender to divine will, and communal rituals of fasting or seclusion all echo the womb's suspension of responsibility. They restore the sense of being carried rather than burdened.

Clinical implication: Therapists must assess whether suspension is being used to recalibrate identity or to indefinitely escape confrontation. When suspension becomes permanent, it shifts from progressive revisit to stagnation.

5) Integrative Perspectives: Bion, Winnicott, and Attachment

Psychoanalytic and developmental theories provide useful parallels. Bion's concept of containment and Winnicott's holding environment both describe the psychological need for structures that absorb anxiety. *DCΨ* reframes these not as inventions of early caregiving but as derivatives of the womb template. Similarly, attachment theory's emphasis on dependable connection can be enriched by recognizing the prenatal origin of connection-imprints. *DCΨ* thus situates classical insights within a broader developmental arc that begins before birth.

6) Mapping Across DCT Stages

- Stage 1 (Igniter vs. Adaptor): Containment sets expectations for safety. Disrupted prenatal containment predisposes to anxiety or rigidity.
- Stage 2 (Wall vs. Mirror): The womb embodies paradox: absolute boundary with total connection. Later, Wall and Mirror replicate this duality.
- Stage 3 (Flame vs. Mask): The womb's suspension of performance contrasts with later demands for authenticity or concealment. Adults return to the unborn familiar when performance exhausts identity.
- Stage 4 (Seer vs. Wound): The womb is pre-mortal. Later mortality confrontations are colored by this unique condition of existing outside time and death.

Modern Manifestations of Womb Mimicry

1) Abstinence and Purity Practices

In the modern landscape, abstinence movements and purity-centered practices have gained extraordinary visibility. From alcohol-free lifestyles to caffeine avoidance, from sugar elimination to gluten-free or allergen-free regimens, individuals are reshaping daily life around strict filtration of intake. At a surface level, these are health decisions. At a deeper symbolic level, *DCΨ* interprets them as reenactments of the womb's protective filtration system.

The fetus never confronted raw intake; every nutrient was pre-filtered. The symbolic reenactment of this condition appears in adults' efforts to purify what enters the body. "Clean eating" cultures echo the intrauterine environment where everything harmful was excluded. Even where there is no medical necessity, abstinence provides a psychological sense of protection: "I am safe because nothing impure can enter."

Clinical relevance: Clients who pursue purity practices may report increased clarity or relief, but underneath lies the pursuit of existential safety. When such practices are adaptive revisits, they allow temporary recalibration. But when rigidity hardens into compulsive avoidance, they signal stagnation — womb mimicry turned into a substitute for real confrontation.

Cultural echo: Purity laws across traditions (kosher, halal, ritual fasting) demonstrate that womb mimicry is not new. *DCΨ* reframes them not only as religious rules but as developmentally structured replays of prenatal filtration.

2) Wellness Retreats and Industries of Suspension

Retreat culture exemplifies womb mimicry at the collective level. From silent meditation camps to flotation tanks, from detox spas to yoga retreats, the wellness industry promises more than health: it offers containment, rhythm, and suspension of responsibility.

- **Containment:** Retreats isolate participants from daily chaos, reproducing the boundaries of prenatal life.
- **Rhythm:** Programs impose predictable schedules, mirroring the constancy of fetal rhythms.
- **Suspension:** All decisions are outsourced — meals, routines, even speech. The participant simply exists.

These are not luxuries but cultural enactments of womb templates. Participants consistently describe such experiences in rebirth metaphors: "I felt like I was being carried, like I could start over."

Clinical relevance: For some, retreats are adaptive stabilizers, permitting a temporary reset before re-entering confrontation. For others, dependency develops: the client can function only within retreat structures. In such cases, womb mimicry becomes stagnation.

Anthropological continuity: Across cultures, initiation rites employ seclusion, fasting, or immersion in water. DCΨ situates these traditions within the same archetypal logic: rituals of enclosure designed to echo the unborn familiar.

3) Minimalism and the Architecture of Enclosure

Minimalism has grown into a lifestyle movement. Capsule wardrobes, tiny homes, and decluttering manifest as attempts to reduce the external world to bounded essentials. Psychologically, these echo the womb's enclosure — an environment where nothing superfluous exists, where choice is minimal, and safety is derived from simplicity.

Clinical dimension: For individuals overwhelmed by complexity, minimalism can provide stabilizing containment. It reduces decision overload, echoing the womb's suspension of responsibility. But when minimalism hardens into rigidity — rejection of all complexity, avoidance of relational entanglement — it becomes stagnation, replacing confrontation with sterile enclosure.

Architectural resonance: Curved, domed spaces in sacred architecture symbolically replicate the womb's geometry. Modern minimalist interiors — uncluttered, softened, enclosed — can be seen as unconscious continuations of this archetypal longing.

4) Sensory Technologies and Artificial Wombs

Modern technology increasingly manufactures womb-like environments. Weighted blankets mimic amniotic pressure; noise-cancelling headphones mute the auditory field; blackout curtains replicate darkness; virtual reality offers bounded worlds with reduced agency.

Neuroscientific findings: Studies confirm that deep pressure stimulation (weighted blankets) lowers cortisol, echoing the fetus's regulated stress environment. Flotation therapy reduces sympathetic arousal, mimicking amniotic suspension.

Clinical relevance: For clients, these tools may serve adaptive stabilization — symbolic womb revisits that reduce anxiety. But when dependency develops — reliance on devices for all regulation — the unborn familiar is transformed into technological stagnation.

Cultural significance: These technologies illustrate the depth of womb mimicry: entire markets thrive on recreating prenatal containment, even if marketed as "stress relief."

5) Digital Enclosures and Safe Spaces

The digital world offers new arenas for womb mimicry. Curated online communities, algorithmic feeds, and safe spaces create bounded enclosures where threat is minimized and responsibility reduced.

Psychological function: These enclosures mimic containment and filtration. Exposure is carefully curated, creating a sense of safety akin to prenatal life.

Clinical risk: While digital enclaves can provide relief and community, they risk stagnation by trapping individuals in echo chambers. The unborn familiar here extends beyond the body into virtual architectures of avoidance.

6) Clinical Integration

Therapists must recognize womb mimicry not as triviality but as symbolic revisits. By mapping behaviors to the four archetypal features (containment, connection, rhythm, suspension), clinicians can discern whether the client is engaging in progressive revisits (stabilizing, temporary, goal-oriented) or stagnation (rigid, permanent, avoidance-based).

Case formulation approach:

- Identify the archetypal function (containment, connection, rhythm, suspension).
- Assess duration: Is the revisit time-limited or indefinite?
- Evaluate direction: Does it enable re-entry into confrontation or block it?

This framework prevents over-pathologizing adaptive strategies while still identifying risks of developmental arrest.

The Psychology of Womb-Seeking

1) Anxiety Regulation: The Need for Containment

Anxiety is among the strongest drivers of womb-seeking. When the self feels overwhelmed by the unpredictability of life, the psyche instinctively searches for templates that once guaranteed stability. The unborn familiar offers a symbolic containment strategy, promising reduction of chaos.

Phenomenological account: Individuals often describe anxiety in spatial terms — "I feel scattered," "I'm falling apart," "I have no ground." Womb mimicry responds with the opposite imagery: enclosed, bounded, gathered. A flotation tank, a silent retreat, or even curling under a weighted blanket produces the felt sense of being held together.

Case vignette: A client with panic disorder reported relief only when seated in a small, enclosed meditation pod with dim light. The environment, while artificial, echoed the womb's sensory parameters: muted input, rhythmic ventilation, safe enclosure. The pod did not cure the panic, but it stabilized the client enough to tolerate exposure therapy.

Cultural parallel: Collective rituals of chanting, rocking, or synchronized movement similarly soothe anxiety. They are womb strategies at scale: rhythm and enclosure to manage collective overwhelm.

2) Fear of Mortality: Seeking Pre-Mortal Suspension

The womb is the only condition of existence experienced before mortality-awareness. Adults who confront death — through illness, bereavement, or existential fear — often long for the womb's symbolic suspension, a state untouched by finitude.

Phenomenological account: Clients facing terminal illness describe a desire to "rest," "float," or "be carried." These are not simple metaphors but experiential longings for a time when life was sustained without the shadow of death.

Case vignette: A palliative care patient refused aggressive interventions but found comfort in hydrotherapy sessions. Submersion in warm water produced a sense of timeless suspension, interpreted as "returning to where I began." This womb-seeking provided existential comfort, allowing the patient to engage conversations about mortality without terror.

Cultural parallel: Tombs shaped as caves, myths of rebirth, and resurrection rituals across cultures echo this motive. They promise continuity by mimicking womb-like enclosures, reframing death not as an end but as a portal to symbolic return.

3) Relational Collapse: Longing for Boundary and Connection

When human relationships fracture — through abandonment, betrayal, or chronic invalidation — individuals may retreat into womb-seeking. The womb represents the paradox of absolute boundary and total connection: a condition where one is simultaneously enclosed and unconditionally linked.

Phenomenological account: Clients often express relational despair as "I can't trust anyone," "I feel invisible," or "I don't belong anywhere." In response, they create womb-like micro-environments: highly curated online groups, tightly controlled relationships, or rituals of enclosure that provide both protection and recognition.

Case vignette: A young adult with a history of rejection joined an online "safe-space" community. Participation there was experienced as "finally being held and seen at once." The digital enclave functioned as a symbolic womb — bounded from harm, yet ensuring connection. While stabilizing, dependency risked preventing broader relational repair.

Cultural parallel: Traditional rites of passage often involve seclusion followed by reintegration. These practices stage the womb logic: withdrawal for containment, then re-entry into relational life. They reveal that relational collapse has long been answered with womb-seeking rituals.

4) Identity Exhaustion: Relief from Performance

Modern life imposes relentless demands to perform, present, and curate identity. This burden corresponds to Stage 3 dynamics of authenticity and mask. Under such pressures, the unborn familiar becomes attractive because it represents existence without performance.

Phenomenological account: Clients facing burnout describe longing for "a place where I don't have to be anyone." The womb is remembered not as productivity but as unconditional being.

Case vignette: A corporate professional experiencing burnout turned to silence retreats. The appeal was not meditation per se, but the suspension of self-presentation: "No one here knows me, no one asks anything of me, I can just exist." The retreat offered womb-like suspension from identity labor, allowing temporary restoration.

Cultural parallel: Movements like minimalism and digital detox respond to identity fatigue by stripping away demands for curation. These practices are modern womb mimicries designed to temporarily free individuals from the exhausting work of being seen.

5) Integration: The Motives Behind Womb-Seeking

These four motives — anxiety regulation, mortality fear, relational collapse, and identity exhaustion — clarify why womb mimicry recurs across modern and historical contexts. They show that womb-seeking is not random, but systematically arises when core psychological demands overwhelm the individual.

Clinical synthesis: Therapists should inquire not only what womb-like behaviors a client engages in, but why. Is the motive anxiety relief? Mortality fear? Relational despair? Identity fatigue? Identifying the motive helps differentiate adaptive revisits from avoidance stagnation and guides targeted interventions.

Collective & Cultural Dynamics

1) Womb Mimicry in Times of Crisis

At the societal level, womb-seeking behaviors surge most visibly during collective crises. When wars, pandemics, or economic collapses destabilize entire populations, cultures instinctively generate womb-like responses: protective enclosures, restrictions, and suspension of ordinary life.

Phenomenological layer: The COVID-19 pandemic illustrated this globally. Lockdowns, curfews, and enforced isolation recreated womb-like containment. Citizens retreated into homes as symbolic "amniotic sacs," buffered from external threat. Food deliveries, digital connectivity, and structured schedules echoed the womb's unbroken supply and rhythm. While presented as public health measures, they also functioned psychologically as collective womb mimicry, calming existential panic.

Historical layer: During World War II, civilian populations often described bunkers, shelters, and blackout curtains as paradoxically comforting. These enclosures mirrored prenatal security: darkness, protection, suspension of external agency.

Clinical-cultural implication: Therapists working in collective trauma contexts may notice that clients interpret crisis restrictions not only as oppressive but also as strangely reassuring — evidence of womb templates reactivated at scale.

2) Nostalgia Movements and Utopian Politics

Beyond crisis, entire political and cultural movements can be understood as womb mimicry. Nostalgia appeals to a collective memory of safety: a longing for a time when boundaries were clearer, rhythms predictable, and identity less burdened.

Examples:

- Populist politics often frame their promise as "returning" — to national purity, to simpler times, to mythic golden ages. These narratives replicate womb logic: safety achieved through filtering, exclusion, and enclosure.

- Utopian experiments — communes, idealist religious sects, or "back to the land" projects — function as cultural attempts to rebuild womb conditions. Structured rhythms, communal purity, and boundary defense echo prenatal templates.

Cultural psychology: Nostalgia is not merely sentimental. It taps the same psychic drive that sends individuals toward minimalism or abstinence, but applied to entire societies: the wish to recreate the unborn familiar on a collective scale.

3) Rituals of Enclosure and Rebirth

Anthropological research reveals that many cultures employ ritualized womb mimicry during transitions. Initiation rites, funerary practices, and healing rituals often involve seclusion, enclosure, or immersion, followed by symbolic rebirth.

Examples:

- Indigenous rites where adolescents spend days in dark huts or caves before re-entering society.
- Religious practices of fasting, immersion in water, or retreat into monasteries.
- Modern equivalents: detox camps, rebirthing workshops, or even spa rituals that frame themselves explicitly as "renewal."

Interpretation through *DCΨ*: These rituals are not arbitrary. They operationalize the womb archetype as a structure for transformation: containment before confrontation, symbolic rebirth as preparation for new identity.

Clinical implication: Understanding these rituals helps therapists recognize that womb mimicry is not pathology alone. It is also a cultural technology for renewal, harnessed consciously to enable growth.

4) Collective Symbols of the Womb

Cultures also externalize womb imagery in their architecture, myths, and social spaces.

- **Architecture:** Domes, caves, circular sanctuaries, and underground chambers serve as collective womb symbols. Cathedrals and mosques use enclosing geometry to induce awe and safety, mirroring prenatal containment.
- **Mythology:** Creation myths frequently begin with a cosmic egg, a primordial sea, or a dark void — all womb analogues.
- **Social forms:** Festivals of renewal (spring equinox, new year rites) reenact womb rebirth, suspending ordinary rules before reintegration.

These collective symbols allow societies to anchor themselves in the unborn familiar, particularly when identity is threatened.

5) Clinical-Cultural Synthesis

For *DCΨ*, womb mimicry is not confined to individuals but pervades collective life. Societies facing crisis or change instinctively return to the unborn familiar through lockdowns, shelters, nostalgia, utopias, rituals, and symbols.

Clinical relevance: Therapists must remain sensitive to these cultural currents. A client's retreat into womb mimicry may not be an isolated act but part of a broader collective pattern. Recognizing this situates the individual within their cultural womb dynamics, preventing misdiagnosis.

Clinical & Therapeutic Implications

1) Diagnostic Markers of Womb-Seeking

Clinically, womb-seeking behaviors often disguise themselves as lifestyle choices, wellness practices, or even spiritual commitments. The challenge for the therapist is distinguishing progression (temporary revisit that stabilizes confrontation) from stagnation (avoidance that blocks confrontation).

Key markers include:

- Enclosure dependence: preferring controlled spaces, difficulty tolerating unpredictability.
- Purity fixation: strict rituals around food, substances, or media without medical necessity.
- Suspension behaviors: chronic postponement of decisions, withdrawal into passive states.
- Rhythmic reliance: compulsive use of repetitive practices (e.g., breath counts, rocking, ritualized routines) as sole coping method.
- Regressive language: fantasies or statements about being "carried," "protected from everything," or "returning to the beginning."

These markers are not pathological in themselves. They become clinically significant when they dominate functioning, prevent re-engagement with developmental confrontation, or cause impairment.

2) Therapist's Orientation: The "Midwife of Progression"

In *DCΨ*, the therapist is positioned not as an interpreter of resistance, but as a midwife of progression. Womb-seeking is approached as a symbolic stabilizer — a protective enclosure the client creates when direct confrontation feels overwhelming.

Therapeutic stance involves:

- Validation without collusion: respect the stabilizing role of womb mimicry while clarifying its limits.
- Containment with an exit: create a therapeutic space that mirrors womb-like safety but is always oriented toward re-entry into life.
- Gradual re-engagement: scaffold steps that bridge the safety of mimicry into the client's avoided confrontation.
- Symbolic literacy: help the client see their behaviors as archetypal revisits, which reduces shame and enhances agency.

3) Developmental Resolution Therapy (DRT) as the Umbrella

DRT is the core therapeutic model in *DCΨ*. It guides clients back into unresolved confrontations, using womb mimicry as a temporary stabilizer that must ultimately serve progression. Within DRT, three integrated modules provide structure:

A) ART (Analytical Resolution Module)

- Function: make unconscious symbolic revisits explicit; link behaviors to stage confrontations.
- Use: interpret purity rituals as containment, retreats as suspension, or abstinence as filtration.
- Goal: transform hidden avoidance into conscious strategy with defined exit criteria.

B) BRT (Behavioral Resolution Module)

- Function: train stage-specific behaviors to reopen blocked confrontations.
- Use: graded exposures to situations avoided through womb mimicry (social settings, mortality reminders).
- Goal: replace compulsive rituals with deliberate, progressive action.

C) XRT (Experiential Resolution Module)

- Function: provide embodied reenactments of safety → confrontation sequences.
- Use: guided imagery of containment followed immediately by symbolic confrontation (e.g., role-play of relational boundary).
- Goal: consolidate safety in the body, then redirect it toward facing avoided tasks.

In practice, therapists flow flexibly between modules depending on client needs. *DRT* is not fragmented — it is one therapy expressed through analytic, behavioral, and experiential methods.

4) Case Formulation Guidelines

Formulation in womb-seeking cases requires anchoring in *DCT* stage logic and resolution vs distortion polarity:

1. Identify presenting womb-seeking behavior. (e.g., extreme minimalism, abstinence, retreat cycling).

2. Clarify motive. (fear of collapse, mortality anxiety, relational exhaustion, identity fatigue).

3. Map to stage.

    - Stage 1 instability → need for containment.
    - Stage 2 collapse → need for mirrored safety.
    - Stage 3 exhaustion → withdrawal into suspension.
    - Stage 4 terror → symbolic denial of mortality.

4. Differentiate revisit vs stagnation.

    - Revisit = temporary stabilizer, progression possible.
    - Stagnation = permanent avoidance, no confrontation.

5. Select DRT entry point (ART, BRT, or XRT emphasis).

6. Set explicit progression goals. ("Containment → boundary practice," "Suspension → mortality dialogue.")

5) Clinical Challenges

- Over-collusion: risk of therapist becoming the client's permanent "womb," fostering stagnation.
- Premature confrontation: forcing exposure without stabilizing safety risks retraumatization.
- Cultural blindness: failing to recognize collective womb dynamics (e.g., fasting, retreats, rituals) may pathologize normal symbolic revisits.
- Countertransference: therapist overidentifies with protector role, mirroring parental containment.

Therapists must balance validation with progression, ensuring womb mimicry remains a bridge, never a destination.

6) Integration into Broader DCΨ Practice

The unborn familiar is not an isolated clinical idea but a living application of *DCΨ's* architecture:

- In *SRI*: womb-seeking behaviors indicate unresolved stage confrontation, scored as revisit vs stagnation.
- In *DCPTT*: symbolic traits may appear distorted (e.g., Adaptor over-reliant on purity, Mask collapsing into suspension).
- In *SDC-PT*: projective imagery often reveals womb symbols (caves, enclosures, circles) pointing to containment revisits.
- In *DRT*: womb mimicry is directly worked with through *ART*, *BRT*, and *XRT* until the confrontation is consciously re-entered.
- In the Diagnostic Atlas: cultural and clinical womb phenomena are catalogued as predictable distortions or revisits.

Integration & Conclusion

1) The Womb as the First Confrontation Template

Across this chapter, we have traced the unborn familiar not as an incidental metaphor but as the originary template of confrontation. The prenatal condition embodies the duality that defines all of *DCT*:

- Safety and vulnerability.
- Autonomy and dependence.
- Suspension and movement.
- Filtration and exposure.

Every later stage — self vs world, self vs other, emotional identity, mortality and wisdom — echoes this primal paradox. The womb is the zero-point, the first environment where existence demanded resolution: to grow without collapse, to be enclosed yet in relation, to be passive yet preparing for future confrontation.

2) From Archetype to Modern Life

We saw how this template crystallizes into four archetypal features: containment, connection, rhythm, suspension. These archetypes were then traced forward into modern contexts: abstinence rituals, wellness retreats, minimalism, sensory technologies, digital enclosures. The logic of the womb endures because it is not a stage left behind; it is a living imprint woven into all later developmental work.

This shows why womb mimicry is universal: it re-emerges in cultures, technologies, and personal rituals whenever human beings face destabilization. The unborn familiar is not regression but a developmental constant: a stabilizing archive the psyche reopens when threatened.

3) The Psychology of Womb-Seeking

At the psychological level, womb-seeking arises from four core motives:

- Anxiety regulation → the need for containment against overwhelm.
- Fear of mortality → longing for suspension before the awareness of finitude.
- Relational collapse → refuge in the paradox of total boundary + total connection.
- Identity exhaustion → relief from the endless demand to perform.

These motives clarify that womb mimicry is not a childish return, but a survival strategy triggered when existential demands exceed capacity. Each motive aligns with unresolved or destabilized confrontations across the four stages of *DCT.*

4) Societal Womb Mimicry

The unborn familiar is not limited to individuals. Entire societies replay its template during crises and transitions:

- Lockdowns and shelters during pandemics or wars.
- Nostalgia and utopian politics promising filtered, bounded purity.
- Rituals of enclosure and symbolic rebirth found in every culture.
- Collective symbols — domes, caves, cosmic eggs, renewal festivals — expressing the same archetypal longing.

The womb is thus a collective archetype, shaping cultural architectures and myths as much as private coping. *DCΨ* provides the lens to read these not as curiosities but as structured responses to confrontation at scale.

5) Clinical Integration

Within clinical work, womb mimicry is reinterpreted through *DCΨ* not as pathology in itself, but as a developmental revisit. The clinician's role, framed by *DRT*, is to midwife progression:

- Validate the revisit as stabilizing.
- Set boundaries so it remains temporary.
- Use *ART*, *BRT*, and *XRT* modules to transform mimicry into confrontation.
- Prevent stagnation, where the womb becomes destination instead of bridge.

This therapeutic reframing protects against mislabeling adaptive stabilizers as illness, while still guiding clients toward growth. It gives clinicians a structured way to honor archetypal behaviors without colluding with avoidance.

6) Position within DCT

The unborn familiar is more than a symbol; it is the structural anchor of Developmental Confrontation Theory.

- It shows that all confrontations are grounded in a primal logic: safety is never absolute, vulnerability is never absent, growth is always negotiated.

- It demonstrates that progression is not linear abandonment of earlier stages but the ability to revisit earlier templates without collapsing into them.

- It integrates philosophy, psychology, culture, and therapy into one continuous arc: a school of thought that makes visible the unseen architecture of development.

In this way, **the unborn familiar** proves *DCT's* **central thesis**: development is not additive learning, but confrontation, resolution, and the constant negotiation between safety and growth.

DCΨ

Chapter 5

THE FOUR DEVELOPMENTAL STAGES

The Developmental Confrontation Theory (DCT)
A Framework of Structured Human Development

Introduction

The Developmental Confrontation Theory (DCT) is the foundational model of *Developmental Confrontation Psychology*. It proposes that human growth unfolds through sequential confrontations, critical psychological demands that cannot be bypassed without leaving fractures behind. Unlike stage theories that emphasize skills or cognitive milestones, *DCT* frames development as a series of existential confrontations: structured encounters between the self and its limits, its relationships, its emotions, and its mortality.

These stages are **sequential** in their architecture. Stage 1 confronts the world as undivided reality, Stage 2 confronts the other, Stage 3 confronts the uniqueness of self, and Stage 4 confronts mortality. Each builds upon the existential threshold of the prior. **Yet this sequence is not rigid in lived experience**. Entry into a later stage does not require the resolution of earlier ones, and unresolved confrontations remain active across life. A person may grapple with the demands of Stage 4 while still carrying distortions from Stage 1. In this sense, the stages are cumulative fields of confrontation: **they open in order, but they remain simultaneously alive, whether resolved or unresolved.**

This layered structure explains why the *Stage Resolution Index* is necessary. It is not enough to ask whether someone has entered a stage; the question is whether that stage is resolved, distorted, or carried unresolved into later development. Development in *DCΨ* is therefore not a ladder to be climbed and left behind but an unfolding matrix in which the earliest confrontations remain present even as later ones are opened.

In addition to the four stages, *DCΨ* identifies **meta-functions** that mediate every confrontation. Chief among these are the **Rational Self** and the **Emotional Self.** They are not traits or stages but **psychological translators**: one processes the world through structure and function, the other through connection and feeling. These two become visible in Stage 2, when the child distinguishes between objects and people, assigning logic to one and emotion to the other. Once formed, however, they remain active across all later stages, shaping how each confrontation is understood, symbolized, and resolved. They will be introduced in detail in Stage 2, but their presence must be kept in mind as a background process throughout all that follows, for every confrontation is filtered through them, visibly or not.

In the pages ahead, each stage will be presented in turn: its core confrontation, its traits, its pathways of resolution, its distortions, and its clinical implications.

Stage 1: Self vs. World
The Foundational Confrontation of Autonomy and Order

Core Confrontation

Stage 1: Self vs. World establishes the individual's first organized stance toward an external environment that is larger, limiting, and unpredictable. Under this pressure, the infant does not "choose," but organizes a way of meeting the world, an emergent pattern shaped by arousal regulation, caregiving contingencies, and context. Two valid orientations appear, each capable of healthy resolution or distortion:

- **Igniter (Exploratory Orientation)**

Approach-led engagement with the environment: vigilance to novelty, mobilization toward stimuli, trial-and-error contact with obstacles. Resolution builds autonomous agency, initiative, and confidence in effecting change. Distortion appears as scattered activation (impulsivity, hypervigilance, disorganized approach) when exploration is unanchored.

- **Adaptor (Regulatory Orientation)**

Order-led engagement with the environment: preference for predictability, routines, and stabilizing structures (soothing cues, external scaffolds). Resolution builds reliable self-regulation, persistence, and secure use of structure. Distortion appears as rigidity, avoidance, or over-reliance on external order when regulation eclipses contact.

Both orientations are developmentally normative responses to the same confrontation, "How do I stand in a world that can overwhelm me?" The quality of resolution (not the orientation itself) determines later stability: well-anchored Igniter or Adaptor patterns scaffold all subsequent stages; distorted patterns reverberate forward as either uncontained activation or overcontrolled withdrawal.

Resolution Pathways

Unlike simplistic "positive/negative" binaries, *DCT* holds that both traits in Stage 1 are valid orientations toward resolution:

- **Igniter (Exploratory Orientation)**

Confronts the world by igniting curiosity, approaching novelty, and testing limits through initiative. Resolution through this path means the person feels capable of shaping reality by trial, persistence, and discovery.

- **Adaptor (Regulatory Orientation)**

Confronts the world by seeking protective order, aligning with external structures, and stabilizing through predictable routines or caregivers. Resolution through this path means the person experiences safety and coherence by embedding themselves in secure systems.

Both pathways can lead to healthy resolution if they remain flexible and adaptive. The Igniter without distortion produces a bold, exploratory personality capable of initiative. The Adaptor without distortion produces a grounded, reliable personality capable of stability.

Distortions

Failure in Stage 1 does not erase the confrontation; it twists it. Distortion occurs when either orientation becomes exaggerated, collapsed, or disconnected from its developmental task:

A Igniter Distortions (Exploratory Orientation distorted):

- Hyperactive or scattered approach to novelty.
- Impulsivity, oppositional behavior, chronic restlessness.
- Destructive autonomy ("If I cannot lead, I must destroy").
- Clinical anchors: ADHD-like patterns, conduct defiance, disorganized activation.

B Adaptor Distortions (Regulatory Orientation distorted):

- Compulsive order-seeking and rigidity.
- Excessive dependence on external authority or rituals.
- Avoidance of initiative ("I only exist if I am protected").
- Clinical anchors: OCPD traits, dependency symptoms, rigidity-based anxiety.

C Mixed Distortions:

- Oscillation between rebellion and submission.
- Unstable autonomy (periods of explosive initiative alternating with collapse).
- Somatic compulsions or tics (fidgeting, repetitive rituals) representing unresolved grounding.
- Clinical anchors: obsessive-compulsive spectrum, generalized anxiety, conversion patterns.

These distortions do not reflect new pathologies but are Stage 1 fractures reverberating forward. Many adult disorders trace their origins here:

- Generalized Anxiety Disorder (GAD) → uncontained Igniter energy fused with weak Adaptor containment.

- Obsessive-Compulsive Personality Disorder (OCPD) → overextended Adaptor with collapsed Igniter flexibility.

Phenomenology of Stage 1

Stage 1 is lived through the body and environment before language or abstract thought develops. The confrontation of Self vs. World is not theoretical, it is experienced somatically, behaviorally, and symbolically:

1. **Bodily Anchoring**
   - Feeding, sleep, and movement patterns become the first terrain of confrontation.
   - Secure exploration (Igniter) shows as playful curiosity, motor activation, or trial-and-error learning.
   - Secure regulation (Adaptor) shows as soothing, rhythm, and predictable cycles.
   - Distorted forms: fidgeting, compulsive blinking, disrupted sleep, or ritualized feeding behaviors.

2. **Boundary Formation**
   - Early limits (walls, floors, parental "no's") provide the first sense of separation between "self" and "world."
   - Igniter resolution: testing limits without collapse, learning initiative within boundaries.
   - Adaptor resolution: using boundaries as scaffolding for stability.
   - Distorted forms: boundary collapse (fear of engulfment) or overdependence (fear of losing containment).

3. **Autonomy Anxiety**

- The infant begins to sense that without initiative, suffocation occurs; without protection, collapse follows.
- Resolution: balance between initiative and safety.
- Distortion: panic responses, either compulsive control of the environment or complete passivity.

4. **Symbolic Carriers**

- Objects, routines, or rituals (blankets, toys, parental habits) become symbolic containers of safety.
- Resolution: flexible use of transitional objects.
- Distortion: panic or rage when symbolic anchors are disrupted.

Adult Manifestations of Stage 1

Unresolved or distorted Stage 1 patterns continue to echo into adulthood, often disguised as personality traits, compulsions, or anxiety states.

Distorted Manifestations:

- Over-control of environment: compulsive order, perfectionism, ritualized behaviors (Adaptor distortion).
- Explosive autonomy: sudden resignations, reckless rebellion, chronic restlessness (Igniter distortion).
- Grounding anxiety: persistent fear of losing stability, environment perceived as unsafe or overwhelming.
- Somatic expressions: tension, compulsive habits (hair pulling, nail biting), sleep disruption, psychosomatic complaints.

Resolved Manifestations:

- Stable grounding in reality: capacity to feel secure despite external unpredictability.

- Healthy autonomy: ability to initiate actions without collapsing under pressure.

- Balanced integration: fluid alternation between inner initiative (Igniter) and external structure (Adaptor).

- Adaptive resilience: capacity to use structure for support without rigidity, and novelty for growth without chaos.

Resolution at Stage 1 provides the foundation for later stages: a person who feels secure in the world can risk vulnerability in relationships (Stage 2), emotional authenticity (Stage 3), and existential meaning (Stage 4). Distorted Stage 1, however, creates fractures that reverberate forward, often as relational instability, emotional dysregulation, or existential anxiety.

Therapeutic Approaches in Stage 1

Therapeutic work at Stage 1 is not about erasing symptoms, but about restoring the original confrontation: re-engaging the threshold between Self and World so the client can integrate resolution consciously.

1 **DRT–ART (Analytical Resolution Therapy):**

- Focus: uncover symbolic anchors and distorted regulatory/exploratory patterns.
- Examples: identifying compulsive rituals, decoding fidgeting or repetitive actions, analyzing the meaning of "protective objects."
- Goal: awareness of how distorted Igniter or Adaptor responses still shape adult behavior.

2 **DRT–BRT (Behavioral Resolution Therapy):**

- Focus: rebuild healthy routines and controlled autonomy.
- Examples: graded exposure to novelty for Igniter distortion; structured flexibility training for Adaptor distortion.
- Goal: strengthen balance between initiative and external structure.

3 **DRT–XRT (Experiential Resolution Therapy):**

- Focus: direct re-experiencing of the confrontation in safe settings.
- Examples: grounding exercises (breathwork, movement therapy), role-play of confronting environmental triggers, symbolic use of transitional objects.
- Goal: embody a new resolution by integrating both stability and initiative into lived experience.

Therapeutic Principle: The task is not to eliminate anxiety or compulsion but to reopen the confrontation, allowing the client to choose resolution actively rather than remain trapped in distortion.

Stage 2: Self vs. Other
The Confrontation of Boundaries and Reflection

Core Confrontation

Stage 2: Self vs. Other establishes the individual's first organized stance toward human presence. No longer confronting only the impersonal world, the child now meets others who respond, reflect, and intrude. Identity begins to form not in isolation but in dialogue with recognition and separation. The developmental demand is: "How do I exist when another exists beside me?"

Two valid orientations appear, each capable of healthy resolution or distortion:

- **Wall (Boundary Orientation)**

Differentiation-led engagement: the child asserts separateness, learning to say "this is me, this is not me." Resolution builds stable boundaries, integrity, and autonomy. Distortion appears as over-differentiation, rigidity, defensive withdrawal, hostility to intimacy, when boundaries harden against all contact.

- **Mirror (Recognition Orientation)**

Reflection-led engagement: the child internalizes identity through recognition, learning "I am as I am seen." Resolution builds empathy, resonance, and flexible identity. Distortion appears as over-identification, collapse of self into others' views, dependence on validation, or volatility of self-image, when reflection eclipses inner stability.

Both orientations are developmentally normative responses to the same confrontation. The quality of resolution, not the orientation itself, determines stability: a well-anchored Wall or Mirror supports mature relational identity, while distorted forms reverberate forward as either chronic isolation or unstable dependence.

Resolution Pathways

Unlike simplistic "healthy vs. unhealthy" binaries, *DCT* holds that both orientations in Stage 2 are valid routes toward resolution. The confrontation of Self vs. Other can be resolved either by strengthening boundaries (Wall) or by opening to reflection (Mirror). Both are developmentally normative and both can distort if rigid.

- **Wall (Boundary Orientation — Differentiation)**

Confronts the presence of the Other by asserting distinct selfhood. Resolution here creates the ability to say: "This is me, and this is not me." Clinically, it aligns with secure boundary-setting, self-assertion, and autonomy within relationships. Symbolically, the Wall is the protective skin or border, ensuring the self is not erased. A well-resolved Wall produces integrity, dignity, and the capacity to remain intact even under pressure.

- **Mirror (Reflective Orientation — Recognition)**

Confronts the presence of the Other by internalizing their recognition and feedback. Resolution here creates identity through resonance: "I see myself in how you see me." Clinically, it aligns with secure attachment, empathic reciprocity, and adaptive self-image formation. Symbolically, the Mirror is reflection and validation, allowing the self to become visible. A well-resolved Mirror produces flexibility, empathy, and the ability to grow through connection without collapse.

Both orientations are legitimate. Resolution through the Wall provides strength against fusion; resolution through the Mirror provides resonance against isolation. Together they define relational maturity: the ability to stand apart while also being seen.

The Rational and Emotional Selves

Alongside the dual orientations of Wall and Mirror, Stage 2 makes visible a deeper division in the psyche: the differentiation between the **Rational Self** and the **Emotional Self.** These are not additional traits but **meta-functions**, psychological processors that cut across all stages and remain active throughout life. They first emerge here, when the child recognizes that the world of others cannot be grasped only in terms of objects and rules, but also through emotions, connection, and meaning.

The **Rational Self** interprets reality by structure, logic, and function. It asks what things do, what rules govern them, what boundaries define their role. In contrast, the **Emotional Self** interprets through affect and resonance. It asks how the other makes me feel, whether I am safe, loved, or rejected. Together they form a translation system: one makes the external world intelligible, the other makes it meaningful. Their interplay is most apparent when symbols act as bridges between the two. A child who offers a stone as a gift to a parent is engaging both functions: the **Rational Self** chooses the stone as object, while the **Emotional Self** invests it with affection. When received, the object is retranslated back into emotional meaning.

This continuous circulation between **Rational and Emotional** processing forms what can be called the **Symbolic Transfer Loop**. Objects acquire emotional weight, and emotions are externalized through objects, gestures, or words. Far from being incidental, this loop is the mechanism through which recognition and boundary-setting are enacted in daily life. The Wall relies on the Rational Self to sustain structure, but it also requires the Emotional Self to prevent isolation. The Mirror relies on the Emotional Self to resonate with others, but it also needs the Rational Self to stabilize identity so that reflection does not collapse into dependency.

Clinically, the **Rational–Emotional** split explains why distortions in Stage 2 are rarely only structural. An overextended Wall often co-occurs with a Rational Self that dominates affect, producing cold detachment. A collapsed Mirror often reveals an Emotional Self overexposed to external validation, with little rational structure to stabilize identity. In therapy, the recognition of both functions allows the clinician to see that every boundary and reflection is filtered twice: once by the Rational Self, once by the Emotional Self.

By framing them as **meta-functions** rather than stages or traits, *DCΨ* positions the **Rational and Emotional Selves** as enduring translators of confrontation. They are born in the crucible of Stage 2, but they continue to shape how authenticity is expressed in Stage 3 and how mortality is interpreted in Stage 4. To understand them is to understand how the psyche turns experience into meaning, and how meaning is returned to the psyche as confrontation.

Distortions

These distortions appear not only in the structural expressions of Wall and Mirror but also in the imbalances of the Rational and Emotional Selves, where one dominates the other instead of working together.

Failure in Stage 2 does not erase the confrontation; it twists it. Distortion occurs when either orientation becomes exaggerated, collapsed, or disconnected from its developmental task:

A. **Wall Distortions (Boundary Orientation distorted):**

- Excessive rigidity and emotional withdrawal.
- Intimacy experienced as threat; identity defended by exclusion of others.
- Hostility, mistrust, or superiority used as defense ("I only exist if I keep others out").
- Clinical anchors: Avoidant Personality Disorder traits, schizoid detachment, antisocial coldness.

B. **Mirror Distortions (Recognition Orientation distorted):**

- Over-dependence on external validation.
- Collapse of identity without recognition.
- Frantic bids for approval or unstable self-image ("I only exist if you see me").
- Clinical anchors: Borderline instability, Dependent Personality Disorder features, dramatic relational swings.

C. **Mixed Distortions:**

- Oscillation between clinging and rejection.
- Disorganized attachment signals; relational chaos and volatility.
- Boundaries that appear and vanish, producing instability.
- Clinical anchors: borderline push–pull cycles, attachment disorganization, unstable identity states.

These distortions are not "new" disorders but fractures of Stage 2 reverberating forward. Many adult disorders trace their roots here:

- Borderline Personality Disorder (BPD) → collapsed Mirror with weak or absent Wall.
- Dependent Personality Disorder (DPD) → inflated Mirror with no Wall.
- Avoidant Personality Disorder (AvPD) or Schizoid traits → rigid Wall with collapsed Mirror.
- Antisocial Personality Disorder (ASPD) → hardened Wall in absence of reflective Mirror

Phenomenology of Stage 2

Stage 2 is lived through relationships rather than the body alone. The confrontation of Self vs. Other is not abstract; it is experienced in gestures, reflections, and emotional exchanges:

1. **Boundary Testing**
    - Children experiment with closeness and separation through "mine vs. yours," "no vs. yes," and physical distancing.
    - Wall resolution: boundaries affirmed without hostility, capacity to say "this is me" without rejecting others.
    - Mirror resolution: recognition of self through others' acknowledgment, maintaining connection while individuating.
    - Distorted forms: rigid exclusion of others (hardened Wall) or collapse into fusion (collapsed Mirror).

2. **Mirroring and Recognition**

- Facial expressions, vocal tones, and gestures of acknowledgment form the reflective surface of identity.
- Mirror resolution: identity coheres through consistent recognition.
- Wall resolution: develops capacity to internalize reflection while preserving separation.
- Distorted forms: unstable identity, frantic bids for recognition, or defensive blindness to others' acknowledgment.

3. **Attachment Dynamics**

- Early attachments determine whether boundaries and reflections stabilize.
- Secure attachment: flexible balance of Wall and Mirror.
- Avoidant patterns: overextended Wall, relational withdrawal.
- Ambivalent patterns: inflated Mirror, anxious clinging.
- Disorganized patterns: mixed distortion, chaotic oscillation.

4. **Shame and Validation**

- Shame emerges when reflection fails ("you don't see me"); validation arises when mirroring succeeds.
- Resolution: shame regulated by dignity (Wall) or recognition (Mirror).
- Distortion: shame becomes overwhelming, leading to either collapse of self (Mirror) or emotional numbing and contempt (Wall).

Adult Manifestations of Stage 2

Unresolved or distorted Stage 2 patterns continue to echo into adulthood, often disguised as relational styles, attachment strategies, or personality disorders.

Distorted Manifestations:

- Fear of abandonment and unstable attachment: frantic clinging, unstable relationships, alternating idealization and devaluation (Mirror distortion).
- Rigid mistrust and emotional withdrawal: refusal of intimacy, cold detachment, or hostile superiority (Wall distortion).
- Oscillating relational chaos: cycles of clinging and rejection, erratic boundaries, volatile attachment behaviors (Mixed distortion).
- Identity diffusion: self-image collapsing or shifting entirely on others' recognition or rejection.

Resolved Manifestations:

- Healthy boundaries: capacity to say yes/no without collapse, integrity preserved in presence of others.
- Relational resonance: ability to reflect others while keeping identity intact, empathy balanced with selfhood.
- Balanced autonomy-with-connection: self maintained in dialogue, not dissolved or isolated.
- Stable attachment: resilience in closeness without clinging, independence without detachment.

Resolution at Stage 2 provides the relational scaffolding for later stages: a person who can maintain selfhood in the presence of others can risk emotional authenticity (Stage 3) and existential confrontation (Stage 4). Distorted Stage 2, however, fractures into chronic relational instability, attachment dysregulation, or social detachment that reverberates forward into identity and meaning crises.

Therapeutic Approaches in Stage 2

Therapeutic work at Stage 2 is not about bypassing relational wounds, but about restoring the original confrontation: re-engaging the threshold between Self and Other so the client can integrate resolution consciously.

1. **DRT–ART (Analytical Resolution Therapy):**
   - Focus: uncover distorted boundary or mirroring patterns.
   - Examples: analyzing cycles of over-dependence, tracing histories of relational withdrawal, decoding symbolic meanings of "being seen" or "being excluded."
   - Goal: awareness of how distorted Wall or Mirror responses continue to script adult relationships.
2. **DRT–BRT (Behavioral Resolution Therapy):**
   - Focus: rebuild adaptive relational behaviors and boundary-setting.
   - Examples: structured boundary practice (assertive "no" without collapse), graded exposure to intimacy for avoidant tendencies, coaching balanced responsiveness for Mirror distortion.
   - Goal: strengthen flexible boundaries and stable recognition in everyday interactions.

3. **DRT–XRT (Experiential Resolution Therapy):**

- Focus: direct re-experiencing of self–other confrontation in safe therapeutic space.
- Examples: role-play of rejection and recognition scenarios, therapist functioning as a "stable mirror," experiential exercises in closeness and distance.
- Goal: embody new relational patterns by integrating both boundary integrity and reflective recognition into lived experience.

Therapeutic Principle: The task is not to erase dependency or mistrust but to reopen the confrontation, allowing the client to consciously choose resolution — sustaining both the dignity of the Wall and the resonance of the Mirror, rather than remaining trapped in distortion.

Stage 3: Emotional Identity
The Confrontation of Authenticity and Role

Core Confrontation

Stage 3: Emotional Identity establishes the individual's first organized stance toward the inner self as expressed outwardly. No longer confronting only the impersonal world (Stage 1) or the presence of others (Stage 2), the person now faces the confrontation of authenticity: to align inner truth with outer expression. The developmental demand is: "Am I truly myself, or am I only the role I perform?"

Two valid orientations appear, each capable of healthy resolution or distortion:

- **Flame (Authenticity Orientation)**

Emotion-led engagement: the individual asserts identity through passion, vulnerability, and direct expression of inner life. Resolution builds congruence between inner and outer self, capacity for intimacy, and a sense of vitality. Distortion appears as unchecked emotional flooding, instability of self, or worth tethered to volatile feelings, when expression loses anchor in stability.

- **Mask (Role Orientation)**

Function-led engagement: the individual organizes identity through roles, responsibilities, and socially recognized expressions. Resolution builds coherence, reliability, and the ability to sustain selfhood across contexts. Distortion appears as hollow performance, compulsive role-playing, or collapse of self when the role is threatened, when outer function eclipses inner depth.

Both orientations are developmentally normative responses to the same confrontation. The quality of resolution, not the orientation itself, determines identity stability: a well-anchored Flame or Mask supports mature emotional identity, while distorted forms reverberate forward as either emotional chaos or empty performance.

Resolution Pathways

Unlike simplistic notions of "true self" versus "false self," *DCT* holds that both traits in Stage 3 are valid orientations toward resolution. Each represents a developmental strategy for stabilizing identity and sustaining emotional coherence.

- **Flame (Authenticity Orientation)**

Resolution occurs when emotional expression is anchored and integrated into identity. The Flame type develops vitality, intimacy, and congruence between inner experience and outer life. Emotion becomes a resource rather than a flood, fueling creativity and deep connection. A well-resolved Flame allows the individual to be emotionally transparent without collapsing into volatility.

- **Mask (Role Orientation)**

Resolution occurs when roles and functions are inhabited with depth, becoming containers that support identity rather than hollow performances. The Mask type develops stability, coherence, and reliability across contexts. A well-resolved Mask allows the individual to embody responsibility without losing inner depth, and to sustain a consistent self even under external demands.

Both orientations are developmentally normative responses to the same confrontation. The quality of resolution, not the orientation itself, determines stability: a well-anchored Flame or Mask sustains mature emotional identity, while distorted forms reverberate forward as either emotional chaos or empty performance.

Distortions

Failure in Stage 3 does not erase the confrontation; it twists it. Distortion occurs when either orientation becomes exaggerated, collapsed, or disconnected from its developmental task:

A. **Flame Distortions (Authenticity Orientation distorted):**

- Overwhelming intensity of emotion, uncontrolled expression, or explosive reactivity.
- Identity fused with raw feeling ("I am only real when I burn").
- Emotional flooding that destabilizes relationships and personal coherence.
- Clinical anchors: mood instability, histrionic traits, affective dysregulation.

B. **Mask Distortions (Role Orientation distorted):**

- Identity reduced to external functions, roles, or performances.
- Hollow selfhood behind polished appearance, emotional disengagement.
- Dependence on approval for worth; collapse when roles are threatened.
- Clinical anchors: narcissistic traits, depersonalization, performance-based identity disorders.

C. **Mixed Distortions:**

- Oscillation between emotional excess (Flame) and rigid control (Mask).
- Instability of selfhood, moments of raw exposure followed by concealment.
- Relationships marked by alternating passion and detachment.
- Clinical anchors: borderline instability, identity diffusion, dramatic-avoidant cycles.

These distortions are not "new" disorders but fractures of Stage 3 reverberating forward. Many adult disorders trace their roots here:

- Borderline Personality Disorder (BPD): oscillation between Flame excess (affective volatility) and Mask defense (identity diffusion linked to roles).
- Histrionic Personality Disorder (HPD): amplified Flame with externalized self-worth (attention-seeking, dramatization) when authenticity loses anchor.
- Narcissistic Personality Disorder (NPD): inflated Mask (grandiose or vulnerable) with attenuated Flame; self-esteem contingent on role, status, or performance.
- Depersonalization/Derealization presentations: dominant Mask with muted Flame; hollowed sense of self, detachment from felt authenticity.
- Antisocial Personality Disorder (ASPD): Mask without Flame, emotional void behind manipulation.
- Somatic Symptom Disorder: Suppressed Flame redirected into bodily symptoms.

Phenomenology of Stage 3

Stage 3 is lived through the confrontation with emotional identity: the task of answering "Who am I when I feel, and when I act in roles?" This confrontation unfolds in the interplay of expression and performance, vulnerability and function, authenticity and social mask.

1. **Emotional Anchoring**

   - Emotional intensity becomes the terrain of confrontation.
   - Flame resolution: capacity to feel and express passion in a grounded way, emotions fuel intimacy, creativity, and vitality.
   - Mask resolution: capacity to channel emotion into roles and responsibilities without losing inner depth.
   - Distorted forms: explosive outbursts, uncontrolled affect (Flame) or emotional deadness and hollow role performance (Mask).
   - Clinical anchors: affective dysregulation, histrionic intensity, narcissistic detachment.

2. **Identity Through Expression and Role**

   - Selfhood is tested in the balance between authentic expression and assumed roles.
   - Flame resolution: identity feels genuine, congruent, transparent.
   - Mask resolution: identity feels coherent and continuous across contexts.
   - Distorted forms: self reduced either to raw emotion (unstable, chaotic) or to role alone (hollow, depersonalized).
   - Clinical anchors: borderline instability (emotional identity diffusion), performance-based narcissism.

3. **Anxiety of Exposure**

- The central anxiety here is visibility: the fear of being "too exposed" (Flame) or "never truly seen" (Mask).
- Resolution: balance between vulnerability and presentation, the ability to be both known and respected.
- Distortion: panic of exposure (emotional flooding, shame spirals) or panic of invisibility (feeling like a façade).
- Clinical anchors: social anxiety with affective volatility, depersonalization, or dramatic-avoidant cycles.

4. **Symbolic Carriers**

- Symbols of Stage 3 identity emerge in language, art, rituals, uniforms, and roles.
- Resolution: flexible use of symbolic carriers — names, works, roles — as stabilizers of identity.
- Distortion: over-attachment ("Without my title I am nothing") or destructive rejection ("I must destroy the role to prove I am real").
- Clinical anchors: identity crises, role-dependent self-worth, destructive reactivity to labels or symbols.

Adult Manifestations of Stage 3

Unresolved or distorted Stage 3 patterns echo into adulthood as instability of emotional identity, oscillating between raw authenticity without anchor and hollow performance without depth.

Distorted Manifestations:

- Flame distortions (excess of authenticity): uncontrolled affect, mood swings, impulsive intimacy, self-destructive passion, identity tied only to raw emotion.
- Mask distortions (excess of role): rigid adherence to roles or titles, depersonalization, emptiness behind achievement, collapse when performance is threatened.
- Mixed distortions: oscillation between dramatic intensity and detached façade; unstable relationships alternating between overexposure and withdrawal.
- Clinical anchors: Borderline instability, Histrionic features, Narcissistic personality styles (grandiose or vulnerable), depersonalization/derealization states.

Resolved Manifestations:

- Flame resolution: vitality and emotional congruence, the ability to express passion while maintaining stability; creativity and intimacy flourish without chaos.
- Mask resolution: stability through roles that are inhabited with depth, coherent identity across life contexts; responsibility does not erase authenticity.
- Balanced integration: capacity to move fluidly between passion (Flame) and role (Mask), creating a stable yet adaptive identity.
- Adaptive resilience: ability to be emotionally transparent without collapse and socially functional without hollowness.

Resolution at Stage 3 provides the foundation for later existential confrontation: one who has achieved emotional identity can approach mortality and meaning (Stage 4) without collapsing into despair or detachment. Distorted Stage 3, however, reverberates forward as identity diffusion, dramatic-avoidant cycles, and existential emptiness.

Therapeutic Approaches in Stage 3

Therapeutic work at Stage 3 is not about suppressing emotion or reinforcing roles, but about reopening the confrontation of emotional identity, allowing the client to integrate authenticity (Flame) and role (Mask) consciously.

1. **DRT–ART (Analytical Resolution Therapy):**

    - Focus: uncover the symbolic carriers and distorted emotional/role patterns.
    - Examples: analyzing dramatization (Flame excess), exploring depersonalization (Mask excess), decoding creative output or role fixation as symbolic identity anchors.
    - Goal: awareness of how distorted Flame or Mask orientations still dictate identity and relationships.

2. **DRT–BRT (Behavioral Resolution Therapy):**

    - Focus: retrain relational and emotional behaviors, balancing self-expression with role stability.
    - Examples: graded emotional exposure (for Flame distortions), structured role-flexibility training (for Mask distortions).
    - Goal: strengthen adaptive regulation of identity, sustaining both passion and coherence.

3. **DRT–XRT (Experiential Resolution Therapy):**

- Focus: direct re-experiencing of identity confrontation in safe therapeutic contexts.
- Examples: role-play of vulnerable disclosure, expressive arts therapy for Flame distortions, embodied role rehearsal for Mask distortions.
- Goal: embody a new resolution, authenticity without chaos, and role without emptiness.

Therapeutic Principle: The task is not to eliminate emotion or dismantle roles, but to reintegrate them as twin carriers of identity. Resolution comes when the client can consciously inhabit both, living authentically while sustaining coherence across life contexts.

Stage 4: Mortality & Wisdom
The Confrontation of Transcendence and Continuity

Core Confrontation

Stage 4: Mortality & Wisdom emerges once the individual has established grounding (Stage 1), relational identity (Stage 2), and emotional identity (Stage 3). The task now is to live meaningfully under the shadow of mortality. Death becomes not an abstract fact but an existential demand that presses on life with urgency.

Two valid orientations appear, each capable of healthy resolution or distortion:

- **Seer (Clarity Orientation)**

Meaning-led engagement: the individual turns toward mortality directly, seeking wisdom, perspective, and insight. Resolution builds clarity, serenity, and the capacity to integrate finitude into vision. Distortion appears as false transcendence, detachment, or pseudo-spiritual superiority, when clarity becomes escape rather than integration.

- **Wound (Continuity Orientation)**

Legacy-led engagement: the individual bears mortality as a wound and seeks to transform it into continuity, through legacy, creativity, sacrifice, or symbolic survival. Resolution builds depth, generativity, and symbolic presence beyond death. Distortion appears as despair, compulsive legacy-seeking, or destructive fixation on death.

Both orientations are developmentally normative responses to the same confrontation: "How do I live, knowing I will die?" The quality of resolution, not the orientation itself, determines stability. A well-anchored Seer or Wound provides existential wisdom; distorted forms reverberate forward as nihilism, emptiness, or frantic denial.

Resolution Pathways

In Stage 4, two orientations offer valid pathways toward existential resolution. Each provides a distinct but equally necessary way of integrating mortality into life.

- **Seer (Clarity Orientation)**

Resolution occurs when the individual confronts mortality directly and accepts finitude as an inescapable reality. The Seer type develops perspective, serenity, and truth-seeking capacities. Mortality is not erased but woven into wisdom, enabling the person to guide others and to face life's end without collapse.

- **Wound (Continuity Orientation)**

Resolution occurs when the individual bears the scar of mortality yet transforms it into continuity. Instead of despair, the wound becomes a source of depth and generativity: parenting, mentorship, creative legacy, or sacrificial contribution. Mortality is carried forward symbolically, ensuring life echoes beyond the individual's end.

Both orientations are developmentally normative responses to the same confrontation. The quality of resolution, not the orientation itself, determines stability: a well-anchored Seer or Wound integrates mortality into meaning, while distorted forms reverberate as either shallow transcendence or consuming despair.

Distortions

Failure in Stage 4 does not erase the confrontation; it twists it. Distortion occurs when either orientation becomes exaggerated, collapsed, or disconnected from its developmental task:

A. Seer Distortions (Clarity Orientation distorted):

- False transcendence, pseudo-spirituality, or detachment from human reality.
- "All-seeing" arrogance — superiority masked as wisdom.
- Avoidance of mortality through intellectualization or mystical escape.
- Clinical anchors: schizotypal traits, spiritual bypassing, dissociative detachment.

B. Wound Distortions (Continuity Orientation distorted):

- Despair, nihilism, or fixation on mortality as annihilation.
- Compulsive legacy-seeking, frantic productivity to "outrun death."
- Self-destruction or martyrdom without integration.
- Clinical anchors: depressive collapse, self-harm patterns, compulsive achievement under existential fear.

C. Mixed Distortions:

- Oscillation between shallow transcendence (Seer distortion) and paralyzing despair (Wound distortion).

- Existential instability — alternating denial of mortality with compulsive reminders of death.

- Inability to integrate wisdom or continuity into a coherent meaning.

- Clinical anchors: existential crises, severe identity diffusion, chronic despair masked by false serenity.

These distortions are not "new" disorders but fractures of Stage 4 reverberating through adult life. Many adult pathologies trace their roots here:

- Existential depression → collapsed Wound without continuity.
- Nihilistic detachment → distorted Seer without grounding.
- Workaholic legacy compulsion → overextended Wound, collapsed Seer.
- Spiritual bypassing → inflated Seer avoiding mortality's reality.

Phenomenology of Stage 4

Stage 4 is lived through the confrontation with mortality and meaning: the demand to answer "How do I live, knowing I will die?" This confrontation is embodied in awareness of finitude, symbolic continuity, and the need to anchor life in wisdom or legacy.

1. **Mortality Awareness**
   - The individual begins to face death as a reality, not just a concept.
   - Seer resolution: mortality is accepted, fostering clarity, humility, and perspective.
   - Wound resolution: mortality is carried, producing depth and symbolic continuity.
   - Distorted forms: denial of death through pseudo-transcendence (Seer) or collapse into despair (Wound).
   - Clinical anchors: existential anxiety, death phobia, compulsive denial behaviors.

2. **Legacy and Continuity**
   - The drive for symbolic survival emerges, children, works, mentorship, cultural impact.
   - Seer resolution: continuity anchored in truth and wisdom, not compulsion.
   - Wound resolution: continuity through sacrifice, care, and creativity.
   - Distorted forms: compulsive productivity, obsessive legacy-seeking, or rejection of all continuity.
   - Clinical anchors: workaholism, burnout, despair of insignificance.

3. **Anxiety of Finitude**

- Fear emerges around annihilation versus endurance.
- Resolution: balance between clarity (acceptance of limits) and continuity (creation of symbolic life).
- Distortion: panic of erasure ("nothing remains of me") or flight into grandiose transcendence ("I am beyond death").
- Clinical anchors: existential depression, dissociative detachment, obsessive striving.

4. **Symbolic Carriers**

- Mortality and continuity are symbolized through rituals, monuments, texts, art, and spiritual practices.
- Resolution: flexible use of symbolic carriers to embody wisdom or continuity.
- Distortion: over-attachment to symbols ("without my monument, I am nothing") or destruction of them ("to reject death, I must reject all symbols").
- Clinical anchors: religious fanaticism, iconoclasm, obsessive symbolic control.

Adult Manifestations of Stage 4

Unresolved or distorted Stage 4 patterns echo into adulthood as existential instability, either clinging to false transcendence, collapsing into despair, or compulsively seeking legacy without integration.

Distorted Manifestations:

- Seer distortions (clarity inflated): pseudo-spiritual superiority, detachment from ordinary life, intellectualization of death as escape.
- Wound distortions (continuity inflated): compulsive productivity, obsession with legacy, fixation on symbolic survival.
- Mixed distortions: oscillation between shallow transcendence and consuming despair; denial of mortality alternating with panic of annihilation.
- Clinical anchors: existential depression, burnout, spiritual bypassing, compulsive overachievement, nihilistic withdrawal.

Resolved Manifestations:

- Seer resolution: serenity in the face of mortality, perspective rooted in acceptance, ability to guide others with clarity and truth.
- Wound resolution: depth through sacrifice and symbolic continuity, legacy built not from compulsion but from care, creativity, or mentorship.
- Balanced integration: capacity to live meaningfully under mortality by weaving wisdom and continuity together.
- Adaptive resilience: capacity to face finitude without collapse, to create continuity without compulsion, and to embody existential maturity.

Resolution at Stage 4 provides existential wisdom: the ability to live fully under the shadow of death. Distorted Stage 4, however, reverberates as chronic despair, compulsive striving, or hollow transcendence, leaving the person unanchored in meaning.

Therapeutic Approaches in Stage 4

Therapeutic work at Stage 4 is not about removing fear of death or forcing optimism, but about reopening the confrontation with mortality so the client can integrate meaning, wisdom, and continuity consciously.

1. **DRT–ART (Analytical Resolution Therapy):**
   - Focus: uncover symbolic distortions around mortality and legacy.
   - Examples: analyzing compulsive legacy projects, deconstructing pseudo-spiritual defenses, decoding symbolic carriers of continuity (monuments, rituals).
   - Goal: awareness of how distorted Seer or Wound orientations still govern life choices and existential outlook.
2. **DRT–BRT (Behavioral Resolution Therapy):**
   - Focus: retrain adaptive responses to finitude and continuity.
   - Examples: structured legacy projects grounded in meaning rather than compulsion, behavioral pacing for workaholic tendencies, balanced role in caregiving or mentorship.
   - Goal: support continuity without overextension, integrate daily life with existential reality.

3. **DRT–XRT (Experiential Resolution Therapy):**

- Focus: direct re-experiencing of mortality confrontation in safe settings.
- Examples: guided visualization of finitude, ritualized symbolic exercises (letters to future generations, symbolic burial/rebirth practices), role-play of confronting death anxiety.
- Goal: embody new resolution — clarity without detachment, continuity without despair.

Therapeutic Principle: The task is not to erase death anxiety, but to integrate it. Healing occurs when mortality becomes a source of wisdom (Seer) and continuity (Wound), allowing the individual to live meaningfully under the inevitability of finitude.

Comparative Closing of the Four Stages

The four stages of the *Developmental Confrontation Theory (DCT)* form a sequential yet interdependent architecture of human development. Each stage introduces a new existential confrontation, with dual orientations that can either resolve adaptively or distort pathologically.

Stage 1: Self vs. World

- Core Question: How do I stand in a world that overwhelms me?
- Orientations: Igniter (Exploration) vs. Adaptor (Regulation).
- Resolution: balance between initiative and order.
- Distortions: scattered activation, compulsive rigidity, oscillation.

Stage 2: Self vs. Other

- Core Question: How do I exist when another exists beside me?
- Orientations: Wall (Boundary) vs. Mirror (Recognition).
- Resolution: balance between differentiation and reflection.
- Distortions: isolation, dependency, relational chaos.

Stage 3: Emotional Identity

- Core Question: How do I know myself as unique and authentic?
- Orientations: Flame (Authenticity) vs. Mask (Role).
- Resolution: balance between raw expression and symbolic function.
- Distortions: emotional burnout, hollow role-play, identity collapse.

Stage 4: Mortality & Wisdom

- Core Question: How do I live meaningfully under finitude?
- Orientations: Seer (Clarity) vs. Wound (Continuity).
- Resolution: balance between insight and legacy.
- Distortions: pseudo-transcendence, despair, compulsive legacy.

Integrative View

Across all four stages, the principle holds:

- Both orientations are valid paths to resolution. Distortion emerges not from choosing one over the other, but from inflation, collapse, or disconnection.

- Each stage reverberates forward. Early fractures echo into later confrontations, while resolution provides scaffolding for maturity.

- Therapeutic work restores confrontation. Healing does not bypass developmental tasks but reopens them, allowing resolution to be chosen consciously.

Thus, the four stages together constitute the constitutional architecture of *DCΨ*: a system where growth is structured by confrontation, resilience by resolution, and pathology by distortion.

DCΨ

Chapter 6

COMPARATIVE APPROACHES TO DCT

Freud & Erikson

Psychoanalytic Foundations and the Birth of Confrontation

The developmental confrontation model finds one of its earliest roots in psychoanalysis, where both Freud and Erikson sought to map the inner struggles that shape identity. While their theories differ in structure and emphasis, they converge on a central principle: human development unfolds through conflict. Each stage of growth presents a unique tension that demands resolution. The originality of *Developmental Confrontation Theory (DCT)* lies not in denying this legacy but in refining it—removing ambiguities, eliminating cultural limitations, and extending confrontation beyond intrapsychic or social conflict into an existential, structured process.

Freud's Structural Conflicts

Freud's psychosexual stages represent an initial attempt to trace the sequence of human development through bodily zones and instinctual satisfactions. Each stage was framed around a confrontation between instinctual drives and social restrictions. The oral stage, for example, is marked by the confrontation between the infant's need for nourishment and the inevitable frustration of delayed or denied satisfaction. The anal stage introduces control and autonomy, while the phallic stage confronts identity through the Oedipal complex.

What Freud mapped, albeit in terms rooted in drive theory, parallels *DCT's* insistence that development cannot progress without confrontation. Where Freud saw fixation and regression as consequences of failed resolution, *DCT* interprets these phenomena as distortions—pathological residues of unresolved confrontation. The insight of *DCT* is that resolution is not merely about redirecting libido or satisfying instinctual needs but about reorganizing identity itself. Fixations represent not only unintegrated desires but also fractured confrontations that failed to solidify the self in its dialogue with world, other, emotion, and mortality.

Another refinement lies in the symbolic scope. Freud's focus on oral, anal, and phallic stages emphasized bodily pleasure, but *DCT* sees confrontation as extending into symbolic, emotional, and existential dimensions. In this sense, Freud provided the scaffolding of conflict, but *DCT* reconstructs the building: it is not drive against prohibition, but self against confrontation—existentially necessary and universal.

Erikson's Psychosocial Reframing

Erikson extended Freud's framework by detaching development from purely instinctual processes and grounding it in psychosocial confrontations. His stages—from trust vs. mistrust to integrity vs. despair—each describe a polarity that the individual must negotiate. This shift brings Freud's drive-based theory closer to the *DCT* model, as Erikson emphasized identity formation through crisis.

For example, Erikson's stage of autonomy vs. shame and doubt parallels *DCT's* Stage 1: Self vs. World. The child must assert independence while also recognizing external order. Resolution generates autonomy; failure produces shame, dependency, or withdrawal. Similarly, Erikson's identity vs. role confusion resonates with *DCT's* Stage 3: Emotional Identity, where the self must embrace authenticity or collapse into performance and mask.

Yet Erikson's framework often diluted confrontation into balance. His language of "crisis" suggests turning points, but he also implied that partial or delayed resolution was possible, leaving ambiguity in outcomes. *DCT* sharpens this into a stricter structure: confrontation is not optional, and avoidance produces distortions that linger. Resolution is not merely balancing two poles—it is establishing a coherent identity through direct engagement with confrontation.

DCT's Refinement of the Psychoanalytic Tradition

The confrontation lens in *DCT* builds directly on what Freud and Erikson only partially realized. *DCT* differs in three essential ways:

1. **Universality of Confrontation**: Freud tied stages to bodily zones; Erikson tied them to social expectations. *DCT* instead asserts that confrontations are universal existential demands—self vs. world, self vs. other, emotional identity, and mortality. These are not cultural or bodily accidents but fundamental structures of being.

2. **Resolution vs. Distortion**: Freud spoke of fixation and regression; Erikson spoke of crisis and partial resolution. *DCT* sharpens this into a dual outcome: confrontation either leads to resolution (healthy reorganization of identity) or distortion (pathological fracture). This dualism eliminates the gray ambiguity of "partial success."

3. **Symbolic and Therapeutic Integration**: Freud and Erikson's models remained descriptive. *DCT* integrates diagnostic (Stage Resolution Index), symbolic (*DCPTT*), and therapeutic (*DRT*, *ART*, *BRT*, *XRT*) tools that operationalize confrontation in clinical practice.

In this way, Freud and Erikson provided necessary but incomplete maps. *DCT* absorbs their insights, translates them into existential terms, and builds a structured school that is simultaneously diagnostic, therapeutic, and symbolic.

Freud's Clinical Parallels with DCT

Freud's patients often revealed patterns that *DCT* now interprets as distortions of confrontation. Hysterical paralysis, obsessive rituals, or phobic avoidance were not random neuroses but echoes of unresolved developmental struggles.

- **Oral Fixations**: Patients who remained dependent, overly trusting, or chronically seeking external soothing mirror a Stage 1 distortion. Instead of igniting autonomy (Igniter) or building adaptive order (Adaptor), they remained bound to infantile dependency, unable to confront the world independently.

- **Anal Fixations**: Excessive control, rigidity, or messiness correspond to distortions of boundary-making in Stage 2. These patients were trapped between the need to assert their will (Wall) and the need to seek approval (Mirror).

- **Oedipal Conflicts**: At the phallic stage, unresolved identity struggles foreshadow Stage 3 distortions—either burning with misplaced flame (exhibitionism, narcissism) or collapsing into masks of repression and false conformity.

Freud lacked the symbolic precision to map these distortions systematically. *DCT*, by contrast, interprets such patterns as predictable outcomes of confrontation avoidance. In modern terms, Freud diagnosed symptoms; *DCT* diagnoses distortions.

Erikson's Psychosocial Expansion Revisited

Erikson, unlike Freud, paid closer attention to the social mirror. His concept of identity crisis emphasized the relational and cultural dimensions of confrontation. For instance:

- **Trust vs. Mistrust (infancy):** Echoes the earliest grounding of self vs. world.
- **Autonomy vs. Shame (toddlerhood):** Parallel to Stage 1 in DCT, where confrontation with external order tests autonomy.
- **Initiative vs. Guilt (early childhood):** Resonates with early aspects of Stage-2, where social interaction tests boundaries.
- **Identity vs. Role Confusion (adolescence):** A clear precursor to Stage 3: Emotional Identity in DCT.

Erikson recognized the symbolic and social weight of each stage but left outcomes open-ended. A person could re-encounter a crisis later in life, potentially resolving it retroactively. DCT narrows this flexibility: unresolved confrontations do not simply "wait" but actively distort future development. For example, a fractured Stage 2 confrontation (failure of Wall or Mirror) will not only reappear in adolescence but will distort Stage 3 identity formation, producing unstable emotional authenticity.

Neuroscientific Support for Freud and Erikson's Legacy

Modern neuroscience lends surprising support to both Freud's intuitions and Erikson's expansions, and by extension validates *DCT's* framework.

- **Attachment and the Orbitofrontal Cortex:** Research shows that early attachment interactions shape neural circuitry in the orbitofrontal cortex, responsible for emotional regulation and social attunement. Secure attachment strengthens the child's ability to mirror and be mirrored—directly supporting *DCT's* Stage 2 confrontation (Wall vs. Mirror).

- **Memory and Trauma in the Hippocampus and Amygdala:** Freud intuited that unresolved conflicts leave psychic residues. Contemporary neuroscience shows how trauma disrupts hippocampal memory integration and heightens amygdala reactivity, producing distortions that resemble *DCT's* unresolved confrontations. A child who fails Stage 1 grounding, for example, may carry hypervigilance and insecurity into every later stage.

- **Adolescence and the Prefrontal Cortex:** Erikson emphasized the identity crisis of adolescence. Neuroscience confirms that the prefrontal cortex, which integrates emotional identity with long-term planning, is not fully developed until early adulthood. This aligns with *DCT's* Stage 3 confrontation: the adolescent struggles to integrate authentic flame or risk collapsing into performance masks.

These findings suggest that Freud and Erikson's theories were not mere speculation but early recognition of confrontation-driven development. *DCT* absorbs these insights, restructuring them into a precise model that can integrate psychological, symbolic, and neuroscientific evidence.

Mapping Freud's Stages to DCT

Freud's psychosexual stages, when reframed through the lens of *Developmental Confrontation Theory*, can be interpreted not as literal fixations on erogenous zones, but as symbolic encounters with confrontation.

- **Oral Stage → Stage 1 (Self vs. World):**
Freud described dependency on oral gratification as central to early life. *DCT* refines this into a confrontation: the infant must ignite its own autonomy (Igniter) or adaptively integrate order (Adaptor). Fixations here, seen in adults who are overly dependent, passive, or compulsively consuming, reflect distortions of this confrontation.

- **Anal Stage → Stage 2 (Self vs. Other):**
Freud viewed anal fixations as about control, order, and defiance. *DCT* interprets this more structurally: the individual must build a Wall (boundaries) or form identity through Mirror (reflection). Distortions here map onto obsessive rigidity, oppositionalism, or dependency on others' approval.

- **Phallic Stage → Stage 3 (Emotional Identity):**
Freud emphasized Oedipal struggles, but *DCT* reframes this as the confrontation of authentic emotional Flame versus the protective Mask. Exhibitionism, narcissism, or compulsive role-playing represent distorted confrontations at this level.

- **Latency & Genital Stages → Stage 4 (Mortality & Wisdom):**
Freud considered these final stages as consolidation and reproductive maturity. *DCT* instead sees them as existential confrontation: facing mortality and achieving symbolic legacy. The Seer accepts finitude and transforms it into wisdom; the Wound denies mortality, producing aggression, denial, or destructive despair.

By restructuring Freud's stages into confrontation-driven terms, *DCT* both preserves his clinical insights and transcends their limitations. What Freud saw as instinctual fixations are, in *DCT*, psychological stand-offs between resolution and distortion.

Mapping Erikson's Stages to DCT

Erikson's psychosocial crises overlap even more directly with *DCT's* structure. His eight stages can be streamlined into DCT's four confrontations:

- **Trust vs. Mistrust → Stage 1 (Self vs. World):**
  Parallels the need for grounding in Igniter/Adaptor. Secure trust enables exploration; mistrust creates distorted dependency or avoidance.

- **Autonomy vs. Shame → Stage 1 (Self vs. World):**
  Aligns with autonomy-building. Shame emerges when Igniter is suppressed or Adaptor becomes rigid.

- **Initiative vs. Guilt → Stage 2 (Self vs. Other):**
  Equivalent to the confrontation of Wall and Mirror. Initiative reflects healthy assertion of boundaries; guilt reflects distorted mirroring or collapse.

- **Industry vs. Inferiority → Stage 2/3 bridge:**
  The child compares self to peers. Resolution involves balanced mirroring; distortion leads to feelings of incompetence or excessive self-criticism.

- **Identity vs. Role Confusion → Stage 3 (Emotional Identity):**
  The central adolescent confrontation of Flame vs. Mask. Authentic identity requires burning with genuine expression; distortion collapses into confusion or superficial role-playing.

- **Intimacy vs. Isolation → Stage 3/4 bridge:**
  Healthy flame extends into relational intimacy; distorted Mask produces isolation or shallow relationships.

- **Generativity vs. Stagnation → Stage 4 (Mortality & Wisdom):**
  Aligns with the Seer trait—leaving symbolic legacy through nurturing, teaching, or creating. Stagnation corresponds to the Wound, a collapse into emptiness and futility.

- **Integrity vs. Despair → Stage 4 (Mortality & Wisdom):**
  Final confrontation of Seer vs. Wound. Integrity transforms mortality into wisdom; despair rejects finitude and collapses into bitterness.

Unlike Erikson's model, which allows crises to remain "open," DCT insists that unresolved confrontations distort all subsequent development. For example, failure at Stage 2 (Wall/Mirror) leads to relational instability that directly undermines Stage 3's capacity for authentic identity.

Neuroscientific Corroboration of Stage Mapping

Recent findings strengthen this alignment:

- **Stage 1 (Self vs. World):**
  Infant brain studies show how sensorimotor grounding and early caregiver regulation shape the ventromedial prefrontal cortex and limbic system. Secure grounding strengthens Igniter (autonomy) and Adaptor (order integration).

- **Stage 2 (Self vs. Other):**
  Mirror neuron systems, particularly in the inferior frontal gyrus and superior temporal sulcus, support recognition and reflection. These neural mechanisms directly underpin *DCT's* Mirror function. Boundary formation (Wall) correlates with maturation of inhibitory control in the dorsolateral prefrontal cortex.

- **Stage 3 (Emotional Identity):**
  Limbic-prefrontal integration during adolescence explains the volatility of Flame vs. Mask. A balanced prefrontal cortex enables authentic expression; hyperactive amygdala + weak regulation produces role confusion or emotional distortions.

- **Stage 4 (Mortality & Wisdom):**
  Neuroscience of aging highlights the shift toward meaning-making and symbolic legacy. Frontal lobe networks adapt to compensate for cognitive decline, supporting reflective integration (Seer). When distorted, the same decline can lead to rigidity, despair, or destructive denial (Wound).

Comparative Synthesis: Freud, Erikson, and the Refinement of DCT

Freud and Erikson remain foundational to developmental psychology, yet both frameworks contain structural gaps that *Developmental Confrontation Theory (DCT)* systematically addresses. The synthesis demonstrates how *DCT* neither discards nor merely borrows from these traditions but instead reformulates their partial insights into a coherent confrontation-driven structure.

1. From Instinct to Confrontation

Freud's view of development emphasized instinctual zones and libidinal energies. While this framework provided valuable clinical metaphors, it often reduced human development to drives that lacked psychological agency. *DCT* reframes these so-called fixations as structured confrontations. Instead of an oral fixation representing unresolved dependency, *DCT* interprets it as the failure to resolve the confrontation of autonomy versus adaptive order in Stage 1. This translation preserves Freud's observations while grounding them in existential and psychological dynamics rather than biological determinism.

2. From Social Crisis to Confrontation

Erikson, by contrast, expanded Freud's framework into psychosocial stages, highlighting identity, intimacy, and legacy. Yet Erikson's stages remain somewhat descriptive, with crises that may or may not be "resolved" without clear structural consequences. *DCT* advances this by insisting that every confrontation is decisive. An unresolved confrontation does not simply linger but distorts subsequent development, cascading into predictable fractures across later stages. For instance, failure to establish boundaries in Stage 2 (Wall) undermines authentic identity in Stage 3 (Flame vs. Mask) and destabilizes mortality confrontation in Stage 4 (Seer vs. Wound).

3. Structural Precision: Four Core Confrontations

Where Freud proposed five to six stages and Erikson eight, *DCT* reduces these proliferations into four universal confrontations. Each stage in *DCT* carries a precise internal opposition—Igniter vs. Adaptor, Wall vs. Mirror, Flame vs. Mask, Seer vs. Wound—that either resolves or distorts. This duality is absent in both Freud and Erikson. Their models account for growth but insufficiently for distortion. *DCT* defines not only what successful resolution looks like but also the predictable forms of collapse, grounding pathology in the same developmental logic as healthy growth.

4. Neuroscientific Integration

Modern neuroscience reinforces *DCT's* confrontation-driven framework. Freud lacked access to neurobiological evidence, relying on metaphorical drives. Erikson, while attentive to social context, could not explain the neural mechanisms underlying attachment, reflection, or identity consolidation. *DCT* integrates findings from brain development: the role of the prefrontal cortex in boundary-setting, the mirror neuron system in reflection, limbic-prefrontal regulation in emotional identity, and compensatory frontal mechanisms in meaning-making during aging. These neural structures correspond directly to the confrontations mapped by *DCT*, offering biological grounding for what Freud and Erikson observed but could not fully explain.

5. Therapeutic Implications

Freud's psychoanalysis sought to uncover unconscious fixations; Erikson emphasized supportive environments for crisis navigation. *DCT*, by contrast, prescribes confrontation as therapeutic necessity. The therapist's role is not only to uncover past failures but to re-engage the client in the unresolved confrontation, within a structured framework. For example, a client with borderline pathology (Stage 2 distortion) cannot simply be reassured (Erikson's solution) or analyzed for early dependency (Freud's approach). They must actively reconstruct Wall (boundaries) and Mirror (reflection) within therapeutic confrontation. *DCT* thus provides both diagnostic precision and a confrontation-based intervention strategy.

6. Comparative Summary

- **Freud** → Drives without structure

DCT preserves clinical insights but replaces drives with confrontation dynamics.

- **Erikson** → Crises without necessity

DCT preserves psychosocial insights but introduces structural inevitability and distortion.

- **DCT** → Confrontations with dual outcomes

Growth is not optional but demanded; failure produces distortion, success produces resolution.

By drawing from both Freud and Erikson, *DCT* reveals itself as the next structural synthesis in developmental theory: grounded in observation, sharpened by confrontation logic, and corroborated by neuroscience. Freud mapped instinct, Erikson mapped crisis, but *DCT* maps confrontation as the essential engine of human development.

Piaget & Vygotsky

Piaget and the Cognitive Architecture of Confrontation

Jean Piaget's contribution to developmental psychology is the systematic mapping of cognitive structures across childhood and adolescence. His theory demonstrates that children do not merely accumulate information; rather, they reconstruct their mental world through stages characterized by distinct logical forms: sensorimotor, preoperational, concrete operational, and formal operational. Although Piaget did not frame development in explicitly existential terms, his stage theory can be reinterpreted through the lens of *Developmental Confrontation Theory* (*DCT*) as an account of how the mind equips itself to meet and metabolize the four great confrontations of life.

Sensorimotor Intelligence and DCT Stage 1: Self vs. World

During the sensorimotor period, the infant learns the invariants of the world through action—grasping, tracking, object permanence, means–end coordination. Piaget described this as the birth of the object and the stabilization of schemas through assimilation and accommodation. *DCT* reads this achievement as the earliest resolution of the Self vs. World confrontation. The child must acquire enough internal agency to act (Igniter) while simultaneously discovering a stable external order that can be relied upon and gradually internalized (Adaptor). When the sensorimotor world resists or overwhelms—through neglect, chaos, or inconsistent caregiving—cognitive schemas do not simply lag; the self's engagement with the world becomes distorted. Hypervigilance, withdrawal, or ritualized reliance on external cues later in life can be understood as sequelae of an unresolved Stage 1 confrontation rather than merely a cognitive delay.

Piaget's core mechanisms—assimilation (fitting the world into current schemas) and accommodation (altering schemas to fit the world)—map neatly onto the *DCT* dialectic. Assimilation without accommodation corresponds to a rigid Adaptor overreliance (clinging to prior structure even when the world changes). Accommodation without adequate assimilation corresponds to an undisciplined Igniter overreach (acting without the stability of an internalized frame). Balanced equilibration is, in *DCT* terms, resolution: the world is neither swallowed by the self nor the self dissolved into the world, but a negotiated, stable relationship is achieved.

Preoperational Thought and DCT Stage 2: Self vs. Other

The preoperational period introduces symbolic function, language, and representational play, yet is characterized by egocentrism, centration, and difficulty with perspective-taking. *DCT* recognizes this as the cognitive prelude to the Self vs. Other confrontation. As representational thought blossoms, the child begins to encounter others not simply as sources of stimulation but as mirrors in which identity is reflected and as boundaries against which the self differentiates. Piaget's egocentrism is not merely a cognitive limitation; it expresses a developmental task: the child must cultivate the capacity to see the other's point of view (the seed of Mirror) and to maintain self-continuity against the other's difference (the foundation of Wall).

Failures in decentration—difficulty stepping into another's perspective—are not only logical deficits but early signs of a relational distortion. Some children compensate by fusing with the other (a distorted over-reliance on Mirror), while others protect themselves by withdrawing behind impermeable boundaries (a distorted exaggeration of Wall). Seen in this way, Piaget's "errors" become *DCT's* clinically meaningful markers: cognitive indices of how the child is faring in the second developmental confrontation.

Concrete Operations and the Stabilization of Social Reality

Concrete operational thought, with its capacity for reversibility, conservation, class inclusion, and seriation, corresponds to a marked strengthening of internal structure. Children at this stage can entertain multiple perspectives within concrete limits, resolve contradictions in simple domains, and apply rules consistently. For *DCT*, this consolidation is crucial because it supports the sustained negotiation of boundaries and reflection: Wall becomes less brittle (it can bend without breaking), and Mirror becomes less volatile (reflection can occur without collapse into the other). Concrete operations thus provide the cognitive spine that allows relational confrontations to be held, examined, and reworked without panic. When concrete operations remain fragile, relational life tends to become either rule-bound and inflexible (over-structured Adaptor/Wall) or unstable and conformist (over-reactive Mirror without a stabilizing Wall).

Formal Operations and the Entrance to DCT Stage 3 and Stage 4

Piaget's formal operational stage introduces hypothetico–deductive reasoning, second-order thinking, and the capacity to abstract beyond the immediately given. Adolescents can imagine possible worlds and reason about meta-level relationships. This cognitive expansion opens the door to *DCT's* final two confrontations. In Stage 3 (Emotional Identity), the self must align authentic feeling and expression; formal reasoning allows the adolescent to reflect on the authenticity of emotions, the gap between inner conviction and outer display. It furnishes the conceptual tools to integrate Flame (authentic affect) with the social realities that demand adjustment—without dissolving into Mask (merely resonating with external signals at the cost of inner truth). In Stage 4 (Mortality & Wisdom), formal thought makes it possible to contemplate finitude, legacy, and symbolic continuity—prerequisites for the emergence of the Seer. In the absence of stable cognitive scaffolding, mortality confrontation inclines toward denial, magical thinking, or despair, all forms of the Wound as Stage 4 distortion.

Piaget's model, in short, describes the cognitive scaffolding required to mount *DCT's* existential confrontations. Where Piaget explained what logical forms must be in place, *DCT* explains what those forms are for: the metabolization of world, other, emotion, and death. Cognitive success is not equivalent to existential resolution, but without adequate cognitive structure, resolution becomes precarious; with it, resolution becomes durable.

Case Illustrations across Piagetian Stages Reinterpreted by DCT

Consider a child with robust sensorimotor exploration who nevertheless shows extreme distress when routines are disrupted. Piaget might note uneven consolidation across sub-stages; *DCT* identifies a Stage 1 imbalance: the child over-privileges Adaptor (external order) and struggles to ignite autonomous action without a fixed script. In adolescence, imagine a high-achieving formal reasoner who constructs impressive arguments for life goals that shift with peer approval. Cognitively, this is a formal thinker; existentially, *DCT* sees a Stage 3 distortion toward Mask, where the capacity for abstraction has been pressed into the service of external resonance rather than authentic self-definition. In both cases, *DCT* reframes cognitive competence as necessary but insufficient; the salient question is whether cognitive structure is enlisted in the service of confrontation and resolution or co-opted into maintaining distortions.

Methodological Convergences

Piaget's methods—clinical interviews, conservation tasks, error analysis—demonstrate that development is best revealed when the child is asked to explain their reasoning under strain. *DCT* shares this methodological instinct. The scanner and assessment components aligned with *DCT* (e.g., *Stage Resolution Index*) similarly examine how individuals confront destabilizing prompts rather than how they perform in neutral contexts. Both systems privilege the point of breakdown as diagnostic: Piaget for cognitive structure, *DCT* for existential organization.

Limits of Cognitivism and DCT's Existential Supplement

Piaget powerfully established that children think differently from adults and that their logic evolves in structured sequences. Yet children can display formal reasoning in constrained domains while remaining existentially fragile. *DCT* clarifies why: cognitive operations do not guarantee that the four confrontations have been authentically engaged. A precocious formal thinker may rationalize avoidance—construct elaborate justifications to circumvent Stage 2 intimacy or Stage 3 authenticity—thus enlisting cognition to fortify distortion. This explains the clinically familiar case of highly intelligent individuals collapsing under relational or existential pressure.

Cognitivism also underestimates the symbolic dimension of development. For *DCT*, symbols such as Igniter, Adaptor, Wall, Mirror, Flame, Mask, Seer, Wound are not poetic labels but compressed functional descriptions of how the self organizes confrontation. Piaget rightly focuses on how the child comes to conserve physical quantity; *DCT* asks how the person comes to conserve identity under pressure from world, other, emotion, and mortality. Cognitive conservation without identity conservation leaves the person logically consistent but structurally unresolved.

Vygotsky and the Social Genesis of Resolution

Lev Vygotsky's sociocultural theory complements *DCT* by foregrounding the role of social mediation in development. Higher mental functions are internalized through dialogue with more capable others within the zone of proximal development (ZPD). Tools and signs—language foremost—transform the child's thought from outside in, then from inside out. This process is not accidental to *DCT*; it is the mechanism by which Stage 2 (Self vs. Other) is most visibly negotiated.

Mirroring and Scaffolding: Convergence with DCT Stage 2

In *DCT* terms, the Mirror pathway draws strength from sensitive scaffolding. When adults track the child's intent, amplify initiative, and provide graded assistance, they create a reflective field in which the child can see themselves doing more than they could alone. This revelation is not just cognitive; it is ontological—the child discovers who they are by witnessing their capacity reflected in another's gaze and language. Conversely, over-intrusive or indifferent scaffolding distorts mirroring: the self either fuses with the guide's intention or withdraws from a field that offers no recognition. Both produce relational distortions later described clinically as dependency, identity diffusion, or oscillation between clinging and rage.

Boundary Formation within Social Mediation: Convergence with DCT Wall

Vygotsky's emphasis on internalization risks being mistaken for pure fusion. *DCT* clarifies that internalization must be bounded by a developing Wall—a capacity to take in tools and language without losing self–other distinction. Effective scaffolding includes planned withdrawal: the adult recedes as the child's Wall strengthens. When withdrawal never occurs, scaffolding becomes colonization and the person later shows an "other-directed" pattern: fluent, compliant, yet structurally hollow.

Private Speech, Self-Regulation, and Stage Intersections

Vygotsky's analysis of private speech as a bridge to self-regulation provides a powerful microcosm of *DCT's* first two stages. The child's whispered instructions to self are both an internal Mirror (adopting the caregiver's voice) and a rehearsal of Wall (taking command of action). Over time, private speech condenses into inner speech, a core element of executive function. When this process is disrupted, the person retains dependence on external prompts (distorted Mirror) or avoids guidance altogether (distorted Wall), with downstream effects on Stage 3 authenticity and Stage 4 meaning-making.

ZPD and the Ethics of Confrontation

The ZPD concept also carries an implicit ethics aligned with *DCT*: optimal development occurs when challenge slightly exceeds current capacity in a reliable relational field. This is exactly the clinical logic of DCT-guided intervention: to re-enter unresolved confrontations under graded demand, within a stable alliance, so that resolution can be rehearsed, consolidated, and internalized.

Case Vignettes: Vygotskian Mediation Re-read by DCT

A school-age child who excels when the teacher sits beside them but falters when asked to work independently shows a strong Mirror response with underdeveloped Wall. Vygotsky notes scaffold-dependence; *DCT* specifies a Stage 2 distortion likely to manifest later as relational over-reliance or identity diffusion under separation. Conversely, a child who resists any assistance, insists on solitary problem-solving, and melts down when corrected may be consolidating Wall prematurely at the expense of Mirror—a different Stage 2 distortion that hardens into avoidant intimacy patterns.

From Social Mediation to Emotional Identity: Preparing Stage 3

Vygotsky's insistence that higher functions are fundamentally social sets the stage for understanding Stage 3 (Emotional Identity) in *DCT.* Authenticity (Flame) presupposes an adequate history of mirroring: the self must have been seen well enough to dare to be seen truly. At the same time, authenticity requires a developed Wall: the capacity to remain oneself even when resonance with others is strong. Vygotsky explains the route of internalization; *DCT* defines the target—a self able to articulate and own affect without either submission to or rejection of the social field.

Theory of Mind, Perspective-Taking, and Mirror

The maturation of theory of mind—recognizing that others have beliefs and desires distinct from one's own—has been linked to language exposure, conversational scaffolding, and family discourse about mental states. These findings align with *DCT's* Mirror pathway: the more richly the child encounters reflective talk, the more robustly they construct a self-in-relation-to-others. When mental-state discourse is scarce or punitive, Mirror development falters, and later emotional identity struggles often present as hypersensitivity to others' judgments or dependency on external esteem.

Executive Functions, Boundary Control, and Wall

Advances in executive function research (working memory, inhibitory control, cognitive flexibility) show that boundary maintenance is not only psychological but also neurocognitive. *DCT's* Wall resonates with inhibitory control and goal maintenance; its absence predicts both behavioral disinhibition and relational permeability. Adolescents with weak executive function are particularly vulnerable to Stage 3 distortions: rather than expressing a coherent Flame, they oscillate between signals from peers, partners, and media, amplifying Mask at the expense of authenticity.

Information-Processing Perspectives and DCT

Information-processing models emphasize attentional control, encoding, storage, and retrieval. From a *DCT* standpoint, these mechanisms are either enlisted for confrontation and resolution or co-opted against them. Rumination, for example, is a sophisticated information-processing strategy used to avoid Stage 3 confrontation: it preserves self-narrative coherence by rehearsing explanations while never risking authentic exposure. Skill becomes the servant of distortion.

Educational and Clinical Implications

Reinterpreting Piaget and Vygotsky through DCT yields concrete guidance. Educationally, instruction should be designed not only to promote cognitive mastery but also to exercise confrontation: structured opportunities to set boundaries (Wall), to receive and offer reflection (Mirror), to risk authentic expression (Flame) without collapsing into pleasing (Mask), and to link learning to meaning beyond self-interest (Seer vs. Wound). Clinically, treatment plans should evaluate whether cognitive and social strengths are being used to fortify distortions (e.g., using superior reasoning to rationalize avoidance) or to support resolution (e.g., using planning skills to structure graded exposure to feared relational tasks).

Clinical Integration and Pathological Mapping

The strength of *Developmental Confrontation Theory (DCT)* does not lie solely in its philosophical depth or symbolic mapping, but also in its ability to be clinically operationalized. By articulating both resolution and distortion, *DCT* provides a scaffold that enables researchers, therapists, and diagnosticians to trace the origins of pathology across the lifespan. In this sense, *DCT* functions as both a developmental model and a diagnostic compass, guiding clinical interventions toward the unresolved confrontations that fracture identity.

Neuropsychological Foundations of Distortion

Distortions within each stage are not abstractions; they are grounded in the very architecture of the human brain:

- **Stage 1 (Self vs. World):**
  The Igniter and Adaptor are linked to regulatory systems of the brainstem and early prefrontal control. Distortions here can be understood through hypervigilance in the amygdala or underdevelopment of regulatory circuits in the dorsolateral prefrontal cortex, producing either overwhelming impulsivity (Igniter distortion) or paralytic over-compliance (Adaptor distortion).

- **Stage 2 (Self vs. Other):**
  The Wall and Mirror depend on the social brain, particularly the temporoparietal junction and anterior cingulate cortex. Distorted Walls show hypoactivation of empathic circuits, while distorted Mirrors reveal hyperactivation of mirror neuron systems, causing identity enmeshment and unstable attachment. These distortions echo in borderline, dependent, and avoidant personality structures.

- **Stage 3 (Emotional Identity):**
  The Flame and Mask correlate with the limbic system and ventromedial prefrontal cortex, where affective resonance and inhibition balance one another. Distorted Flames manifest as affective overload (mania, rage, or hysteria), while distorted Masks show excessive inhibitory control, producing flattened affect, rigid performance, or histrionic dramatization.

- **Stage 4 (Mortality and Wisdom):**
  The Seer and Wound rely heavily on default mode network (DMN) connectivity. Resolution in the Seer corresponds to integrated self-referential processing, while Wound distortions reveal disrupted DMN synchrony, producing existential despair, nihilism, or derealization phenomena.

This alignment between symbolic confrontation and neurological substrate demonstrates that DCT is not a mere metaphorical model, but a biologically traceable framework.

Comparative Clinical Models

DCT aligns with, but also surpasses, major developmental frameworks:

- **Erikson:** Stage 2 in *DCT* (Self vs. Other) overlaps with Erikson's autonomy/shame and initiative/guilt stages, but *DCT* extends the analysis into distortions that manifest as personality disorders rather than simply *"failure to resolve."*

- **Freud:** Introjection (Stage 1) and identification (Stage 2) are reinterpreted through confrontation rather than mere instinctual development.

- **Attachment Theory:** Bowlby and Ainsworth provide empirical evidence of mirroring and boundary failures that validate Stage 2 distortions. Secure, avoidant, ambivalent, and disorganized attachment styles correspond directly to Wall/Mirror resolution and collapse.

- **Object Relations:** *DCT* integrates object constancy and splitting into its confrontation framework, explaining why unresolved boundaries (Wall collapse) lead to chronic splitting dynamics.

- **Existential Psychology:** Stage 4 resonates with existentialist themes of finitude (Heidegger), freedom (Sartre), and symbolic immortality (Becker). Unlike existential theories, however, *DCT* offers predictive mapping of distortions rather than descriptive phenomenology alone.

By linking with these traditions, *DCT* not only situates itself within the history of psychology but also corrects the blind spots of its predecessors.

Mapping Pathologies to Confrontational Distortions

A central contribution of *DCT* is its capacity to classify psychopathology not as arbitrary clusters of symptoms but as predictable distortions of confrontation:

- **Borderline Personality Disorder (BPD):** Mirror collapse + unstable Wall. Identity is fractured because validation from others never stabilizes into an internal structure.

- **Narcissistic Personality Disorder (NPD):** Distorted Flame + rigid Mask. Emotional identity is inflated outward but internally fragile.

- **Antisocial Personality Disorder (ASPD):** Hardened Wall + collapsed Mirror. Absence of reflective resonance produces predation without conscience.

- **Avoidant Personality Disorder (AvPD):** Inflated Mirror + weak Wall. Others' judgment becomes unbearable, producing withdrawal.

- **Dependent Personality Disorder (DPD):** Mirror inflation collapses selfhood entirely into external recognition.

- **Obsessive-Compulsive Personality Disorder (OCPD):** Distorted Adaptor dominates, producing compulsive reliance on external order.

- **Depersonalization/Derealization Disorder:** Stage 1–4 collapse, severing Igniter from Seer, producing radical alienation from self and world.

- **Post-Traumatic Stress Disorder (PTSD):** Stage 1 rupture, where Igniter collapses and Wall fails to shield the self. The psyche replays unresolved confrontation in flashbacks and hyperarousal.

These mappings provide both diagnostic clarity and therapeutic direction, showing that pathology is not random but the consequence of developmental confrontation avoided, mishandled, or prematurely foreclosed.

From Symbol to Science

In the symbolic language of *DCΨ*, each metaphor carries a direct psychological correlate. A "collapsed Wall" refers clinically to a breakdown of ego-boundaries and defense mechanisms, leaving the self overexposed to external pressures and unable to regulate interpersonal intrusion. An "unstable Wall" signals fragile ego defenses, where boundaries exist but are inconsistent, producing oscillation between dependency and withdrawal. A "hardened Wall" corresponds to rigid, overdeveloped defenses, resulting in emotional detachment and diminished empathy. The "Mirror", when "collapsed", indicates failure of self-image consolidation, often manifesting as identity diffusion or dependence on external validation; when "inflated", it reflects distorted self-appraisal dominated by external reflection without internal grounding. The "Flame", when "distorted", points to dysregulated affective energy—emotions either exaggerated or suppressed—producing instability of self-worth. The "Mask", when "rigid", symbolizes over-identification with social roles and suppression of authentic affect, clinically aligning with compulsive role-conformity. The "Adaptor", when "distorted", describes over-reliance on environmental order and control, as seen in compulsive or perfectionistic traits. A "Stage 1–4 collapse" refers to reversional progression across all developmental confrontations, clinically akin to dissociation and derealization. The "Igniter severed from the Seer" captures disconnection between instinctive drive (somatic vitality) and existential meaning, producing alienation from both self and world. Finally, "Igniter collapse" signals shutdown of vitality, with diminished spontaneity and hypoactivity, while the "Wall fails" underlines the psyche's inability to contain traumatic intrusion, resulting in flashbacks, hyperarousal, and fragmentation of the self.

Therapeutic Reorganization

Therapy, when guided by *DCT,* is not symptom management but confrontation reinstatement. Each stage requires the client to re-engage the confrontation they once avoided:

- Stage 1 Therapy: Grounding exercises, somatic awareness, reactivation of Igniter autonomy in controlled environments.

- Stage 2 Therapy: Boundary training and reflective dialogues. The therapist oscillates between being a Wall (offering firm structure) and a Mirror (providing reflective validation).

- Stage 3 Therapy: Emotional regulation combined with symbolic exploration. Clients learn to express the authentic Flame while discarding distorted Masks.

- Stage 4 Therapy: Existential dialogue, legacy creation, symbolic acts of continuity. Clients transform the fear of Wound into Seer's acceptance of finitude and symbolic immortality.

By treating confrontation as the locus of growth, therapy enables re-entry into the unresolved conflict. Healing, therefore, is not avoidance of the confrontation but its conscious resolution.

Humanistic, Existential, and Constructivist Perspectives

Humanistic Psychology and the Logic of Confrontation

The Humanistic Horizon of Confrontation

Humanistic psychology, as developed in the mid-20th century by Abraham Maslow, Carl Rogers, Rollo May, Gordon Allport, and others, emerged as a “third force” in psychology against the determinism of psychoanalysis and the mechanistic reductionism of behaviorism. Its central conviction is that human beings are active, intentional, meaning-seeking organisms. To be human is not merely to be driven by instincts (as Freud claimed) or conditioned by reinforcement (as Skinner argued), but to be propelled by a self-directed tendency toward growth, creativity, and authenticity.

This humanistic vision intersects profoundly with the principles of *Developmental Confrontation Theory (DCT).* Both share the conviction that growth cannot occur without crisis, disruption, and the testing of the self against limits. In Maslow’s language, the “deficiency needs” (safety, belonging, esteem) and “growth needs” (self-actualization, transcendence) are not passive layers of a pyramid but zones of confrontation. Safety is not a condition that simply appears — it is wrestled from danger. Belonging is not given — it emerges from the confrontation with rejection. Esteem does not arrive ready-made — it is born out of repeated testing of competence and failure. And self-actualization, the summit of Maslow’s model, is not a tranquil endpoint but the highest confrontation with freedom, meaning, and responsibility.

DCT takes this insight further by formalizing these struggles into four sequential stages. Each stage is not simply a "need" but a structural confrontation, demanding a resolution that reorganizes identity:

- **Stage 1: Self vs. World** – The humanistic principle of exploratory drive (curiosity, openness) appears in the Igniter trait. Yet the need for safety and order corresponds to the Adaptor trait. Maslow described early safety needs as basic; *DCT* shows they are existential confrontations where autonomy or dependency becomes patterned.

- **Stage 2: Self vs. Other** – Rogers' theory of the self resonates directly here. His concept of unconditional positive regard mirrors *DCT's* Mirror trait: the self is validated through empathic reflection. But his insistence on boundaries and congruence reflects the Wall trait: the capacity to assert "this is me, and not you." Humanistic theory provides empirical confirmation of *DCT's* second stage, where identity crystallizes between autonomy and reflection.

- **Stage 3: Emotional Identity** – Humanistic psychology highlights authenticity as the refusal to wear masks for others. *DCT* translates this into the confrontation between Flame (authentic emotional expression) and Mask (defensive performance of emotion). Rogers described incongruence as the split between the real self and the ideal self; *DCT* frames it as the structural distortion of confrontation in Stage 3.

- **Stage 4: Mortality and Wisdom** – Maslow's later writings (often ignored) moved beyond self-actualization to what he called self-transcendence: confronting death, legacy, and spiritual meaning. This is exactly the terrain of *DCT's* Seer and Wound traits. Where Maslow spoke of "peak experiences" and "transcendence," *DCT* grounds this in the final confrontation with finitude, either resolved through symbolic vision (Seer) or distorted into denial, aggression, or despair (Wound).

Thus, humanistic psychology provides not only a philosophical ally to *DCT* but also a theoretical bridge confirming that confrontation is growth.

Rogers and the Confrontation with Self vs. Other

Carl Rogers provides the most precise humanistic lens for Stage 2. His framework is built around three principles:

1. **Unconditional Positive Regard** – the experience of being accepted without conditions. In *DCT*, this is the fertile soil for the Mirror trait: the ability to form identity through reflection without collapsing into dependency.

2. **Congruence** – the alignment between the individual's self-concept and their lived experience. In *DCT*, congruence is a marker of resolution. Incongruence is a distortion: the Mask of Stage 3 or the collapsed Wall of Stage 2.

3. **Empathic Understanding** – the therapist's role in mirroring the client accurately. This practice aligns with *DCT's* therapeutic model (*DRT–XRT*), where the therapist temporarily becomes the "Mirror," restoring resolution through accurate reflection.

Rogers' clinical insights confirm *DCT's* structural claim: identity is not formed in isolation but in the confrontation between self and other. If unconditional regard is absent, the child develops distorted strategies — excessive clinging (Mirror distortion) or rigid withdrawal (Wall distortion). *DCT* thus reframes Rogers' humanistic optimism into a structured developmental law: resolution emerges from confrontation; distortion emerges from avoidance or conditionality.

Maslow and the Confrontation with Need

Maslow's hierarchy of needs is often simplified into a static pyramid. Yet his actual writings describe human development as a dynamic struggle. Each "need" arises when its absence destabilizes the self, forcing a confrontation:

- **Physiological & Safety Needs** – These align with Stage 1: the confrontation of Self vs. World. Hunger, danger, instability — these threaten existence and demand that the individual ignite initiative or adapt to structures.

- **Love & Belonging Needs** – These align with Stage 2: Self vs. Other. Belonging is not the absence of loneliness but the confrontation with rejection, shame, and recognition.

- **Esteem Needs** – These align with Stage 3: Emotional Identity. Authentic esteem arises from Flame (true expression); distorted esteem arises from Mask (performative self).

- **Self-Actualization & Transcendence** – These align with Stage 4: Mortality & Wisdom. Maslow's later emphasis on self-transcendence explicitly acknowledges the confrontation with mortality, meaning, and legacy.

In short, Maslow confirms that each stage of *DCT* is not only developmental but existential. Needs are confrontations — and the higher the stage, the deeper the confrontation.

Humanistic Therapy and DCT's Interventions

Humanistic therapies, particularly person-centered therapy, Gestalt therapy, and existential-humanistic practices, can be understood as modalities of re-entering confrontation. For example:

- **Gestalt therapy (Perls)** emphasizes awareness and the "here and now." This mirrors *DCT's* call to return to the confrontation instead of bypassing it. A distorted Wall must confront the immediacy of withdrawal. A distorted Flame must confront the authenticity of feeling.

- **Existential-humanistic therapy** emphasizes choice and responsibility. In *DCT*, this is the therapeutic equivalent of resolution over distortion: choosing to re-engage the confrontation rather than avoid it.

- **Positive psychology (Seligman, Csikszentmihalyi)**, a descendant of humanism, empirically confirms that flourishing arises from engagement, not avoidance. Flow states, resilience, and character strengths are all markers of resolution of confrontation, not escape from it.

By mapping these therapies onto *DCT*, we see that humanistic practice provides the clinical embodiment of confrontation-driven growth.

The Existential Roots of Confrontation

Existential psychology arose from the philosophical tradition of Kierkegaard, Nietzsche, Heidegger, and Sartre, later developed clinically by Viktor Frankl, Rollo May, Irvin Yalom, Medard Boss, and others. Its core claim is that human beings are defined not only by instincts or needs but by the fundamental givens of existence: death, freedom, isolation, and meaning.

Existentialists insist that psychological suffering emerges not simply from trauma or repression but from the denial of these givens. Anxiety is not a symptom to be eliminated but a signal that the self is in confrontation with the real conditions of existence. Thus, to live is to confront.

This existential foundation dovetails directly with Developmental Confrontation Theory (DCT). Where existential psychology speaks of the "givens of existence," *DCT* operationalizes them into structured stages of confrontation. Each stage introduces a universal existential demand:

- **Stage 1:** confrontation with the world (security vs. chaos).
- **Stage 2:** confrontation with the other (recognition vs. collapse).
- **Stage 3:** confrontation with the self's emotions (authenticity vs. distortion).
- **Stage 4:** confrontation with mortality and transcendence (wisdom vs. despair).

In this way, *DCT* is not only compatible with existential psychology — it provides a developmental map of when and how these existential confrontations emerge, repeat, and distort across the lifespan.

Anxiety as a Developmental Signal

For existential thinkers such as Kierkegaard and Heidegger, anxiety is not merely a negative state but a gateway to freedom. Heidegger distinguished fear (a reaction to a specific object) from anxiety (a response to the nothingness underlying existence). Rollo May later reframed this as existential anxiety: the signal that we are free, finite, and responsible.

DCT interprets anxiety as the subjective affect of confrontation. Each stage produces its own existential anxiety:

- **Stage 1 (Self vs. World):** anxiety of abandonment or annihilation — *"Will the world support me, or will it crush me?"*
- **Stage 2 (Self vs. Other):** anxiety of rejection or engulfment — *"Will I be recognized as myself, or will I dissolve into you?"*
- **Stage 3 (Emotional Identity):** anxiety of inauthenticity — *"Will I burn with my own flame, or live behind a mask?"*
- **Stage 4 (Mortality & Wisdom):** anxiety of finitude — *"Can I face death and still affirm life?"*

Avoidance of these anxieties leads to distortions (e.g., rigid walls, collapsed mirrors, false masks, denial of mortality). Resolution occurs when the individual tolerates and integrates the anxiety into growth.

Thus, existential anxiety in *DCT* is not pathology but a necessary developmental signal. Its absence (through repression, avoidance, or numbing) is more dangerous than its presence, because it prevents confrontation and guarantees distortion.

Freedom, Responsibility, and Choice

Existential psychology insists that freedom is both a gift and a burden. Sartre described humans as "condemned to be free": unable to escape responsibility for their choices, even when they refuse to choose. Viktor Frankl, through his experiences in Nazi concentration camps, emphasized that even when everything is taken, one freedom remains: the freedom to choose one's stance toward reality.

DCT locates this existential freedom within its sequential confrontations. Each stage provides a field of choice, and the resolution depends on whether the individual assumes responsibility for that choice:

- **Stage 1:** choosing to ignite autonomy (Igniter) or adapt to order (Adaptor). Both are legitimate; avoidance collapses into helplessness.
- **Stage 2:** choosing to build boundaries (Wall) or seek reflection (Mirror). Both resolve identity; avoidance distorts into dependency or alienation.
- **Stage 3:** choosing authenticity (Flame) or self-presentation (Mask). Both can resolve if conscious; distortion arises when the Mask replaces the self.
- **Stage 4:** choosing to face mortality (Seer) or to deny it (Wound). The confrontation is unavoidable, but only the assumption of responsibility produces wisdom.

In this sense, existential psychology provides the philosophical justification for *DCT's* structural law: confrontation cannot be bypassed. Freedom demands responsibility, and responsibility requires entering the confrontation.

Death and the Final Confrontation

Among the existential "givens," death holds a privileged place. Heidegger argued that authentic existence begins only when the individual anticipates their own death — what he called "being-toward-death." Irvin Yalom later described death anxiety as the background music of life, shaping human motivation in ways often denied.

DCT makes this the explicit focus of Stage 4 (Mortality and Wisdom). Death is not merely an external event but a developmental confrontation that reorganizes the psyche. Those who deny death distort into:

- Aggressive clinging to power (Wound distortion).
- Projection of immortality into children (maladaptive generativity).
- Denial through endless distraction or shallow religiosity.

Those who resolve the confrontation become Seers: individuals capable of symbolic vision, legacy, and transcendence. In this way, *DCT* formalizes existential claims: death is the ultimate confrontation, and its resolution determines whether life closes in wisdom or in distortion.

Isolation and the Relational Dimension

Existential psychology also emphasizes isolation — the recognition that no matter how close we come to others, we are ultimately alone. Yalom distinguishes three types of isolation: interpersonal, intrapersonal, and existential. *DCT* integrates this into Stage 2 (Self vs. Other), where the self learns to maintain boundaries (Wall) while seeking reflection (Mirror).

- Failure to accept existential isolation leads to dependency (Mirror distortion).
- Overreaction to isolation leads to withdrawal and hostility (Wall distortion).
- Resolution lies in acknowledging isolation while still seeking connection — a dialectic central to both existential psychology and *DCT.*

Meaning and Confrontation

For Frankl, the search for meaning is the deepest motivation of human life. He argued that despair arises not from suffering itself but from suffering without meaning. *DCT* locates meaning-making in every stage:

- **Stage 1:** meaning arises from mastery of the world ("I can survive").
- **Stage 2:** meaning arises from recognition by others ("I am seen").
- **Stage 3:** meaning arises from authenticity ("I am true").
- **Stage 4:** meaning arises from mortality ("I will be remembered, or I transcend").

Distortion, conversely, produces meaninglessness — the existential vacuum Frankl described. Thus, *DCT* operationalizes meaning as the outcome of resolution, and meaninglessness as the symptom of distortion.

Existential Therapy and DCT's Therapeutic Framework

Existential therapy aims to help clients confront rather than avoid the givens of existence. Yalom outlined four ultimate concerns: death, freedom, isolation, and meaninglessness. Each corresponds directly to *DCT's* stages:

- Death → Stage 4 (Mortality & Wisdom).
- Freedom → Stage 1 (Self vs. World).
- Isolation → Stage 2 (Self vs. Other).
- Meaninglessness → Stage 3 (Emotional Identity).

DCT's Developmental Resolution Therapy (*DRT*) builds on this by embedding existential confrontation within a developmental sequence. Therapy is not only about facing the givens but also about locating which stage's confrontation has been avoided and re-entering it consciously.

For example:

- A client paralyzed by death anxiety (Stage 4 distortion) may also reveal unresolved dependency needs in Stage 2.

- A client inauthentic in relationships (Stage 3 Mask distortion) may be avoiding rejection from Stage 2.

Thus, existential therapy provides the clinical practice of confrontation, while *DCT* provides the structural map to locate, time, and sequence these confrontations.

Summary

Existential psychology confirms and deepens the foundations of DCT:

- Anxiety is developmental → Each stage produces existential anxiety as a signal of growth.
- Freedom is choice under confrontation → Resolution requires assuming responsibility for the existential choice at each stage.
- Death is the final confrontation → Resolution transforms it into wisdom; distortion denies it.
- Isolation and meaning → Integrated in Stage 2 and Stage 3, shaping identity and authenticity.
- Therapy as confrontation → *DCT* provides the developmental scaffolding for existential practice.

In this light, existential psychology does not merely parallel *DCT* but confirms its core premise: development is structured by confrontation, and resolution of existential givens is the measure of psychological health.

Constructivism and the Human Drive to Make Sense

Constructivist psychology emerged as a counter to the idea that knowledge is simply absorbed from the environment. Instead, thinkers like Jean Piaget, Lev Vygotsky, George Kelly, Jerome Bruner, and Ernst von Glasersfeld emphasized that human beings actively construct reality. The mind is not a mirror of the world but a builder of frameworks, concepts, and narratives.

In this perspective, learning, identity, and even truth are not fixed givens but products of confrontation between the self and experience. Knowledge is always relational, provisional, and structured by how individuals negotiate contradictions, conflicts, and challenges.

This fits seamlessly with *DCT's* framework. If existential psychology highlights the givens of existence, constructivist psychology emphasizes the process of sense-making. *DCT* brings these together: every developmental stage confrontation is simultaneously an existential challenge (death, freedom, isolation, authenticity) and an epistemological task (building models of self, other, and world).

Piaget: Cognitive Structures as Confrontation

Jean Piaget's stages of cognitive development already highlight the role of conflict and disequilibrium. For Piaget, knowledge advances when existing schemas fail to assimilate new experience, forcing accommodation. This disequilibrium is not a flaw but the engine of development.

DCT reframes this within its own confrontational map:

- Stage 1 (Self vs. World) → parallel to sensorimotor + early preoperational thought. The child must confront the environment to distinguish self from world. Igniter and Adaptor traits are not just psychological styles but epistemological strategies: either actively imposing action (Igniter) or absorbing external patterns (Adaptor).

- Stage 2 (Self vs. Other) → parallel to the social cognition of concrete operations. Here the confrontation is not with objects but with others' perspectives. Wall and Mirror traits correspond to epistemic orientations: either preserving one's conceptual boundaries (Wall) or reorganizing through others' feedback (Mirror).

- Stage 3 (Emotional Identity) → parallel to formal operations, but reframed. Here the confrontation is self-reflexive: how to construct models of authenticity. Flame builds inwardly consistent systems of self-understanding, while Mask adapts identity strategically to fit social schemas.

- Stage 4 (Mortality & Wisdom) → goes beyond Piaget. This is where epistemology turns existential: the confrontation with finitude reorganizes not just knowledge but the very grounds of meaning-making. Seer and Wound reflect whether one constructs knowledge of mortality as vision or as denial.

Thus, Piaget's assimilation–accommodation cycle is reframed by *DCT* as the mechanism of confrontation: growth occurs when the schema of identity fails and must be reorganized.

Vygotsky: The Zone of Proximal Confrontation

Lev Vygotsky introduced the Zone of Proximal Development (ZPD) — the gap between what a child can do alone and what they can do with guidance. For *DCT*, this zone is the arena of confrontation: a structured field where self, other, and world meet.

- In Stage 1, the ZPD is confrontation with the environment — guided by caregivers who scaffold the child's autonomy.
- In Stage 2, the ZPD is confrontation with otherness — guided by recognition, dialogue, and mutual reflection.
- In Stage 3, the ZPD is confrontation with emotional authenticity — scaffolded by safe spaces that allow the flame of self to emerge without immediate collapse into masking.
- In Stage 4, the ZPD is confrontation with mortality — scaffolded by cultural traditions, religion, philosophy, and symbolic practices that allow the self to face finitude without despair.

Vygotsky's insight that development is socially mediated resonates with DCT's claim that confrontation is relationally structured. No confrontation is endured in isolation; every stage is mediated by external mirrors, boundaries, narratives, and rituals.

George Kelly: Personal Construct Theory

George Kelly's Personal Construct Theory (PCT) proposed that people act as "scientists," building constructs (mental templates) to interpret the world. When a construct fails to predict, the person faces anxiety and must revise it.

Here again, *DCT* provides a developmental sequencing of this principle:

- In Stage 1, constructs are primitive — "the world supports me" vs. "the world abandons me."
- In Stage 2, constructs are relational — "I am recognized" vs. "I am rejected."
- In Stage 3, constructs are reflexive — "I am authentic" vs. "I am false."
- In Stage 4, constructs are existential — "I die and vanish" vs. "I transcend symbolically."

Kelly's view of anxiety as failed prediction is almost identical to *DCT's* framing of distortion as failed confrontation. Both require reorganization of constructs/traits for resolution.

Bruner and Narrative Construction

Jerome Bruner emphasized the narrative mode of thought: humans do not live by logic alone but by stories that give coherence to experience. For Bruner, development is the increasing ability to place the self within broader symbolic narratives.

***DCT* echoes this by embedding narrative confrontation into each stage:**

- Stage 1 → survival stories: "I am safe" or "I am vulnerable."
- Stage 2 → relational stories: "I am loved" or "I am invisible."
- Stage 3 → identity stories: "I am true" or "I wear a mask."
- Stage 4 → legacy stories: "I live on in wisdom" or "I am erased."

Distortions create fragmented narratives (e.g., trauma narratives, self-denying scripts). Resolution produces coherent life stories integrated into broader cultural-symbolic frameworks.

Thus, Bruner's insight that humans are storytelling beings supports *DCT's* symbolic system: the symbolic names of the *DCPTT* (Igniter, Wall, Flame, Seer, etc.) are not decorative but narrative anchors, giving form to otherwise chaotic confrontations.

Radical Constructivism and Relativism

Later constructivists (e.g., von Glasersfeld) argued that knowledge is never objective but always constructed relative to the knower's framework. While critics warn this risks relativism, *DCT* resolves the issue:

- Not all constructions are equal, because some resolve confrontation while others avoid it.

- A distorted Wall or Mask may construct a "reality," but it is fragile, unstable, and maladaptive.

- Resolution-based constructs integrate confrontation and therefore achieve a higher level of coherence across self, other, and world.

Thus, *DCT* is not relativist but evaluative: it provides criteria (resolution vs. distortion) for judging the adequacy of constructions.

Constructivist Therapy and DCT

Constructivist therapies (e.g., narrative therapy, constructivist CBT, personal construct therapy) focus on reframing narratives and reconstructing meaning. *DCT* enriches this by providing a developmental map of confrontation:

- Therapy identifies which stage confrontation was avoided (e.g., abandonment → Stage 1; rejection → Stage 2).
- The client is guided to reconstruct meaning by re-entering confrontation with support.
- Narrative reorganization becomes not just a technique but a developmental necessity.

In this sense, *DCT* gives constructivist therapy structural grounding: every reconstruction is tied to a developmental confrontation and evaluated by whether it resolves or distorts.

Summary

Constructivism validates *DCT's* claim that development is confrontation-driven:

- Piaget shows that disequilibrium (failed schemas) drives development → parallel to *DCT's* confrontations.
- Vygotsky shows that social scaffolding mediates growth → parallel to *DCT's* relational nature.
- Kelly shows that failed constructs produce anxiety → parallel to *DCT's* distortions.
- Bruner shows that narratives hold identity → parallel to *DCT's* symbolic typology.
- Radical constructivists highlight subjectivity → *DCT* resolves relativism by distinguishing resolution from distortion.

In conclusion, *DCT* can be seen as the existential–constructivist synthesis: a model where confrontation drives both meaning-making and knowledge construction, producing either coherent resolution or fragmented distortion.

Humanistic–Existential–Constructivist Synthesis into DCT

1. The Humanistic Turn: Self-Actualization and Authenticity

The humanistic revolution in psychology, led by Abraham Maslow and Carl Rogers, shifted attention away from pathology toward potential, growth, and authenticity. Where psychoanalysis stressed unconscious conflict and behaviorism stressed conditioning, humanistic thought proposed that every human being is oriented toward growth if conditions of safety, acceptance, and congruence are provided.

- Maslow's Hierarchy of Needs: Development was framed as a progressive satisfaction of needs—physiological, safety, love/belonging, esteem, and finally self-actualization. Although criticized for its linearity, the hierarchy resonates with *DCT's* sequential confrontations. Each stage in DCT can be mapped onto a specific cluster of Maslovian needs:

  - Stage 1 (Self vs. World) → safety and autonomy needs.
  - Stage 2 (Self vs. Other) → belonging and esteem needs.
  - Stage 3 (Emotional Identity) → authenticity and recognition needs.
  - Stage 4 (Mortality & Wisdom) → transcendence and symbolic legacy needs.

  - Carl Rogers' Person-Centered Therapy: Rogers emphasized unconditional positive regard, empathy, and congruence as the conditions that allow the self to emerge authentically. This overlaps directly with Stage 2 and Stage 3 in *DCT*: the Mirror requires accurate empathy to develop without distortion, and the Flame requires conditions of acceptance to burn without collapsing into shame or pretense.

In *DCT* terms, the humanistic perspective validates resolution: resolution occurs when the environment provides enough empathic recognition for the individual to confront the stage task without collapsing into distortion.

2. Existential Depth: Confrontation with Freedom and Death

Existential psychologists (Frankl, May, Yalom) took development beyond social and personal growth into the realm of ultimate concerns: death, freedom, isolation, and meaning. Their contribution to *DCT* is profound because Stage 4 explicitly revolves around mortality.

- Viktor Frankl: His logotherapy held that the will to meaning is the central human drive. Stage 4 in *DCT* (*"Self vs. Mortality"*) echoes this: the confrontation with finitude demands a symbolic or existential resolution. Distortion occurs when meaning is evaded—through nihilism, denial, or destructive acting out.

- Rollo May: Highlighted that anxiety is the inevitable companion of freedom and death. *DCT* frames this as distortion: if mortality confrontation is avoided, anxiety festers and collapses identity.

- Irvin Yalom: Named the four existential givens (death, freedom, isolation, meaninglessness). Each aligns with a *DCT* stage:

    - Death → Stage 4 (Mortality & Wisdom).
    - Freedom → Stage 1 (Self vs. World autonomy).
    - Isolation → Stage 2 (Self vs. Other).
    - Meaninglessness → Stage 3 (Emotional Identity).

Thus, existential thought can be read as a parallel map of the very same confrontations *DCT* formalizes.

3. Constructivist Epistemology Revisited

Piaget, Vygotsky, and constructivists framed development as the active construction of knowledge. *DCT* extends this: it is not merely knowledge that is constructed but selfhood itself through confrontation.

- Piaget emphasized equilibration between assimilation and accommodation. *DCT* reframes this as confrontation between resolution vs. distortion. Assimilation that resists reality produces distortion; accommodation that reorganizes identity leads to resolution.

- Vygotsky's ZPD highlighted that development occurs in the tension between what the child can do alone and what they can achieve with guidance. This parallels Stage 2: the Mirror develops within the field of another's recognition. Without scaffolding, the Mirror collapses; with guidance, it resolves.

- Jerome Bruner emphasized narrative construction of reality. In Stage 3, narrative identity becomes central: the Flame's authenticity vs. the Mask's distortion is expressed in the stories individuals tell about themselves.

Constructivism therefore underlines the epistemic ground of *DCT*: each confrontation is not just a psychological crisis but a knowledge-making act where the individual re-constructs reality and self.

4. Integration of Humanistic, Existential, and Constructivist Currents

When synthesized, these traditions confirm *DCT's* originality while providing multiple lines of validation:

- Humanistic validation: Demonstrates that resolution pathways (Wall, Mirror, Flame, Seer) represent the conditions for authentic growth, congruence, and self-actualization.
- Existential validation: Confirms that avoidance of confrontation leads to anxiety, fragmentation, and despair—exactly what *DCT* names as distortion.
- Constructivist validation: Grounds the sequential stages in developmental science, showing how confrontation builds both identity and reality itself.

Together, they transform *DCT* from a novel framework into a grand integrative model: psychoanalytic roots, attachment and neuroscience evidence, humanistic authenticity, existential givens, and constructivist epistemology converge on the same claim—human beings grow through confrontation, or they distort through avoidance.

5. Implications for DCΨ as a School

The fusion of these traditions in *DCT* anchors the wider *Developmental Confrontation Psychology (DCΨ):*

1. Therapeutic Praxis: *DRT (Developmental Resolution Therapy)* gains depth by combining Rogers' empathy, Frankl's meaning, and Vygotsky's scaffolding as specific tools for guiding confrontation.

2. Diagnostic Precision: Distortions at each stage can be understood as existential defenses (denial of death, collapse of freedom), attachment failures (lack of mirroring), or constructivist breakdowns (failure of equilibration).

3. Symbolic Extension: The *DCPTT* typology (Igniter, Adaptor, Wall, Mirror, Flame, Mask, Seer, Wound, etc.) becomes not only symbolic but empirically mapped to traditions of psychology spanning a century.

This chapter closes by affirming: *DCT* is not in competition with humanistic, existential, or constructivist psychology. It is the framework that reveals their hidden unity.

The Comparative Framework of DCT

1. The Need for Comparative Integration

Psychology has long been divided into schools—psychoanalysis, behaviorism, cognitive science, humanistic, existential, systems theory, neuroscience, and more. Each developed its own vocabulary, methods, and favored domain of human experience. Yet, despite their differences, all share a concern with how humans grow, adapt, and fracture under pressure.
Developmental Confrontation Theory (DCT) provides a unifying lens by reframing growth as structured confrontation. The theory does not erase the distinctions of other schools; instead, it integrates them by showing how each school illuminates a particular aspect of the same developmental struggle.

- Psychoanalysis revealed the depth of unconscious conflict.
- Attachment theory highlighted the centrality of early relationships.
- Neuroscience mapped the biological scaffolding of emotion and cognition.
- Humanistic and existential thought emphasized freedom, meaning, and authenticity.
- Constructivism demonstrated that knowledge and self are co-created through interaction.

Where these traditions often appeared fragmented, *DCT* shows them as layers of one architecture: each corresponds to how humans face the core confrontations of the four stages.

2. The Principle of Resolution vs. Distortion as a Meta-Concept

One of *DCT's* strongest contributions is the resolution/distortion duality. Other traditions often recognize growth and pathology but treat them as separate topics. *DCT* reframes them as two sides of the same confrontation:

- Resolution = the successful reorganization of identity through confrontation.
- Distortion = avoidance, collapse, or defensive displacement of the confrontation.

This duality allows comparisons:

- Freud's defense mechanisms (denial, projection, repression) are reinterpreted as distortions.
- Erikson's "virtues" at each psychosocial stage align with resolutions.
- Attachment insecurity (avoidant, ambivalent, disorganized) are distortions of Stage 2 confrontation.
- Self-actualization in Maslow or congruence in Rogers = Stage 3 resolution.
- Existential anxiety in Yalom = Stage 4 distortion.

Thus, the resolution/distortion principle becomes the bridge concept that allows all psychological schools to be compared under one system.

3. Sequentiality as Developmental Law

Another axis of comparison is sequentiality. Nearly all developmental theories propose stages or sequences, but they disagree on number, order, and emphasis.

- Freud described psychosexual stages.
- Erikson proposed eight psychosocial stages.
- Piaget mapped cognitive development.
- Maslow arranged needs hierarchically.
- Kohlberg charted moral stages.

DCT affirms the sequential view but reduces it to four essential existential confrontations. This makes DCT parsimonious (not eight or twelve stages), yet expansive because all other stage theories can be located within its framework:

- Freud's oral stage = Stage 1 confrontation (Self vs. World).
- Erikson's trust vs. mistrust, autonomy vs. shame = Stage 1 and Stage 2.
- Piaget's sensorimotor and preoperational → align with Stage 1 and 2 confrontations.
- Maslow's esteem and belongingness = Stage 2.
- Kohlberg's early moral stages (obedience, interpersonal harmony) → Stage 2.

Instead of fragmenting developmental maps, *DCT* absorbs them into a single sequence. It shows that all traditions were describing aspects of the same confrontations but lacked the unifying frame.

4. Symbolism and Scientific Validation

DCT also distinguishes itself by integrating symbolism (Igniter, Adaptor, Wall, Mirror, Flame, Mask, Seer, Wound) into a scientifically comparable system.

Other schools often use abstract language (ego, superego; schemas; drives; needs), whereas *DCT* uses symbolic traits that are both descriptive and diagnostic.

- The Igniter symbolizes autonomy: parallels with Piaget's object permanence and Erikson's autonomy.
- The Wall symbolizes boundaries: parallels with attachment security and self/other distinction in social neuroscience.
- The Flame symbolizes authenticity: parallels with Rogers' congruence and Maslow's self-actualization.
- The Seer symbolizes mortality integration: parallels with existential philosophy and logotherapy.

The symbolic system allows *DCT* to bridge scientific discourse and therapeutic language. Where other theories are either too clinical or too metaphorical, *DCT* unites both into a functional diagnostic model.

5. Toward a Comparative Matrix

By combining resolution/distortion, sequentiality, and symbolism, *DCT* can produce a comparative matrix where each psychological school finds its rightful place. This is not eclecticism or surface comparison—it is structural integration.

- Psychoanalysis maps onto the distortion mechanisms.
- Behaviorism and cognitive-behavioral approaches map onto adaptive vs. maladaptive strategies of confrontation.
- Humanistic and existential schools illuminate the resolution outcomes.
- Neuroscience anchors the stages in brain development and affect regulation.

This matrix allows practitioners, researchers, and theorists to see *DCT* as the architecture of psychology itself: a meta-framework where all prior theories are housed as parts of the same building.

Attachment Science, Relational Neuroscience, and the DCT Relational Map

Introduction

If Freud and Erikson mapped the psychodynamic and psychosocial scaffolding of development, it is attachment theory and relational neuroscience that have provided the empirical and biological grounding of how human beings actually form, maintain, and distort their connections to others. *Developmental Confrontation Theory (DCT)*, with its Stage 2 confrontation of Self vs. Other, aligns directly with this body of work, while also transcending its limitations. The scientific findings of attachment studies and neurobiological research confirm *DCT's* premise: that confrontation is not optional. The human organism is wired to face the Other, either by establishing boundaries (Wall) or by internalizing reflection (Mirror). When this confrontation is mishandled, distortions reverberate through both psyche and biology.

Attachment Theory and Stage 2

John Bowlby's attachment theory revolutionized psychology by reframing the infant's tie to the caregiver not as secondary to feeding, but as a primary need for safety and regulation. Secure attachment develops when the caregiver provides consistent responsiveness; insecure attachment (avoidant, ambivalent, disorganized) arises from inconsistent, rejecting, or traumatic caregiving.

Within DCT, Bowlby's insight maps directly onto the confrontation of Self vs. Other:

- The Wall orientation aligns with the developmental demand for boundary integrity. A securely attached child with healthy Wall resolution can separate without fear of annihilation and can say "no" without collapsing. By contrast, avoidant attachment reflects a distorted Wall: withdrawal, emotional numbing, premature autonomy.

- The Mirror orientation aligns with the need for recognition and reflection. A securely attached child with healthy Mirror resolution feels seen and valued, internalizing a stable self-image. Ambivalent and disorganized attachment reflect distorted Mirror processes: hypervigilance to others' reactions, identity collapse, or chaotic oscillation between seeking and rejecting connection.

Thus, attachment research provides the observable behavioral correlates of the abstract confrontation *DCT* describes. Where Bowlby spoke of attachment security, *DCT* specifies the developmental mechanism: confrontation with Otherness and the resolution or distortion of Wall and Mirror.

Neuroscience of Relational Confrontation

Recent advances in neuroscience reinforce the biological substrate of *DCT's* claims. Three domains are particularly relevant:

1. Mirror Neurons and Resonance Systems
   Discovered in the premotor cortex of macaque monkeys (Rizzolatti, 1990s), mirror neurons fire both when performing an action and when observing another perform it. In humans, this system underpins empathy, imitation, and resonance. The Mirror orientation of Stage 2 directly engages this neural circuitry. When functioning well, it enables identification and shared affect. When distorted, it produces over-identification (collapse of self-other distinction) or absence of resonance (emotional detachment).

2. Polyvagal Theory and Social Safety
   Stephen Porges' polyvagal theory describes how the vagus nerve modulates physiological states of safety, mobilization, or shutdown. Secure connection activates the ventral vagal system, supporting social engagement. *DCT's* Wall orientation requires precisely this state: the ability to assert boundaries without dropping into fight/flight (sympathetic) or collapse (dorsal vagal shutdown). Distorted Walls—hyper-rigid or absent—mirror dysregulation in these circuits.

3. Oxytocin and Neurochemistry of Bonding
   Oxytocin, the so-called "bonding hormone," facilitates trust, attachment, and maternal-infant bonding. High oxytocin states correlate with healthy mirroring, while disrupted oxytocin systems are implicated in borderline and dependent patterns. Thus, the Mirror orientation is not only symbolic but biochemical, rooted in measurable neurochemistry.

Pathology as Confrontational Distortion

Integrating neuroscience and attachment science sharpens the diagnostic edge of *DCT.* Common relational pathologies reveal themselves as predictable distortions of Wall and Mirror:

- Borderline Personality Disorder (BPD): collapse of Wall, hyperactivation of Mirror. This produces unstable selfhood, frantic efforts to avoid abandonment, and volatile attachment bonds.

- Avoidant Personality Disorder (AvPD): overdeveloped Wall (rigidity), underdeveloped Mirror. Avoidant individuals maintain distance at the cost of intimacy, mirroring early attachment avoidance patterns.

- Dependent Personality Disorder (DPD): inflated Mirror without Wall support. Self collapses into Other's reflection, producing submissive and clinging behavior.

- Antisocial Personality Disorder (ASPD): hardened Wall, absence of Mirror circuitry. Empathy deficits and exploitation reflect both relational distortion and possible neurobiological underactivation of resonance systems.

In each case, pathology is not random but the predictable consequence of failed confrontation at Stage 2, now supported by both psychological observation and neuroscientific evidence.

The Clinical Implications

Where attachment science alone prescribes caregiver sensitivity, and neuroscience alone maps brain systems, *DCT* provides the structural integration: these are not isolated mechanisms, but manifestations of a deeper confrontation. Therapy, therefore, is not merely about reconditioning behaviors or medicating symptoms, but about guiding the client back into the unresolved confrontation of Self vs. Other.

- For Wall distortions: strengthening boundaries without rigidity, teaching the nervous system to tolerate proximity without collapse.
- For Mirror distortions: restoring accurate reflection, rebuilding the resonance systems that affirm selfhood without dependency.

Neuroscientific tools (biofeedback, vagal stimulation, oxytocin research) may one day supplement therapeutic work, but without the *DCT* framework, they risk being fragmented interventions. *DCT* ensures they remain embedded in the confrontational structure of development.

Conclusion

Attachment science and relational neuroscience confirm what *DCT* posits: human development hinges on facing the Other. Secure attachment, healthy neurobiology, and coherent identity all depend on successful confrontation at Stage 2. Distortions reverberate in both psychology and biology, producing predictable pathologies. By integrating Bowlby's observations, Porges' polyvagal theory, mirror neuron research, and oxytocin studies into its map of Wall and Mirror, *DCT* provides the most comprehensive account of relational development to date.

In this way, *DCT* does not discard attachment theory or neuroscience; it reveals their common structure. Both are tributaries flowing into the larger river of developmental confrontation, where the self must face, and not avoid, the presence of the Other.

Humanistic, Existential, and Constructivist Integrations into DCT

Introduction

If attachment science and neuroscience ground *Developmental Confrontation Theory (DCT)* in biology and relational experience, then the humanistic, existential, and constructivist traditions situate it in the realm of meaning, freedom, and lived experience. These traditions emerged in the 20th century as a response to the perceived reductionism of psychoanalysis and behaviorism. Rather than treating the human as a machine driven by instincts or conditioned reflexes, they sought to recover what makes the human experience irreducibly unique: subjectivity, choice, confrontation with mortality, and the construction of meaning.

DCT aligns profoundly with this lineage. At its core, *DCT* asserts that human development unfolds not merely through adaptation but through structured confrontations that demand reorganization of the self. This is precisely where humanistic and existential thinkers located the essence of growth: the capacity to face the givens of existence and to make meaning within them. Constructivist psychology extends this by emphasizing the interpretive frameworks through which the self narrates and re-narrates its confrontations.

Humanistic Psychology and the Call to Self-Actualization

Carl Rogers and Abraham Maslow framed human development as a process of moving toward authentic selfhood. Rogers described the fully functioning person as one who can live congruently with their inner experience, while Maslow articulated the hierarchy of needs culminating in self-actualization.

DCT's framework of staged confrontations parallels this movement:

- Stage 1 (Self vs. World): echoes Maslow's foundational physiological and safety needs. A distorted Igniter/Adaptor resolution parallels failure at the base of the hierarchy.

- Stage 2 (Self vs. Other): maps onto belongingness and love needs. The confrontation with Wall and Mirror reflects Rogers' demand for unconditional positive regard and the risk of conditions of worth.

- Stage 3 (Emotional Identity): aligns with esteem needs and authenticity. The Flame/Mask confrontation mirrors Rogers' congruence vs. incongruence.

- Stage 4 (Mortality & Wisdom): resonates with self-actualization and Maslow's later notion of self-transcendence. The Seer/Wound confrontation expresses the ultimate humanistic project: integrating finitude into a meaningful life.

Where humanistic psychology describes the direction of growth, *DCT* provides the mechanism: resolution or distortion of confrontation.

Existential Psychology and the Confrontation with the Givens

Rollo May, Irvin Yalom, and Viktor Frankl deepened psychology by emphasizing the existential givens: death, freedom, isolation, and meaninglessness. *DCT's* staged confrontations directly engage these givens, not abstractly but developmentally.

- Death / Mortality: Stage 4 is explicitly structured as the confrontation with finitude. The Seer orientation integrates death into wisdom, while the Wound orientation denies or resists mortality, producing neurosis.

- Freedom: Every confrontation in *DCT* is also a freedom crisis. To ignite autonomy (Stage 1), to assert boundaries (Stage 2), to choose authentic flame (Stage 3), and to accept mortality (Stage 4) — all are choices that expose the individual to responsibility.

- Isolation vs. Connection: Stage 2 is existential isolation confronted. The Mirror resolves it through resonance, the Wall through boundary integrity. Distortions here mirror existential aloneness or fusion without identity.

- Meaninglessness: Frankl's logotherapy placed meaning at the center of psychological survival. Stage 4 again reveals its centrality: meaning transforms mortality from annihilation into legacy, symbol, or transcendence.

Thus, existential psychology provides *DCT* with philosophical depth. Where *DCT* names the sequential confrontations, existential psychology provides the ontological gravity of what is at stake.

Constructivist Approaches and the Narrative of Confrontation

Constructivist psychology, associated with George Kelly (personal construct theory), Jerome Bruner (narrative psychology), and social constructivists, argues that reality is not simply received but constructed. Human beings interpret, narrate, and re-narrate their experiences, building frameworks that shape perception and identity.

DCT dovetails with constructivism by demonstrating that each confrontation is not only an event but also a story-making process:

- **Stage 1 (Igniter/Adaptor):** The child constructs a story of self vs. world — "I can act" or "I must conform."
- **Stage 2 (Wall/Mirror):** The narrative becomes relational — "I am separate" or "I exist through others' reflection."
- **Stage 3 (Flame/Mask):** The story centers on authenticity — "I am my inner fire" or "I must perform."
- **Stage 4 (Seer/Wound):** The ultimate narrative is existential — "I transform mortality into meaning" or "I am undone by death."

Constructivism underscores that resolution is not only behavioral but symbolic: the meaning the individual assigns to confrontation determines whether it is resolved or distorted. Therapy, therefore, is often an act of re-storying — constructing new narratives that allow confrontation to be faced rather than evaded.

Clinical Implications of Humanistic, Existential, and Constructivist Integration

When brought together, these traditions illuminate why *DCT* is not only a diagnostic tool but also a therapeutic compass:

- Humanistic: Emphasizes the growth potential inherent in each confrontation and the importance of conditions that allow resolution (unconditional regard, safety, authenticity).
- Existential: Highlights the gravity of unresolved confrontations, showing that avoidance is not benign but a refusal of the very conditions of existence.
- Constructivist: Demonstrates that distortions are often maintained by rigid or collapsed narratives, which can be restructured through therapeutic dialogue.

Therapies aligned with these perspectives (person-centered therapy, logotherapy, narrative therapy) become more powerful when embedded in *DCT.* They no longer float as separate modalities but serve as stage-specific interventions:

- Stage 1: person-centered grounding to ignite agency.
- Stage 2: narrative restructuring of relational identity.
- Stage 3: existential confrontation of authenticity.
- Stage 4: logotherapeutic meaning-making around mortality.

Conclusion

The integration of humanistic, existential, and constructivist perspectives into *DCT* demonstrates the theory's breadth of resonance. Humanistic psychology offers the language of growth, existential psychology the confrontation with ultimate concerns, and constructivism the process of narrative meaning-making. *DCT* weaves them into a sequential map, showing not just that confrontation matters, but which confrontation arises when, how it can resolve, and what distortions result when it does not.

By integrating these traditions, *DCT* becomes not only a structural map of psychological development but also a philosophical psychology that honors human freedom, responsibility, and meaning. In this way, *DCT* stands as a bridge: empirically grounded in science, but also alive to the existential depth of human life.

Comparative Integration and Synthesis into DCT

Introduction

The strength of a theory is measured not only by its internal coherence but also by its ability to synthesize insights from other traditions into a framework that is at once explanatory, predictive, and clinically useful. Developmental Confrontation Theory (*DCT*) stands out because it does not merely echo earlier schools of thought; it organizes them into a developmental architecture where their insights find precise placement. Freud, Erikson, Bowlby, Piaget, Rogers, May, Vygotsky, Bruner — each contributed fragments of truth. *DCT* provides the structure in which these fragments interlock.

This synthesis is not eclecticism. Eclectic models often assemble tools without a unifying spine. *DCT*, by contrast, demonstrates that human development is propelled by staged confrontations. Every tradition that has ever grappled with identity, relationship, cognition, or mortality was touching upon one of these confrontations. The comparative task is therefore not additive, but integrative: showing how diverse theories converge when seen through the lens of confrontation.

Psychoanalysis and DCT: From Drives to Confrontations

Freud framed development in terms of instinctual drives (oral, anal, phallic, latency, genital). Erikson refined this into psychosocial crises (trust vs. mistrust, autonomy vs. shame, etc.). Both intuited that growth is structured around conflictual thresholds.

DCT refines this insight:

- Freud's oral stage → reframed as Stage 1: Self vs. World (Igniter/Adaptor). The question is not oral gratification but how the self ignites autonomy or conforms to external order.

- Erikson's identity vs. role confusion → reframed as Stage 3: Emotional Identity (Flame/Mask). The issue is not mere ego synthesis but whether emotional selfhood burns authentically or distorts into performance.

Thus, psychoanalysis gestured toward the existence of confrontations; *DCT* names, sequences, and diagnoses them with greater precision.

Attachment and Object Relations: Relational Confrontations

Attachment theory and object relations emphasized that human beings are fundamentally relational. Secure attachment provides resilience; failures in mirroring, containment, or attunement generate pathology.

DCT situates these findings within Stage 2: Self vs. Other (Wall/Mirror). Attachment is not just about safety; it is the confrontation between boundary and reflection. Distortions here produce predictable relational disorders (BPD, AvPD, DPD, ASPD). Object relations theory explains the micro-processes (internalized objects, good/bad splits), but *DCT* shows their developmental placement.

Cognitive-Developmental Theories: The Constructive Mind

Jean Piaget mapped stages of cognitive growth (sensorimotor, preoperational, concrete, formal operations). Vygotsky highlighted the zone of proximal development and the role of scaffolding.

DCT reframes these as the cognitive tools of confrontation:

- Stage 1 confrontations emerge alongside sensorimotor mastery.
- Stage 2 mirrors appear in symbolic play and early social comparison.
- Stage 3 authenticity corresponds to formal operations, the ability to think hypothetically and reflectively.
- Stage 4 meaning construction parallels advanced dialectical and post-formal thinking.

Thus, cognitive-developmental theories describe the thinking capacities that make confrontation possible. *DCT* explains the existential stakes that require those capacities.

Humanistic and Existential Schools: Freedom and Mortality

Humanistic psychology (Rogers, Maslow) and existential psychology (May, Yalom, Frankl) emphasized authenticity, choice, and mortality. *DCT* integrates them by showing that each stage of confrontation is an existential threshold:

- Stage 1 → Freedom vs. conformity.
- Stage 2 → Isolation vs. connection.
- Stage 3 → Authenticity vs. performance.
- Stage 4 → Mortality vs. transcendence.

Humanistic psychology describes the potential for growth; existential psychology names the weight of the challenge. *DCT* situates both within a developmental sequence.

Constructivist Perspectives: The Narrative of Confrontation

Constructivist thinkers (Kelly, Bruner, narrative psychology) insisted that humans build meaning through interpretive frameworks. *DCT* shows that each confrontation demands a new narrative integration:

- Stage 1 → *"I act in a world that resists me."*
- Stage 2 → *"I am both boundary and reflection."*
- Stage 3 → *"I must live my truth or wear a mask."*
- Stage 4 → *"I die, but my meaning remains."*

Constructivism explains the form of meaning-making. *DCT* explains the content and sequence of what must be narrated.

Neuroscience: Biological Correlates of Confrontation

Neuroscience demonstrates that confrontation is not metaphorical but embodied:

- Stage 1 confrontations are tied to sensorimotor cortex and early regulatory circuits.

- Stage 2 involves social brain networks (mirror neurons, prefrontal cortex).

- Stage 3 engages limbic–prefrontal integration, governing authenticity and emotion regulation.

- Stage 4 activates the default mode network, where selfhood and mortality are contemplated.

DCT thus integrates neuroscience by demonstrating that existential thresholds map onto neurobiological development.

What DCT Contributes Uniquely

From this comparative integration, three unique contributions of *DCT* stand out:

1. Sequential Universality: Where other theories offer partial maps (cognition, attachment, identity), *DCT* shows that all humans face four structured confrontations.

2. Resolution vs. Distortion: Other models describe stages or needs but often lack a mechanism to explain pathology. *DCT* demonstrates how avoidance of confrontation creates distortions that echo throughout life.

3. Therapeutic Precision: By linking each distortion to a developmental confrontation, *DCT* allows stage-specific therapeutic interventions (*DRT* and its branches).

In this way, *DCT* is not merely compatible with other traditions — it synthesizes them into a unified developmental-existential framework.

Conclusion

The comparative task reveals that every major psychological tradition — psychoanalytic, attachment, cognitive, humanistic, existential, constructivist, neuroscientific — was circling around a truth that *DCT* crystallizes: to be human is to confront. Each stage is a threshold that must be faced, resolved, and integrated. Avoidance generates pathology; resolution generates growth.

By integrating these traditions, *DCT* positions itself as both a culmination of the history of psychology and a launchpad for future therapeutic innovation. It is not an alternative among many, but a framework in which the many can find their place.

DCΨ

Chapter 7

THE FAMILIAR FOSSIL

ANCIENT HISTORY THROUGH THE EYES OF DCΨ

Fossils as Psychological Archives

Human culture does not disappear; it condenses into artifacts. What is left behind in stone, bone, wood, or ritual inscription is more than functional residue — it is a psychological record. Just as paleontologists read bones to reconstruct the anatomy of an extinct creature, psychologists can read artifacts to reconstruct the anxieties, defenses, and resolutions of a civilization.

Developmental Confrontational Psychology (DCΨ) treats these artifacts as "familiar fossils" — externalized remains of humanity's confrontation with its four stages:

1. Self vs World
2. Self vs Other
3. Emotional Identity
4. Mortality & Wisdom

Every tool, wall, carving, or tomb is a snapshot of confrontation at the cultural level. Where individuals carry unresolved distortions forward into adulthood, cultures carry theirs into material legacies.

Fossils as Carriers of Resolution or Distortion

From the *DCΨ* lens, familiar fossils fall into two broad categories:

Fossils of Resolution

- Evidence of progression.
- Artifacts that embody balance: cave art expressing self-in-world, communal fire pits signifying shared identity, wise funerary traditions acknowledging mortality.
- These fossils show that a society integrated confrontation into growth.

Fossils of Distortion

- Evidence of stagnation or avoidance.
- Artifacts that embody fracture: obsessive fortifications revealing unresolved Stage 1 fear, masks erasing individuality in Stage 2 collapse, pyramids built to deny death in Stage 4 avoidance.
- These fossils show that a society, like an individual, can freeze in avoidance.

This distinction is crucial: without it, archaeology reduces artifacts to mere utility, while *DCΨ* reveals them as psychological footprints.

Why Fossils Matter in DCΨ

DCΨ holds that psychological confrontations leave material residues. These residues matter for three reasons:

1. **They anchor the universality of the stages.**
    - The same developmental struggles individuals face are visible in every culture's artifacts.
    - Cave walls, masks, pyramids → each mirrors the same inner confrontations.
2. **They preserve distortions.**
    - A wall built out of paranoia remains long after the fear has passed.
    - Civilizations fossilize their unresolved anxieties into stone, passing distortions to the next generations.
3. **They preserve wisdom.**
    - Philosophical inscriptions, balanced art, symbolic rituals → fossils of resolution.
    - These embody humanity's capacity not only to fear, but to transcend fear.

Thus, familiar fossils are psychological archives of humanity — chronicling not just what we built, but why we built it, and what unresolved struggles were being carried forward.

Why DCΨ Offers a New Lens

Archaeology and anthropology have long studied the remnants of human history. Yet their focus is typically functional or symbolic in a non-developmental sense:

- Archaeology interprets walls as defense, tools as survival, tombs as burial.
- Anthropology interprets masks as ritual identity, myths as cultural narrative.

While these approaches have immense value, they stop at description. They explain what artifacts are and how they were used, but not what developmental confrontation they express.

The Limits of Functionalist Readings

- A fortress wall described as "defense" misses the psychological truth: it is also a projection of Stage 1 confrontation with the world. It can represent resolution (balanced protection) or distortion (paranoid enclosure).

- A mask described as "ritual symbol" misses that it fossilizes Stage 2 confrontation with recognition and mirroring. Is the mask authentic expression, or collapse into cultic dependency?

- A pyramid described as "tomb" misses the existential reality: it is an attempt to solve Stage 4 confrontation with mortality. Is it acceptance or denial?

By reducing artifacts to function, traditional archaeology overlooks their psychological depth.

The Limits of Purely Symbolic Readings

Anthropologists like Lévi-Strauss and Eliade emphasized myth and symbolism. They recognized that rituals and artifacts are not only functional but also express meaning. Yet without a developmental structure, symbolic interpretation floats:

- A cave is "a womb symbol."
- A mask is "a transformation symbol."
- A pyramid is "a symbol of ascent."

These insights are true but unsystematic. They lack the precision of staging: which confrontation is expressed, how it resolves, how it distorts.

The Contribution of DCΨ

DCΨ provides the missing link: a developmental architecture for interpreting cultural fossils.

1. **Stage mapping:** Every artifact can be placed within one of the four confrontations.

2. **Resolution vs distortion:** Each fossil reveals whether a society progressed or stagnated at that stage.

3. **Continuity with therapy:** The same structures appear in modern clinical cases; thus, fossils connect ancient culture with present psychology.

This lens does not discard archaeology or anthropology — it completes them. Where archaeology describes and anthropology interprets, *DCΨ* diagnoses: it reads fossils as psychological footprints of developmental confrontations.

Why This Matters

Without a developmental lens, cultural remnants risk being misunderstood as static curiosities. With *DCΨ*, they become evidence of humanity's inner evolution — showing that civilizations, like individuals, carry unresolved anxieties, construct defenses, project distortions, and at times, achieve resolution.

In this way, *DCΨ* transforms artifacts into living evidence of the psyche across time.

Fossils as Evidence of Resolution vs Distortion

From the *DCΨ* perspective, fossils are not neutral remains of history. They are diagnostic markers of how a civilization confronted — or failed to confront — its developmental stages. They carry within their form the echo of resolution or distortion.

Fossils of Resolution

Fossils of resolution are material signs that a society confronted developmental challenges and integrated them into growth.

- **Stage 1 examples:**
    - Cave art that transforms raw survival into symbolic expression of self-in-world.
    - Tools designed not only for protection but for creative expansion (fire for warmth, not only for fear).
- **Stage 2 examples:**
    - Burials with personal items that recognize individuality within community.
    - Statues that preserve the presence of leaders without collapsing identity into dependency.

- **Stage 3 examples:**
    - Totems that symbolize shared emotional identity, uniting community without erasing authenticity.
    - Early theater that channels emotion into creative, communal experience.
- **Stage 4 examples:**
    - Philosophical inscriptions or wisdom traditions that accept mortality as part of life.
    - Rituals of remembrance that honor death without denying it.

These fossils embody balance — signs that confrontation has produced cultural resilience.

Fossils of Distortion

By contrast, fossils of distortion reveal when societies collapsed into avoidance or overcompensation.

- **Stage 1 examples:**
    - Massive fortifications signaling paranoia rather than balanced protection.
    - Tools used obsessively for control, leading to domination instead of survival.
- **Stage 2 examples:**
    - Idols that absorb all identity, erasing individual recognition.
    - Ritual masks that enforce conformity, preventing authentic mirroring.

- **Stage 3 examples:**
    - Theatrical excess where spectacle replaces authenticity.
    - Totems used for exclusion, fueling tribal aggression rather than identity cohesion.
- **Stage 4 examples:**
    - Pyramids or tombs built as grand denials of death.
    - Mummification practices that embody obsession with immortality.

These fossils embody stagnation — signs of unresolved confrontation preserved in stone and ritual.

Diagnostic Value of Fossils

The distinction between resolution and distortion makes familiar fossils more than cultural curiosities. They are diagnostic tools that allow psychologists to trace the mental health of entire civilizations.

- They show where collective development advanced.
- They show where it stalled or distorted.
- They show how distortions can be carried forward, shaping later societies.

Thus, fossils are clinical evidence at the cultural scale — the externalized remains of unresolved or integrated confrontation.

Purpose of the Chapter & Reader's Gain

Every chapter in this work adds a new dimension to Developmental Confrontation Theory. Where Chapter 4 revealed the womb as the first confrontation template, Chapter 7 expands the scope from the personal to the historical, showing that entire civilizations leave behind psychological footprints in their artifacts.

The purpose of this chapter is threefold:

1. **To demonstrate continuity between individual and collective development.**

    - Just as individuals carry unresolved stages forward, civilizations carry unresolved anxieties into their material culture.

    - Fossils become a collective mirror of humanity's psychological journey.

2. **To reinterpret cultural remnants through DCΨ.**

    - A wall is not only a defense; it is a fossil of confrontation with the world.
    - A mask is not only a ritual object; it is a fossil of confrontation with the other.
    - A totem is not only symbolic art; it is a fossil of confrontation with identity.
    - A pyramid is not only a tomb; it is a fossil of confrontation with mortality.
    - This interpretive framework transforms archaeology into psychology.

3. **To offer clinical and cultural relevance.**

    - For therapists: fossils show how distortions are not only personal but collective, and how inherited anxieties may shape modern clients.
    - For scholars: fossils provide evidence that psychological development is not abstract but leaves lasting imprints in stone, ritual, and symbol.

What the Reader Will Gain

By the end of this chapter, the reader will be able to:

- Recognize ancient artifacts as expressions of developmental confrontations.
- Distinguish between fossils of resolution and fossils of distortion.
- Understand how collective stagnations in history echo into modern culture.
- See that the psychological development of humanity is as tangible as its physical history.

The familiar fossil is more than a metaphor; it is the archaeological residue of the psyche. By studying caves, masks, totems, and pyramids, we are not merely looking into the past — we are looking into the developmental confrontations of humanity itself.

The following sections will examine each stage of *DCT* in turn, tracing its ancient fossils and interpreting them as evidence of confrontation, stagnation, or resolution.

Stage 1: Caves & Enclosures as Containment Fossils

In Stage 1 of *Developmental Confrontation Theory*, the individual confronts the world itself: the need for protection, grounding, and survival in the face of exposure. At the collective level, this confrontation is preserved in the earliest human enclosures — caves, huts, and shelters that stand as the first material expressions of containment.

Caves as the First Containment Fossils

Prehistoric caves were not simply dwellings of convenience. They embody the psychological need for containment against the overwhelming outside.

- **Resolution:** The cave provided balance — safety from predators, moderated climate, and symbolic grounding. Cave walls often became canvases for expression, turning the site of protection into a site of creativity. The art itself is evidence that the confrontation with the world did not remain at the level of fear, but expanded into symbolic mastery.

- **Distortion:** In some contexts, caves also embody withdrawal and over-reliance on enclosure. Tribes that remained bound to caves without developing mobility or external adaptation reflect stagnation: the cave becomes not a base for engaging the world but a prison of avoidance.

Thus, the cave fossilizes Stage 1's tension: containment as a base for life vs containment as collapse into avoidance.

Early Huts and Dwellings

With the emergence of portable shelters, the confrontation with the world shifted from natural caves to human-made enclosures.

- **Resolution:** Portable huts, tents, and wooden dwellings represent the progression of containment — humans no longer depended solely on nature's enclosures but created their own. This transition marks autonomy: the self learns not only to seek safety but to build it consciously.

- **Distortion:** When enclosures became excessively sealed, cutting communities off from their environment, the fossil reveals defensive paranoia rather than adaptive protection.

The architectural leap from caves to huts illustrates the psychological movement from dependence on nature's containment to creation of one's own boundaries.

Symbolism of Darkness and Interior

The inner darkness of caves and enclosed huts has enduring symbolic resonance. Darkness is not only absence of light but also the womb-like return — an archetypal template of safety. This explains why early humans gravitated toward inner sanctuaries, and why so many rituals of initiation and healing across cultures returned to caves or enclosed darkness.

- **Resolution:** Darkness became a place of renewal and ritual transformation.

- **Distortion:** Darkness became fear, superstition, or fixation on withdrawal.

Clinical Parallel

Modern clients who seek excessive enclosure — isolating in rooms, retreating into virtual spaces, shutting out unpredictability — replay the same confrontation fossilized in caves. By recognizing caves as Stage 1 fossils, therapists gain perspective: the instinct for enclosure is ancient, but must be used as a base for progression, not stagnation.

Tools & Survival Artifacts as Extensions of Confrontation with the World

If caves and enclosures represent the search for containment, then tools represent the extension of the self outward into the world.

Stage 1 is defined by the confrontation between vulnerability and autonomy: the infant must establish grounding in a world that overwhelms. At the cultural level, early humans externalized this confrontation by shaping stone, bone, and wood into tools — objects that fossilize the effort to balance exposure with control.

Tools as Psychological Extensions

The first tools — hand axes, spears, scrapers — were more than mechanical aids. They were extensions of the body designed to mediate the self–world boundary.

- **Resolution:** Tools as adaptive partners. They allowed early humans to hunt, build, and create fire, extending autonomy without severing relation to the environment. This reflects Stage 1 progression: the individual does not collapse before the world but learns to stand against it with constructed boundaries.

- **Distortion:** Tools as instruments of domination or obsessive reliance. When entire cultural focus narrowed to weaponry or tool-hoarding, the fossil reveals unresolved fear of the world — control sought not for balance but for paranoid mastery.

Fire as a Dual Fossil

Fire stands among the most important Stage 1 artifacts.

- **Resolution:** Fire contained in hearths represented safety, warmth, and continuity. Communal fire pits became centers of gathering, symbolizing that the confrontation with the world was being integrated into social life.

- **Distortion:** Fire uncontrolled or fetishized becomes destructive. Rituals of burning without purpose, or fire-as-punishment, show the fossil of fear turned outward as aggression.

Fire thus embodies Stage 1's paradox: protection from the cold world vs destructive overreach.

Tools as Creative Expansion

Beyond survival, tools also signaled the capacity to transform the world creatively. Carvings, engravings, and early ornaments demonstrate that containment was not the end goal. The self, once grounded, could turn outward not only to defend but to express. These artifacts are fossils of resolution: proof that confrontation with the world can give birth to culture.

Clinical Parallel

Modern parallels exist in how individuals use "tools" psychologically. Healthy use of tools — routines, coping strategies, creative outlets — mirrors progression. Over-reliance on substances, rituals, or technological "weapons" reflects distortion. The fossil of the hand axe lives on in every anxious grip of the modern phone or ritualized behavior intended to keep the world at bay.

Fortifications & Walls as Distortions vs Balanced Protection

If caves and tools mark the beginnings of containment and extension, then walls and fortifications mark the cultural solidification of Stage 1 confrontation. With the rise of agriculture and settlements, humans faced a new dilemma: how to protect permanence without collapsing into fear. The wall, whether in mud brick, stone, or timber, is a fossil of this confrontation between the self (or community) and the external world.

Walls as Balanced Protection

At their healthiest, walls represent resolved containment:

- They mark boundaries between inside and outside, self and other, without erasing the possibility of exchange.
- They enable communities to cultivate land, build homes, and establish identity in relation to the environment.
- Open gates and porous fortifications reveal that the wall was not built to eliminate the world but to mediate interaction.

Such walls are fossils of progression: they show that Stage 1 can be resolved by balancing openness with protection.

Fortifications as Fossils of Fear

When walls become excessive, monumental, or obsessive, they fossilize distortion:

- Fortresses with no windows or openings mirror paranoia — the world is not engaged, only excluded.
- Endless rebuilding of thicker walls signals an unresolved Stage 1 fear of collapse.
- Archaeological remains of abandoned fortifications show stagnation: communities that enclosed themselves to the point of isolation often withered when exchange was cut off.

The wall, once a tool for survival, becomes a prison of avoidance.

The Symbolism of Separation

Walls fossilize the psychological act of drawing a line: "this is me, that is the world."

- **Resolution:** The line is flexible — it affirms identity without annihilating relation.
- **Distortion:** The line hardens into obsession, denying interaction and freezing development.

Even in myth and religion, walls symbolize the threshold between safety and danger, purity and contamination. When balanced, they structure life. When distorted, they embody fear of dissolution.

Clinical Parallel

In therapy, clients often construct psychological walls. Healthy boundaries mirror resolved Stage 1 fortifications: they allow safety while enabling connection. But rigid defenses — avoidance of intimacy, paranoia, hypervigilance — mirror distorted fortifications. Just as ancient fortresses sometimes fell because their builders could not adapt, individuals who rely on rigid psychological walls risk collapse when life inevitably penetrates their defenses.

Cultural Resolutions

Stage 1 is often remembered in its defensive fossils — caves, tools, fortifications. Yet equally important are the fossils of resolution: moments where humanity confronted the world without collapsing into fear, transforming containment into a platform for creativity.

Cave Art: From Shelter to Expression

Caves were not only refuges from danger. Their walls became canvases, turning survival sites into symbolic spaces. The paintings of animals, hunts, and symbols at sites such as Lascaux and Altamira reveal that humans could engage the world not only with weapons, but with imagination.

- **Resolution:** The cave shifted from a site of hiding to a site of self-expression. This shows progression: the confrontation with the world was not frozen in fear but translated into art.
- **Distortion avoided:** Instead of obsessively retreating into caves, communities used them as cultural anchors — proof that containment can support outward expression.

These paintings are among the earliest fossils of humanity's ability to balance fear with creativity.

Open Dwellings and Settlements

The emergence of villages and open dwellings marked a shift in how humans engaged the world. Not every community chose impregnable fortresses. Many built semi-open settlements with permeable boundaries, where protection coexisted with interaction.

- **Resolution:** These communities showed confidence in balancing inside and outside, affirming identity without erasing exchange.
- **Cultural impact:** Such openness fostered trade, cooperation, and cultural flourishing.

Where rigid fortifications fossilize paranoia, open dwellings fossilize trust in relation to the world.

Creative Balance: Tools for Expression

Some tools were not for hunting or defense but for symbolic and aesthetic purposes. Engraved bones, decorated tools, and ornaments show that the confrontation with the world could give rise not only to control but to beauty.

- **Resolution:** The same impulse that shaped a hand axe also shaped jewelry — proof that autonomy and safety could lead to expression rather than domination.

These creative fossils reveal that Stage 1, when resolved, is not primitive but foundational to culture.

Clinical Parallel

In therapy, Stage 1 resolutions appear when clients use containment not as escape but as a base for expression. A safe home, routine, or grounding practice enables them to face the world creatively. Just as cave art transformed fear into imagery, modern clients can transform survival into meaning when containment is resolved.

Stage 2: Masks & Statues (Mirroring, Identity Projection)

Stage 2 of *Developmental Confrontation Theory* revolves around the confrontation with the Other: the recognition that identity is shaped not only internally, but in reflection. At the collective level, this confrontation fossilized in masks, statues, and early figurative art, where humanity sought to see and be seen.

Masks as Fossils of Mirroring

Masks appear across ancient cultures, from ritual masks in Africa to shamanic masks in Asia and death masks in Egypt. Beyond function, they are fossils of the human need for recognition.

- **Resolution:** Masks allowed communities to embody roles, express shared identities, and reflect collective emotion. In rituals, they created resonance — individuals saw themselves mirrored in symbolic figures.

- **Distortion:** Masks could erase individuality, forcing conformity to collective identity. When worn to suppress selfhood rather than enrich it, they fossilize Stage 2 distortion: collapse of self into the Other.

Thus, masks embody the dual potential of Stage 2 — authentic resonance vs dependent conformity.

Statues and Figurines

From the Venus figurines of the Paleolithic to monumental statues of rulers, early figurative art represents another form of fossilized mirroring.

- **Resolution:** Figurines often celebrated fertility, continuity, and individuality within community. Statues of leaders or deities could function as anchors of identity, helping people locate themselves in relation to others.
- **Distortion:** When statues became idols demanding total devotion, they fossilize collapse into external validation. Identity becomes dependent on an image, not on reciprocal recognition.

Statues thus mark humanity's effort to stabilize identity through the gaze of the other — an effort that could lead to progression or stagnation.

Clinical Parallel

In therapy, clients often replay these same dynamics. Some seek recognition in healthy resonance (authentic relationships, symbolic roles). Others collapse into masks that hide or statues that dominate, leaving them trapped in external validation. Ancient masks and statues remind us that the confrontation with the Other is as old as civilization itself — and its fossils still shape identity today.

Twin Motifs, Kinship Carvings, and Early Myths

The confrontation of Stage 2 — Self vs Other — does not end with masks or statues. At the cultural level, this confrontation expanded into twin motifs, kinship carvings, and early myths that sought to stabilize identity by embedding it within relationships. These artifacts function as relational fossils: reminders that selfhood is always discovered in dialogue with another.

Twin Motifs

Across ancient cultures, twin figures appear with striking frequency: mythological twins in Mesopotamia, mirrored figures in Mesoamerican art, dual gods in Egypt. Twins fossilize the Stage 2 truth: "I see myself in another."

- **Resolution:** Twin motifs celebrate complementarity, suggesting that identity emerges not in isolation but in partnership. The fossil here represents progression: a recognition that the self is strengthened, not erased, by reflection.

- **Distortion:** Twins can also symbolize collapse — the individual reduced to a copy, unable to differentiate from the other. Where one twin dominates or both merge without boundary, the fossil reveals Stage 2 stagnation.

Kinship Carvings

In graves, temples, and totems, carvings often depict family groups or lineages. These artifacts fossilize the effort to stabilize selfhood by anchoring it in kinship ties.

- **Resolution:** Such carvings embody healthy recognition — identity confirmed through belonging without annihilation of individuality.

- **Distortion:** When kinship fossils emphasize hierarchy or subordination, they fossilize Stage 2 distortion: the self valued only through obedience to relational authority.

Early Myths

Narratives preserved in oral and written form are also fossils of relational confrontation. Stories of siblings, rivalries, parental gods, and child-heroes reflect humanity's effort to grasp identity through relational drama.

- **Resolution:** Myths of reconciliation or partnership reveal progression: identity is affirmed in cooperative reflection.
- **Distortion:** Myths of endless rivalry, jealousy, or fusion reveal stagnation: identity lost in destructive mirroring.

Clinical Parallel

Modern relational struggles mirror these fossils. Clients may repeat twin dynamics (fusion vs complementarity), kinship struggles (identity bound to family approval), or mythic rivalries (competition for recognition). Stage 2 fossils show that these dilemmas are not new — they are woven into the very fabric of human history.

Distortions (Idolatry, Collapse of Self into Cultic Dependency)

Not all Stage 2 fossils reflect progression. Many civilizations left behind remnants of distortion, where the confrontation with the Other collapsed into dependency or subjugation. These fossils embody the danger of Stage 2: when recognition becomes obsession and identity dissolves into the gaze of the Other.

Idolatry as Fossil of Collapse

Monuments, idols, and divine statues often reveal Stage 2 distortion. Instead of functioning as symbols that enrich identity, they became objects of absolute devotion.

- **Resolution avoided:** A statue could affirm identity by anchoring communal values. But in distortion, the statue absorbs identity entirely. The people exist only as worshippers, reflected solely in the idol.
- **Psychological meaning:** This fossil reveals collapse of boundaries — the individual "I" is erased, existing only as part of the Other's image.

Thus, idolatry fossilizes Stage 2 stagnation: identity surrendered to external recognition.

Cultic Dependency

Beyond idols, entire cults fossilize the distortion of Stage 2. Archaeological evidence of ritual complexes, repetitive offerings, or forced conformity indicates that identity became entirely dependent on collective mirroring.

- **Resolution avoided:** Rituals can unify and affirm identity. Distortion occurs when ritual enforces sameness, preventing authentic reflection.
- **Psychological meaning:** The cult becomes the Other whose gaze is absolute — to belong is to obey, to disobey is to vanish.

Cultic fossils, then, are reminders that unresolved confrontation with the Other leads to conformity without selfhood.

Masks of Suppression

Where earlier masks allowed creative resonance, some masks functioned as instruments of suppression. These fossils show identity not reflected but hidden — erased beneath the collective demand.

- **Distortion:** The mask here becomes a barrier, cutting off recognition rather than enabling it.

Clinical Parallel

In therapy, distorted Stage 2 fossils echo in clients who collapse into dependency: those who cannot define themselves without constant validation, or who submit entirely to controlling others. The cultic idol of antiquity finds its modern equivalent in authoritarian relationships, social media validation, or identity swallowed by groupthink.

Resolutions (Personal Burials, Recognition Systems, Kinship Orders)

Despite the distortions fossilized in idols and cults, many ancient remnants also testify to resolution in Stage 2 — moments where civilizations found balance between self and other, recognition and individuality. These fossils reveal how humanity progressed beyond collapse, learning to build identity through authentic relational structures.

Personal Burials

Archaeological discoveries of burials with personal items — tools, ornaments, or tokens — represent more than ritual. They are fossils of recognition: acknowledgment that the individual mattered in death as in life.

- **Resolution:** The buried were not erased into anonymity but affirmed as unique persons within community.
- **Psychological meaning:** This fossil reflects Stage 2 resolution: identity confirmed in relation to others, without collapsing into dependency.

Recognition Systems

Inscriptions, seals, or early naming systems functioned as cultural recognition tools. They fossilize humanity's effort to grant individuality while affirming belonging.

- **Resolution:** Names or symbols serve as mirrors — "I am recognized by others, yet I remain myself."
- **Psychological meaning:** The fossil here is balance: the self gains identity in relation, but not at the cost of erasure.

Kinship Orders

Lineage carvings, family depictions, and early kinship structures show how civilizations stabilized identity through structured belonging.

- **Resolution:** Kinship fossils affirm the individual's place within a web of relations, anchoring identity without suffocating it.
- **Psychological meaning:** Stage 2 confrontation here reaches harmony: boundaries exist, but so does connection.

Clinical Parallel

In therapy, Stage 2 resolution appears when clients establish boundaries while sustaining recognition. Just as personal burials honored individuality within community, modern clients progress when they can say: "I exist in relationship, but I am not erased by it."

Stage 3: Totems & Fire Rituals (Communal Identity Markers)

Stage 3 of Developmental Confrontation Theory revolves around Emotional Identity: the struggle to live authentically, to express emotion, and to find cohesion without collapsing into performance or pretense. At the cultural level, this confrontation is fossilized in totems and fire rituals — communal markers that bound groups together through shared symbols and practices.

Totems as Fossils of Identity

Totems are among the clearest Stage 3 fossils. Whether carved poles, animal symbols, or clan emblems, totems externalize a group's emotional identity.

- **Resolution:** Totems served as authentic anchors of belonging. They affirmed individuality while uniting people through shared symbolism. Each clan had its totem, but individuals retained their humanity beyond the symbol.

- **Distortion:** Totems also fossilized exclusion. When used to enforce rigid tribal identity or fuel intergroup aggression, they reveal Stage 3 stagnation — identity hardened into spectacle, emotion channeled into rivalry.

Thus, totems stand at the intersection of resolution and distortion: they can embody authentic belonging or rigid division.

Fire Rituals

Communal fires were not merely practical. They became emotional centers where groups sang, danced, and enacted rituals.

- **Resolution:** The fire pit as fossil reflects emotional authenticity shared communally. Around the fire, people expressed joy, grief, and solidarity.
- **Distortion:** Fire rituals distorted into empty spectacle, where emotion was manipulated or ritualized without sincerity. In such fossils, authenticity was lost to performance.

Fire rituals therefore fossilize the capacity — and risk — of using shared symbols to bind emotional identity.

Clinical Parallel

Stage 3 struggles persist in modern life:

- **Resolution:** Clients who form authentic groups (family bonds, friendships, communities) experience totemic belonging without erasure.
- **Distortion:** Clients who collapse into group labels, tribal conflicts, or performative emotional displays mirror the fossil of distorted totems and hollow rituals.

Ancient totems and fires show that the confrontation with emotional identity is not modern — it is a recurring challenge, leaving fossils in culture as surely as in stone.

Early Theater, Dramatic Masks, and Ritual Performances

As civilizations grew, emotional identity was no longer only carried in totems or fire rituals. It evolved into theater, dramatic masks, and ritual performances — fossils of humanity's attempt to express, transform, and stabilize emotional life. Stage 3's central confrontation is whether emotions can be lived authentically or are reduced to performance. These cultural remnants capture both possibilities.

Theater as Fossil of Expression

The origins of theater in Greece, Egypt, and ritual societies show a universal impulse: to embody emotion before others.

- **Resolution:** Early theater allowed communities to process grief, joy, and conflict collectively. Tragedy and comedy reflected real human struggles, offering catharsis — the release and integration of emotion.

- **Distortion:** Theater could also fossilize spectacle. When performances became hollow displays, serving only entertainment or manipulation, authenticity was lost. The fossil here is not lived emotion but its mask.

Dramatic Masks

Distinct from Stage 2 ritual masks, Stage 3 dramatic masks fossilize not the confrontation with recognition, but with emotional identity.

- **Resolution:** Masks helped amplify emotions to be shared communally — joy, sorrow, fear — creating resonance that affirmed shared humanity.

- **Distortion:** When the mask detached from authentic feeling, it fossilized the reduction of emotion to appearance. Emotion became exaggerated, but hollow.

Ritual Performances

Dance, song, and staged ritual expanded the fossil of emotional identity.

- **Resolution:** They created authentic bonding. Grief rituals, seasonal dances, or healing chants affirmed emotion as real and communal.
- **Distortion:** When ritual became rigid or theatricalized for domination, it lost its authenticity. The fossil here is emotional performance without depth.

Clinical Parallel

Clients often struggle with the same tension:

- **Resolution:** Authentic emotional sharing creates catharsis and connection.
- **Distortion:** Performative displays — exaggerated but insincere emotion — mirror the fossil of empty theater.

Ancient drama, masks, and rituals thus preserve the confrontation of Stage 3: whether emotion becomes true identity or mere spectacle.

Distortions (Spectacle Over Substance, Theatricality as Mask)

While theater, ritual, and performance had the potential to resolve Stage 3 by enabling authentic expression, they also carried the danger of distortion. In distortion, emotion becomes detached from authenticity and reduced to display. These fossils reveal societies where identity was not lived, but performed — where spectacle triumphed over substance.

The Rise of Spectacle

Archaeological and historical records show many cultures where performance grew excessive.

- **Distortion:** In late-stage Greek theater, plays were sometimes staged more for competition and acclaim than for catharsis. The performance became about winning favor, not expressing truth.
- **Distortion:** Roman amphitheaters fossilize this distortion at scale. Gladiatorial combat and staged executions were spectacles designed to stir emotion without depth. Identity and emotion were reduced to entertainment and control.

These fossils show Stage 3 collapse: the mask of emotion without its soul.

Ritual as Hollow Performance

Rituals can be powerful when authentic, but fossil evidence also reveals when they became mechanical repetitions.

- **Distortion:** Repetitive sacrifices, staged dances, or chants performed without emotional engagement reflect stagnation.
- **Psychological meaning:** The ritual mask hides emptiness. What should have been an authentic emotional bond becomes a duty, a show.

In these fossils, the community performs emotion but no longer feels it.

Theatricality as Social Mask

Beyond art, entire cultures sometimes fossilized emotional life into theatricality.

- Court life in ancient kingdoms often demanded exaggerated displays of loyalty or grief. Funerary rituals that required loud mourning, even from hired mourners, reveal fossilized performance.

- **Distortion:** Here, emotion is commodified. Grief or loyalty is staged because it is expected, not because it is lived.

The fossil that remains is one of inauthenticity: the mask overtakes the face.

Clinical Parallel

Modern parallels abound. Clients may:

- Perform happiness on social media while feeling empty.

- Display exaggerated loyalty in groups while inwardly detached.

- Collapse into identities that are performances — "masks" demanded by society.

These behaviors echo the ancient fossil of spectacle. Just as amphitheaters fossilized emotion turned into entertainment, today's culture often fossilizes performance over authenticity.

Resolutions (Authentic Ritual Bonding, Expressive Art)

Stage 3 is not only remembered for its distortions of spectacle and hollow performance. Many fossils testify to the successful resolution of emotional identity, where communities used art and ritual to express authentic emotion and strengthen collective bonds. These artifacts show how humanity, when confronting the demands of authenticity, can achieve balance rather than collapse.

Authentic Ritual Bonding

Archaeological evidence points to rituals that were deeply tied to lived emotion.

- **Resolution:** Seasonal festivals, harvest rituals, and mourning practices often created genuine shared catharsis. Communities gathered not to perform emotion for show, but to feel it together.
- **Psychological meaning:** These fossils represent resolution: emotion expressed, recognized, and validated in community.

Unlike hollow repetition, authentic ritual shows that culture can hold space for grief, joy, and transformation without losing sincerity.

Expressive Art

Beyond ritual, Stage 3 resolution appears in the flourishing of expressive art.

- Cave paintings evolved into symbolic engravings, murals, and statues that carried real emotional depth.
- Ancient music, instruments, and dance forms reveal fossils of identity expressed through beauty and creativity, not control or spectacle.
- **Resolution:** Expressive art reflects identity made visible. It does not conceal behind masks, nor collapse into theatricality. It becomes a mirror of authentic feeling shared with others.

Theater as Catharsis

While theater could collapse into spectacle, many early dramas served as genuine catharsis. Greek tragedies, for example, offered communities a way to process loss, fate, and conflict collectively.

- **Resolution:** Theater at its best is a fossil of emotional authenticity — grief, guilt, or joy made visible and metabolized together.

Clinical Parallel

Modern clients can find the same kind of resolution in authentic expression.

- **Resolution:** Journaling, music, art therapy, or genuine communal rituals allow authentic emotion to surface.
- **Distortion avoided:** When performance is not for show but for truth, the fossil of authenticity is revived.

Stage 3 resolutions remind us that emotional identity can be lived, not acted. The fossils of authentic ritual and expressive art are proof that humanity has always sought ways to embody emotion truthfully.

Stage 4: Tombs, Pyramids, Mummies (Immortality Projects)

Stage 4 of *Developmental Confrontation Theory* centers on the confrontation with mortality and wisdom. Individuals — and civilizations — must face the inevitability of death, and either distort it through denial or resolve it through acceptance. Across ancient cultures, this confrontation fossilized most visibly in tombs, pyramids, and mummification practices.

Tombs as Fossils of Mortality

From simple stone cairns to elaborate burial chambers, tombs represent humanity's attempt to preserve identity beyond death.

- **Resolution:** Modest burials with symbolic items reflect acceptance of mortality. The individual is honored, remembered, and integrated into continuity without excess.

- **Distortion:** Monumental tombs built to overwhelm death reflect denial — an attempt to defy finitude through scale. In these fossils, mortality is not accepted but resisted through overcompensation.

Thus, tombs fossilize the spectrum between wisdom and denial in the face of death.

Pyramids and Monumental Architecture

The pyramids of Egypt, ziggurats of Mesopotamia, and similar structures worldwide are among the clearest Stage 4 fossils.

- **Resolution:** At times, monuments symbolized cosmic order — aligning with stars, seasons, or cycles, reflecting wisdom traditions that embraced life's transience.

- **Distortion:** More often, pyramids represent the obsession with immortality. Their sheer scale reflects humanity's refusal to accept death, fossilizing denial into stone.

Monuments thus reveal whether civilizations turned mortality into philosophy or fought it with hubris.

Mummification and Preservation Practices

In Egypt and elsewhere, practices of embalming and mummification show humanity's urge to extend life beyond its natural limit.

- **Resolution:** At their symbolic best, these practices honored continuity — the belief that the dead journey onward, leaving wisdom for the living.

- **Distortion:** When embalming became fixation, the fossil reveals Stage 4 collapse: denial of mortality, identity frozen rather than integrated.

Clinical Parallel

Modern parallels echo these fossils. Clients may confront mortality through wisdom — accepting finitude, finding meaning in legacy — or through distortion, denying aging, obsessing over youth, or clinging to permanence. Just as pyramids fossilized immortality projects, so too do modern obsessions with preservation fossilize denial.

Ancestor Worship and the Myth of Eternal Return

Beyond tombs and monuments, many civilizations confronted mortality through ancestor worship and myths of eternal return. These fossils reveal how cultures sought to transform death from absolute loss into continuity — either wisely integrated or distorted into denial.

Ancestor Worship as Fossil of Continuity

Archaeological and anthropological records show widespread practices of ancestor veneration:

- Shrines built within homes.
- Offerings placed at graves.
- Ritual invocations of the dead in seasonal ceremonies.

- **Resolution:** Ancestor worship can embody Stage 4 progression. It acknowledges mortality while affirming continuity — the dead are remembered, integrated into family identity, and honored as sources of wisdom.

- **Distortion:** Ancestor worship could also fossilize dependency. When the living surrendered agency to the imagined authority of the dead, identity was frozen. Instead of continuity, the ancestor became an idol, obstructing progression.

These fossils show the duality of Stage 4: mortality can inspire humility and wisdom, or collapse into fixation.

The Myth of Eternal Return

Myths across cultures reveal a cyclical vision of time: life, death, and rebirth repeating endlessly. Agricultural societies in particular fossilized mortality through cyclical symbolism — the dying and rising god, the annual harvest sacrifice, the endless cycle of seasons.

- **Resolution:** Cyclical myths offer reconciliation with mortality, embedding death within life's rhythm. They provide symbolic acceptance: death is not annihilation but transformation.

- **Distortion:** When myths became rigid systems promising literal escape from death, they fossilize denial. The promise of return becomes obsession with eternal repetition, refusing the uniqueness of mortality.

Clinical Parallel

Clients today echo these fossils:

- **Resolution:** Some find peace in continuity — seeing themselves as part of family, community, or natural cycles.

- **Distortion:** Others deny mortality by clinging to fantasies of literal return or refusing to face the finality of death.

Ancestor worship and cyclical myths remind us that the confrontation with mortality is never abstract. It is always lived — fossilized in rituals that either integrate wisdom or perpetuate denial.

Distortions (Denial of Death Through Monumentality and Immortality Projects)

Stage 4 confronts mortality — the recognition that life is finite. But many civilizations responded to this confrontation not with wisdom, but with denial. Their fossils reveal monumental attempts to overcome death through architecture, ritual, and fantasy. These distortions show what happens when fear of mortality drives cultures into excess.

Monumentality as Fossil of Denial

The sheer scale of ancient monuments often signals unresolved confrontation with death.

- **Distortion:** Pyramids built to dwarf time, megaliths raised to defy decay, temples constructed to project eternal order, each reflects a refusal to accept impermanence.
- **Psychological meaning:** The larger the monument, the deeper the anxiety fossilized in stone. These artifacts are not only achievements but also defenses against mortality.

Immortality Projects

Across cultures, evidence shows obsessions with preserving the body or projecting legacy beyond death.

- **Distortion:** Elaborate embalming, treasures buried for the afterlife, or rulers immortalized in exaggerated statues reveal fixation. These fossils embody the attempt to freeze identity rather than integrate finitude.
- **Resolution avoided:** Instead of using mortality as a source of wisdom, civilizations collapsed into fantasies of permanence.

Hubris and Collapse

Ironically, monuments built to deny death often became fossils of cultural mortality. Many civilizations invested immense resources in immortality projects, only to decline as living needs were neglected. The ruins themselves are paradoxical fossils: reminders that denial of death hastens cultural death.

Clinical Parallel

Modern parallels echo these ancient distortions:

- Obsessions with youth, cosmetic immortality, or digital legacies reflect Stage 4 denial.
- **Distortion:** Clients who refuse to face mortality may build psychological "monuments" — obsessions, collections, or identities meant to outlast them.
- **Wisdom avoided:** Just as ancient monuments fossilized denial, modern defenses fossilize avoidance rather than progression.

Resolutions (Wisdom Traditions, Acceptance of Mortality, Philosophy)

Despite the distortions fossilized in monuments and immortality projects, many civilizations also left behind fossils of resolution at Stage 4. These are not artifacts of denial, but of acceptance — cultural practices that transformed mortality into wisdom and continuity.

Wisdom Traditions

Philosophical schools, spiritual texts, and oral traditions often reflect resolution.

- **Resolution:** Instead of denying death, they sought to integrate it into life. Examples include Egyptian Book of the Dead passages affirming the journey of the soul, Stoic meditations on mortality, and Eastern traditions that frame death as transformation.

- **Psychological meaning:** These traditions fossilize wisdom: mortality acknowledged as inevitable, used as a guide for living well.

Rituals of Acceptance

Not all rituals sought to freeze or preserve. Many celebrated the cycle of life and death.

- **Resolution:** Seasonal festivals, ancestor remembrance, and symbolic burials affirmed continuity without excess. These fossils show that death can be marked with dignity, not denial.

- **Psychological meaning:** Mortality becomes a teacher, not an enemy.

Philosophy as Fossil of Reflection

The emergence of philosophy itself is a Stage 4 resolution. From Socrates' calm acceptance of death to Eastern meditations on impermanence, philosophical writings fossilize humanity's progression.

- **Resolution:** Philosophy turns mortality into reflection. Instead of fear, it produces meaning — the individual learns to live wisely because life is finite.

Clinical Parallel

Stage 4 resolutions remind us that clients can integrate mortality into their identity.

- **Resolution:** Acceptance of finitude, pursuit of legacy, and commitment to wisdom represent progression.
- **Therapeutic task:** To guide clients from denial (immortality projects) into wisdom (acceptance).

Just as civilizations fossilized their wisdom into texts, rituals, and philosophies, individuals can carry mortality as a source of depth and meaning.

Integration Across Eras: Fossilized Stagnations

When viewed across eras, familiar fossils reveal a striking pattern: distortions do not vanish. Once a civilization collapses into avoidance at any stage, the fossil remains as a cultural imprint. Later societies inherit not only wisdom, but also stagnation, carried forward like psychological scar tissue.

Stage 1 Stagnations → Walls as Paranoia

Defensive fortifications began as balanced protection but often fossilized into paranoia.

- **Carried forward:** Later civilizations inherited this instinct, repeatedly building impenetrable cities even when threats were minimal.
- **Psychological meaning:** Fear of the world became architectural destiny. The fossil of Stage 1 stagnation shaped cultures that valued exclusion over exchange.

Stage 2 Stagnations → Idols and Cultic Dependency

Collapse into idolatry and cultic mirroring left fossils that repeated across eras.

- **Carried forward:** Successive cultures reproduced statues, ritual complexes, and systems of blind devotion.
- **Psychological meaning:** The fossil of collapsed recognition hardened into cultural expectation — identity bound to authority or image.

Stage 3 Stagnations → Spectacle Over Substance

Theatrical distortions became recurring fossils.

- **Carried forward:** Gladiatorial games in Rome, hollow rituals in declining empires, and staged displays in royal courts repeated the same collapse.
- **Psychological meaning:** Emotional identity became fossilized as performance, not lived authenticity.

Stage 4 Stagnations → Monuments of Denial

Mortality denial fossilized into monumental architecture.

- **Carried forward:** From pyramids to mausoleums, from temples to modern skyscrapers built as legacies, cultures repeated the same fixation: stone as denial of death.
- **Psychological meaning:** Fear of mortality hardened into monuments that outlasted their builders but froze their anxieties into history.

Integration

Across eras, distortions show continuity. Each stage's stagnations became templates that later cultures repeated, often unconsciously. The fossil of paranoia, idolatry, spectacle, or denial carried forward not as progression but as repetition of unresolved confrontation.

Integration Across Eras: Resolutions as Engines of Culture

Just as distortions fossilized into recurring stagnations, resolutions also left their imprint. These fossils reveal not avoidance but transformation, where civilizations carried forward structures that propelled cultural growth, creativity, and wisdom.

Stage 1 Resolutions → From Shelter to Settlement

When containment was resolved, caves became canvases, and huts became foundations for open settlements.

- **Carried forward:** Agricultural villages with permeable boundaries fostered trade, exchange, and cooperation.
- **Psychological meaning:** Resolution of self vs world created the conditions for civilization itself. Containment became base, not prison.

Stage 2 Resolutions → Systems of Recognition

Personal burials, naming systems, and kinship orders fossilized the resolution of relational confrontation.

- **Carried forward:** These became the precursors of legal identity, record-keeping, and governance.
- **Psychological meaning:** Resolution of self vs other laid the groundwork for societies where individuals were recognized within communities, sustaining both autonomy and belonging.

Stage 3 Resolutions → Authentic Art and Collective Catharsis

Resolved emotional identity fossilized in authentic rituals, expressive art, and cathartic theater.

- **Carried forward:** These traditions evolved into literature, music, and philosophy.
- **Psychological meaning:** Resolution of Stage 3 gave humanity tools for processing emotion communally, allowing depth rather than spectacle to define culture.

Stage 4 Resolutions → Wisdom Traditions

Resolved confrontation with mortality produced philosophy, spiritual traditions, and rituals of remembrance.

- **Carried forward:** Stoic philosophy, Buddhist teachings, and ancestral wisdom are fossils of acceptance that continue to guide humanity.
- **Psychological meaning:** Mortality, once integrated, became a source of guidance, anchoring culture in meaning rather than denial.

Integration

Together, these resolved fossils form the engines of civilization. Where distortions hardened into stagnations, resolutions opened paths to growth. Art, governance, philosophy, and spiritual traditions are not accidents of history but the cultural fruits of resolved developmental confrontations.

Fossils as Psychological Footprints of Civilizations

When all stages are viewed together, familiar fossils reveal themselves as more than isolated artifacts. They are psychological footprints — enduring imprints of how civilizations confronted, avoided, or resolved their developmental tasks.

Fossils as Collective Memory

Every fossil, whether cave wall or pyramid, functions as a memory inscribed in material form.

- **Resolution fossils:** Cave paintings, personal burials, expressive art, wisdom traditions. These preserve the successes of confrontation, testifying that humanity has always been capable of growth.
- **Distortion fossils:** Fortifications of paranoia, idols of dependency, spectacles of emptiness, monuments of denial. These preserve failures, warning that unresolved fears can dominate entire eras.

Civilizations vanish, but their footprints remain. Fossils carry the psyche forward.

Civilizations as Psychological Beings

Through fossils, civilizations can be seen as collective beings undergoing their own developmental journey.

- Some resolved confrontations and thrived.
- Others stagnated, leaving behind grand but brittle monuments.
- Most carried both — wisdom and distortion fossilized side by side.

These psychological footprints allow us to read history not only as politics or economics but as developmental psychology on a civilizational scale.

The Legacy of Fossils

The enduring presence of fossils means that:

1. Humanity is never free from its past — distortions can be inherited unconsciously.

2. Humanity is never without guidance — resolutions remain available as models.

3. Fossils serve as teachers: they show what happens when confrontation is met with courage, and what happens when it is avoided.

Clinical Reflection

For therapists, fossils remind us that the struggles of clients are not only personal but cultural. Modern anxieties echo ancient stagnations; modern creativity echoes ancient resolutions. Fossils show that psychology is written not only in the mind but in stone, ritual, and culture.

Clinical-Cultural Reflection: Fossils and Collective Trauma

The study of fossils in *DCΨ* is not limited to archaeology or history. These remnants hold clinical value, offering insight into how collective distortions shape the psychological lives of individuals today. Fossils reveal that trauma is not only personal but cultural, carried forward through inherited stagnations.

Fossils as Mirrors of Collective Trauma

- **Stage 1 distortions** (walls, fortifications) mirror cultural legacies of paranoia and isolation. Modern clients raised in societies of suspicion carry echoes of these fossils.
- **Stage 2 distortions** (idols, cultic dependency) fossilize the collapse of identity into authority. Clients in rigid cultural systems often struggle with dependency, inherited from these patterns.
- **Stage 3 distortions** (spectacle, hollow rituals) reveal cultures where authenticity was eroded. Clients raised in performance-driven contexts reproduce these fossils in their emotional lives.
- **Stage 4 distortions** (monuments, immortality projects) fossilize denial of mortality. Clients facing death anxiety reflect these inherited distortions.

By recognizing fossils as collective trauma, therapists gain tools to situate the client's struggles in a broader historical context.

Fossils as Clinical Guides

Therapists can use cultural fossils in three ways:

1. **Contextualization:** Helping clients see their struggles not as isolated weakness but as echoes of collective stagnations.

2. **Differentiation:** Identifying whether a client's revisit to ancient patterns (e.g., enclosure, idolization, spectacle) is progression or stagnation.

3. **Transformation:** Using fossils of resolution — art, philosophy, wisdom traditions — as therapeutic resources, showing clients that humanity has always found ways to progress.

The Therapist as Archaeologist of the Psyche

Working with clients through *DCΨ* is like uncovering fossils:

- Some fossils are distortions, showing where identity froze.

- Others are resolutions, offering pathways to healing.

The therapist, like the archaeologist, brushes away the dust to reveal what was left behind — guiding the client from inherited stagnation into renewed progression.

Inherited Stagnations in Modern Cultures

Fossils of distortion are not confined to the past. They continue to echo into the present, shaping cultural norms, institutions, and psychological struggles. Inherited stagnations are fossils carried forward not in stone, but in patterns of thought and behavior that repeat across generations.

Stage 1 Echoes — Fortifications of Fear

The paranoia fossilized in ancient walls lives on in modern societies through:

- Gated communities, border obsessions, and surveillance systems.
- Cultural narratives that cast the outside world as perpetual threat.

Clinical effect: Clients raised in such cultures often exhibit chronic anxiety, mistrust, or over-reliance on defensive routines — modern psychological fortresses.

Stage 2 Echoes — Dependency and Idolatry

Ancient idols and cultic structures echo in today's celebrity worship, political personality cults, and blind institutional loyalty.

- Identity collapses into the gaze of the Other, now in the form of media, leaders, or ideologies.

Clinical effect: Clients struggle with dependency, lack of self-definition, or fear of rejection when separated from authority or group belonging.

Stage 3 Echoes — Spectacle Society

The fossil of spectacle has resurfaced in digital culture.

- Social media, influencer economies, and entertainment-driven politics mirror ancient amphitheaters.
- Emotional authenticity is reduced to curated performance.

Clinical effect: Clients often present with exhaustion, emptiness, or disconnection, caught in cycles of performance without authentic identity.

Stage 4 Echoes — Denial of Mortality

Modern culture mirrors ancient immortality projects through:

- Anti-aging industries, digital legacy preservation, and medicalized attempts to escape death.
- Cultural silence around mortality, as though death can be erased by technology.

Clinical effect: Clients experience intensified death anxiety, obsessive attempts at control, or existential crises when denial collapses.

Integration

Modern culture is not free from fossils. Ancient stagnations have been inherited, transformed by new technologies and contexts, but their psychological structure remains the same. Understanding these echoes allows therapists to recognize that clients do not only confront personal history — they are also inhabiting collective fossils.

From Ancient Fossils to Modern Remnants

The study of familiar fossils demonstrates that civilizations, like individuals, confront developmental stages and leave behind the traces of their resolutions and distortions. From caves to pyramids, masks to monuments, humanity has externalized its inner struggles in forms that endure long after their makers vanish. These remnants are not relics of dead cultures but living witnesses to the universal confrontations of the psyche.

From Fossil to Remnant

The distinction between ancient fossils and modern remnants is not chronological but structural:

- Fossils are the durable material legacies of early civilizations — caves, idols, monuments.
- Remnants are the contemporary expressions of the same structures — skyscrapers as pyramids, social media as amphitheater, gated communities as fortresses.

Seen through *DCΨ*, the past is not gone; it replays itself in new forms.

Why the Transition Matters

This transition is crucial for the continuity of the book:

1. It shows that the developmental stages are not theoretical abstractions but enduring realities visible across history.
2. It prepares the ground for exploring how the same structures appear in today's societies and individual psychologies.
3. It highlights the responsibility of modern psychology: to recognize inherited stagnations and to foster new resolutions.

Closing Chapter 7

The familiar fossil teaches us that every wall, mask, ritual, and monument is more than history — it is psychology preserved. The task of *DCΨ* is to read these fossils, discern resolution from distortion, and apply the lessons to the present.

As we move forward, we leave behind the ancient world without discarding it. The fossils remain, reappearing in modern remnants that continue to shape how individuals and societies confront their stages. The next chapter will follow these remnants into contemporary life, showing that the story of confrontation is ongoing.

Familiar Unearthed

Civilizations and Their Fossils

The previous chapter traced how cultures leave behind fossils of confrontation — walls, idols, rituals, monuments — each a silent witness to humanity's unresolved fears or courageous resolutions. Yet these examples were fragments, glimpses of a greater whole. To understand the depth of developmental confrontation, we must descend further into the ruins themselves, studying not only isolated artifacts but entire civilizations as living psychologies.

Civilizations are not remembered only for their kings and monuments but for the totality of their life: worship and law, war and economy, art and fashion, philosophy and punishment. Each domain becomes a fossil, preserving how a people as a collective confronted the same developmental stages that individuals face.

This section, Familiar Unearthed, is an excavation of cultures across time — from Mesopotamia and Egypt to Greece, Rome, India, China, the Americas, and the Islamic Golden Age. Each is examined as if it were a patient of history, its architecture, myths, and daily life treated as diagnostic fossils. Within them we find both resolutions that propelled humanity forward and distortions that froze identity into stone.

Here, the familiar stages of *DCΨ* will be seen not in theory alone, but in the lived record of civilizations — unearthed, remembered, and interpreted through the lens of confrontation.

Mesopotamia — The First Cities of Confrontation

Worship & Religion

Mesopotamian religion was polytheistic, centered on gods of storm, fertility, and the underworld. Temples (ziggurats) were not only religious centers but mountains of the psyche, bridges between earth and the heavens.

- Resolution: Ziggurats represented an attempt to integrate human life with cosmic order, giving meaning and structure.

- Distortion: Priests often manipulated divine fear, demanding tribute and sacrifices to appease angry gods. Religion fossilized dependency on authority.

Overlooked detail: Inscriptions show kings rewriting myths to place themselves at the center — early evidence of ego fossilized in divine narrative.

Architecture

Mesopotamia invented the walled city. Massive walls of Uruk, Ur, and Babylon fossilize Stage 1 confrontation: the self against the world.

- Resolution: Protection, organization, urban stability.
- Distortion: Paranoia, exclusion of outsiders, constant reinforcement of fear.

Overlooked detail: Babylon's famous walls were rebuilt multiple times, even when the city was not under direct threat — a fossil of anxiety, not necessity.

War & Politics

City-states were perpetually at war. The Assyrians, in particular, left behind carvings showing extreme cruelty: impalements, flaying, beheadings displayed as warnings.

- Resolution: Organized armies created stability, defensive strategies, and centralized administration.
- Distortion: Excessive brutality fossilized unresolved Stage 2 distortion — identity secured only through domination.

Overlooked detail: Assyrian kings had their victories carved in stone reliefs placed in palaces where they themselves lived — daily reminders of cruelty, not for enemies but for their own self-assurance.

Economy & Farming

The Fertile Crescent birthed irrigation systems and surplus farming. Barley, wheat, and date palms supported city populations.

- Resolution: Collective organization of irrigation networks represented Stage 1 resolution — cooperation with the world rather than paranoia against it.
- Distortion: Elite control of water systems fossilized inequality. Farmers became bound to temple bureaucracies, turning survival into dependence.

Overlooked detail: Drought cycles recorded in cuneiform suggest that early ecological anxiety fossilized into divine punishment myths.

Crafts & Technology

Cuneiform writing (on clay tablets), the wheel, and astronomy were invented here.

- Resolution: Writing was a fossil of continuity, transforming memory into permanence.
- Distortion: Bureaucracy used writing to record debts and punishments before it recorded literature — fossilizing power over creativity.

Overlooked detail: The first written word for "freedom" (ama-gi) appears in Sumerian tablets — a fossil of humanity's yearning for release from distortion.

Fashion & Body

Beards and elaborate hairstyles signified power. Jewelry and ornaments were buried with the dead.

- Resolution: Personal adornment fossilized individuality and status as recognition.
- Distortion: Excessive ornamentation tied worth to appearance, fossilizing dependency on external validation.

Philosophy & Art

The Epic of Gilgamesh is the earliest recorded myth confronting mortality. Gilgamesh's journey to escape death fossilizes Stage 4 distortion: denial of mortality. His eventual acceptance — that meaning lies in legacy, not immortality — is Stage 4 resolution.

Overlooked detail: The Flood tablet shows humanity repeatedly retelling destruction myths — a fossil of cultural trauma projected into myth.

Language

Cuneiform served law, myth, trade, and science.

- Resolution: A fossil of memory externalized, allowing culture to progress beyond oral limits.
- Distortion: Used to reinforce hierarchy: most tablets record taxes, debts, punishments.

Torture & Punishment

Hammurabi's Code is the first codified law, famous for "eye for an eye."

- Resolution: Law replaced arbitrary revenge — a fossil of progression from chaos to order.
- Distortion: Laws were class-based (punishments harsher for slaves), fossilizing inequality into justice.

Overlooked detail: Punishments often included drowning or fire — symbolic reenactments of cosmic chaos myths (flood, storm), showing myth fused with law.

DCΨ Integration — Mesopotamia

Mesopotamia is the fossil of humanity's first confrontation with civilization itself.

- Stage 1: Walled cities = paranoia vs containment.
- Stage 2: Priests/kings as mirrors of gods = identity collapse vs recognition.
- Stage 3: Ritual spectacles = emotional manipulation vs communal meaning.
- Stage 4: Gilgamesh's mortality quest = denial vs wisdom.

It is the archetype of how resolution and distortion coexisted from the very beginning — every achievement shadowed by its distortion.

Ancient Egypt — The Civilization of Death and Balance

Worship & Religion

Egyptian religion revolved around cosmic order (Ma'at), fertility, and the afterlife. Gods like Ra (sun), Osiris (death), and Isis (rebirth) structured existence around cycles of life and death.

- Resolution: The myth of Osiris expressed mortality as transformation — death leading to renewal through continuity.
- Distortion: Pharaohs elevated themselves as gods, collapsing divine order into personal authority.

Overlooked detail: The "Negative Confessions" in the Book of the Dead (lists of sins denied by the deceased) fossilize the psychological need to confront guilt, a primitive form of self-analysis tied to Stage 4 confrontation.

Architecture

Egyptian architecture fossilized mortality more than any other culture. The pyramids, tombs, and mortuary temples represent civilization's attempt to make death permanent.

- Resolution: Tomb paintings showing daily life reflect acceptance — preparing the dead for continuity in another form.
- Distortion: Monumentality (pyramids, colossal statues) fossilizes denial — kings refusing finitude, turning anxiety into stone.

Overlooked detail: "False doors" carved into tomb walls were thought to allow spirits passage between worlds. Through DCΨ, these fossilize an unresolved fantasy of escape from mortality.

War & Politics

Egypt oscillated between defensive isolation and expansionist campaigns. Pharaohs used divine kingship to unify politics with religion.

- Resolution: Diplomacy with the Hittites (earliest recorded peace treaty, 1259 BCE) fossilizes progression — war confronted through negotiation.

- Distortion: Pharaoh as god-king fossilizes relational collapse (Stage 2 distortion) — identity of millions bound to one figure.

Overlooked detail: Depictions of conquered enemies carved at temple entrances were less about intimidation of outsiders, more about daily reassurance to Egyptians — a fossil of insecurity beneath the image of power.

Economy & Farming

Egypt's wealth came from the Nile. Annual floods fertilized soil, making Egypt "the breadbasket" of the ancient world.

- Resolution: Communal irrigation and grain storage represented cooperative confrontation with nature (Stage 1 resolution).

- Distortion: Corvée labor (peasants forced into seasonal work on monuments) fossilized inequality — survival converted into elite vanity.

Overlooked detail: Records show grain rations paid to workers, not slaves, on pyramid projects — suggesting a more complex system than pure coercion, blending exploitation with partial recognition.

Crafts & Technology

Papyrus, cosmetics, embalming, and shipbuilding highlight Egyptian ingenuity.

- Resolution: Papyrus fossilized memory and administration into permanence, expanding cultural continuity.
- Distortion: Cosmetics (kohl eyeliner, perfumes) were not just adornment but magical protections — fossilizing fear into daily ritual.

Overlooked detail: Embalming was a chemical science as much as ritual. Recipes preserved in medical papyri reveal technical innovation hidden beneath ritual appearance.

Fashion & Body

Clothing (linen tunics, wigs, ornaments) expressed social order.

- Resolution: Jewelry placed in tombs fossilized continuity of personal identity into the afterlife.
- Distortion: Excessive ornamentation (gold masks, elite wigs) fossilized inequality and identity collapse into status.

Philosophy & Art

Egyptian art was symbolic rather than realistic: rigid poses, idealized proportions.

- Resolution: Symbolism reflected belief in eternal order, fossilizing cultural stability.
- Distortion: Lack of individualism in art fossilized fear of chaos — creativity suppressed to preserve cosmic order.

Overlooked detail: Some rare Amarna-period art under Akhenaten shows elongated, distorted human figures — fossils of cultural rupture when cosmic order collapsed into radical monotheism.

Language & Communication

Hieroglyphs were complex symbolic writing, later simplified into hieratic and demotic scripts.

- Resolution: Hieroglyphs fossilized memory, making Egypt's religious and administrative life transmittable.
- Distortion: Writing was restricted to scribes and priests, fossilizing hierarchy through literacy control.

Overlooked detail: The Rosetta Stone reveals fossilized linguistic confrontation — same decree in three scripts (hieroglyphic, demotic, Greek), showing Egypt's anxiety in preserving identity under foreign rule.

Torture & Punishment

Egyptian law under Ma'at emphasized balance, but punishments could be brutal: mutilation, forced labor, executions.

- Resolution: Law sought harmony, aiming to restore cosmic balance rather than pure vengeance.
- Distortion: Torture and slavery fossilized imbalance, hiding cruelty beneath divine justification.

Overlooked detail: Trials often included public oaths before gods, showing that punishment was staged as cosmic drama — fossilizing law as ritual theater.

DCΨ Integration — Egypt

Egypt is the civilization most defined by Stage 4 confrontation — mortality.

- Resolution: Myths of Osiris, Book of the Dead, tomb paintings, philosophy of Ma'at.
- Distortion: Pyramids, false doors, pharaohs as gods, excessive monumentality.

Egypt fossilized the paradox of human development: wisdom traditions about balance and continuity living side by side with obsessive denial of mortality.

Ancient Egypt — Deeper Excavations

Akhenaten's Monotheistic Revolution

Pharaoh Akhenaten (1353–1336 BCE) introduced worship of Aten, the sun disc, abolishing Egypt's polytheistic pantheon.

- Resolution Attempt: By focusing worship on a single visible force (the sun), Akhenaten fossilized Stage 4 confrontation into a simplified cosmic order: mortality as part of the eternal solar cycle.
- Distortion: In suppressing Egypt's gods and traditions, Akhenaten collapsed cultural identity into his own radical vision. The result was instability, famine, and social unrest.

Overlooked detail: After Akhenaten's death, the old gods were immediately restored, his monuments dismantled, his name chiseled out — a fossil of cultural rejection, revealing how civilizations defend against premature confrontation with mortality by restoring familiarity.

Deir el-Medina — The Workers' Village

The village of Deir el-Medina housed artisans who built royal tombs in the Valley of the Kings. Archaeological records here are unusually detailed.

- Resolution: Workers were paid in grain and enjoyed a structured life, fossilizing recognition of labor as necessary to continuity (Stage 2 resolution).

- Distortion: Strikes occurred when wages were delayed — some of the earliest recorded labor protests. These fossilize collective frustration when recognition collapsed into exploitation.

Overlooked detail: Ostraca (scrap pottery writings) from Deir el-Medina record love poems, jokes, and personal reflections — fossils of individuality in a society otherwise obsessed with cosmic order.

Unfinished Monuments

Numerous pyramids and tombs remain incomplete, often due to sudden death of a ruler or collapse of resources.

- Resolution: Some incomplete tombs reveal improvisation — smaller chapels finished rapidly, fossilizing flexibility in confronting mortality.

- Distortion: Abandoned monuments fossilize the fragility of excessive monumentality — death interrupting denial.

Overlooked detail: The Bent Pyramid at Dahshur, which shifts angle midway, shows engineers adjusting when the original design proved unstable. A fossil of both hubris and adaptation.

Law and Cosmic Balance (Ma'at)

Egyptian justice was tied to Ma'at, the principle of truth, order, and cosmic balance.

- Resolution: The goal of justice was restoration, not vengeance. Even oaths and trials invoked gods as witnesses — fossilizing moral accountability into social life.

- Distortion: Punishments included mutilation (cutting off noses, ears) or exile, fossilizing fear as a deterrent rather than balance.

Overlooked detail: Some court records show women serving as plaintiffs, rare in ancient societies — fossils of relational recognition within an otherwise male-dominated structure.

Medicine and Healing

Papyrus texts (like the Edwin Smith Papyrus) show advanced surgical knowledge: wound treatment, sutures, prosthetics.

- Resolution: Medicine fossilized Stage 3 resolution — emotional care translated into practical healing, acknowledging vulnerability without denial.

- Distortion: Magical spells were often written alongside treatments — fossilizing fear-driven ritual alongside rational science.

Overlooked detail: Dental remains show Egyptians suffered heavily from cavities due to sand in bread — daily suffering fossilized into skeletal evidence, a reminder that even advanced civilizations couldn't escape basic mortality.

Fashion, Body, and Purification

Head shaving, wigs, perfumes, and cosmetics were central to Egyptian identity.

- Resolution: Purification rituals (oils, kohl) fossilized mortality into daily awareness — the body prepared constantly against decay.
- Distortion: Obsession with appearance fossilized external validation and social hierarchy.

Overlooked detail: Wigs were worn not just for beauty but for lice control — fossils of practical confrontation masked by cultural display.

DCΨ Integration — Egypt (Deepened)

Egypt is not just the land of pyramids but a civilization where every domain fossilized the tension between denial and wisdom.

- Akhenaten's revolution → premature wisdom rejected.
- Deir el-Medina → labor as recognition vs exploitation.
- Unfinished monuments → mortality shattering denial.
- Law of Ma'at → balance vs mutilation.
- Medicine → rational healing vs magical distortion.
- Fashion → purification vs obsession.

Egypt shows the most dramatic fossilization of Stage 4 confrontation: mortality simultaneously denied in stone and integrated in philosophy.

Indus Valley Civilization — The Silent Cities

Worship & Religion

The Indus Valley left figurines of fertility goddesses and seals depicting a proto-Shiva figure seated in yogic posture ("Pashupati seal").

- Resolution: Fertility worship fossilized continuity and natural cycles — mortality accepted through regeneration.
- Distortion: Lack of central temples suggests either decentralized worship or loss of records, fossilizing ambiguity — identity without clear symbolic anchoring.

Overlooked detail: No grand monuments (like ziggurats or pyramids) were found, suggesting Stage 4 confrontation took a subtler, communal form — a fossil of balance, not denial.

Architecture

Cities like Mohenjo-Daro and Harappa had advanced urban planning: grid layouts, standardized bricks, drainage, public baths.

- Resolution: The "Great Bath" fossilizes Stage 3 resolution — communal purification, symbolic cleansing, and collective emotional integration.
- Distortion: Sudden abandonment of cities fossilizes unresolved confrontation, perhaps ecological collapse (floods/droughts) overwhelming adaptation.

Overlooked detail: The uniformity of houses across social classes suggests a rare Stage 2 resolution — minimized hierarchy compared to Mesopotamia and Egypt.

War & Politics

Unlike Mesopotamia and Egypt, little evidence of organized warfare exists: no large weapons caches, no glorified battle art.

- Resolution: Absence of militarism fossilizes Stage 2 progression — identity sustained without excessive domination.
- Distortion: Vulnerability to invasion (later Aryan migration) suggests a lack of defensive confrontation, fossilizing naivety.

Overlooked detail: Few skeletal remains show violent trauma — a fossil of relative peace in contrast to contemporaries.

Economy & Farming

Indus farmers cultivated wheat, barley, cotton, and traded with Mesopotamia (Indus seals found in Ur).

- Resolution: Standardized weights and measures fossilized Stage 1 confrontation with world → fairness in trade.
- Distortion: Collapse of trade routes during ecological decline fossilized fragility of dependence on external systems.

Overlooked detail: Cotton textiles were first developed here — fossilizing comfort and adaptation to climate, yet overlooked compared to stone monuments of Egypt.

Crafts & Technology

Bead-making, pottery, and metallurgy were refined crafts. Intricate seals show artistry and literacy.

- Resolution: Seals fossilize identity markers — Stage 2 recognition preserved in trade.
- Distortion: The undeciphered script fossilizes frustration — communication frozen, unresolved.

Overlooked detail: Toys (mini carts, animal figurines) found in ruins suggest childhood was recognized and valued — a fossil of relational care.

Fashion & Body

Female figurines with elaborate headdresses suggest adornment and ritual roles.

- Resolution: Body decoration fossilized communal identity and fertility celebration.
- Distortion: Figurines may fossilize dependency on fertility as sole identity anchor, reducing individuality.

Philosophy & Art

Art was symbolic, not monumental — small seals, figurines, inscriptions.

- Resolution: Miniaturization fossilized intimacy, identity tied to daily life rather than monumentality.
- Distortion: Absence of monumental texts or preserved myths fossilizes silence, leaving identity incomplete to us.

Language & Communication

The Indus script remains undeciphered.

- Resolution: Marks on seals fossilized attempts at continuity in communication.
- Distortion: Its undeciphered state fossilizes a cultural voice silenced, frustrating modern understanding.

Torture & Punishment

No clear evidence of prisons or mass executions.

- Resolution: Fossilizes a society possibly oriented toward cooperation over coercion.
- Distortion: Collapse without resilience suggests that hidden tensions may have existed but left no fossilized trace.

DCΨ Integration — Indus Valley

The Indus Valley fossilizes silence as confrontation.

- Resolution: Communal planning, absence of militarism, equality in housing.
- Distortion: Collapse into obscurity, script undeciphered, myths lost.

The Indus Valley stands as a fossil of what could have been a resolution-heavy civilization, yet one that vanished without passing on its voice — a patient whose symptoms we see, but whose words we cannot hear.

DCΨ

Chapter 8

THE MODERN FAMILIAR

THE PSYCHOLOGICAL ARCHITECTURE OF DAILY LIFE

Chapter Abstract

Having established the theoretical, diagnostic, and historical dimensions of *Developmental Confrontation Psychology (DCΨ)*, this chapter brings the architecture to life. It examines the "Modern Familiar"—the observable, real-time expression of developmental stages and meta-functions within contemporary society. We analyze how the confrontations of Self vs. World, Other, Emotion, and Mortality manifest in modern work, technology, and identity. The chapter culminates in a final synthesis, framing human existence as an interdependent psychological ecosystem and positing the ultimate confrontation: the conscious choice to become an architect of one's own being.

Introduction: The Theory in the Wild

Developmental Confrontation Psychology (DCΨ) is not a relic to be studied but a living lens for interpreting the present. The confrontations detailed in previous chapters are not confined to the clinician's office or the archaeological dig; they are the active, often invisible, architecture of daily life. This chapter turns to the "Living Familiar", the patterns of resolution and distortion visible in our modern ecosystems of work, social media, and civic life. Here, the dual orientations of each stage and the perpetual translation of the Rational and Emotional Selves are not theoretical constructs but the driving forces of culture, innovation, and pathology. We move from diagnosing the past to deciphering the present, revealing how the ancient drama of human development is enacted in the glow of smartphone screens and the architecture of corporate hierarchies.

Part I:

The Living Familiar – The Psychological Architecture of Daily Life

1. Stage 1 in the Wild: Architects of Ground and Horizon

The foundational confrontation between the Self and the World is the engine of modern material and technological culture. The Igniter and Adaptor orientations are the yin and yang of progress and stability.

The Igniter (Exploratory Orientation): The Psychological Pioneer. In the modern context, the resolved Igniter is the entrepreneur, the innovator, the disruptor. Their Emotional Self drives a relentless curiosity and a tolerance for the anxiety of the unknown. This emotional fuel is given direction and structure by a highly developed Rational Self, which builds business plans, prototypes, and systems from raw inspiration. They confront the world by seeking to reshape it.

The Adaptor (Regulatory Orientation): The Psychological Foundation-Builder. The resolved Adaptor is the systematizer, the infrastructure engineer, the long-term planner. Their Rational Self seeks to impose order, predictability, and efficiency on the chaos of the world. This rational drive, however, is ultimately in service to an Emotional Self that craves safety, continuity, and a secure ground from which to operate. They confront the world by seeking to stabilize it.

Distortions in the Wild:

Anxious Control (Adaptor Distortion): This manifests as bureaucratic paralysis, risk-aversion stifling innovation, and compulsive data-tracking. It is the Rational Self in overdrive, attempting to create a perfect, fail-safe system to quell an Emotionally perceived world of constant threat.

Reckless Disregard (Igniter Distortion): Seen in "move fast and break things" cultures that ignore collateral damage, or in speculative bubbles detached from reality. This is the Emotional Self's thrill-seeking impulse unleashed without sufficient Rational containment or consideration of consequences.

2. Stage 2 in the Wild: The Dynamics of Connection and Boundary

The digital age has turned the confrontation of Self vs. Other into a 24/7 global phenomenon. Social media platforms are vast laboratories for the Mirror and the Wall.

The Mirror (Recognition Orientation): The Psychological Bridge-Builder. The resolved Mirror is the diplomat, the collaborator, the community manager. Their Emotional Self is highly attuned to the feelings and needs of others, fostering empathy and connection. This empathic capacity is guided by a Rational Self skilled in the art of negotiation, communication, and building consensus. They facilitate recognition and belonging.

The Wall (Boundary Orientation): The Psychological Fortress Architect. The resolved Wall is the institution-builder, the privacy advocate, the individual who maintains integrity amidst groupthink. Their Rational Self is adept at establishing clear rules, laws, and personal boundaries. This rational structure serves to protect the vulnerability and integrity of the Emotional Self. They ensure differentiation survives amid connection.

Distortions on Social Media:

Validation-Seeking (Mirror Distortion): The curated selfie, the obsession with likes and shares—this is the Emotional Self's need for recognition outsourced to a digital mirror. The Rational Self becomes a tool for optimizing external validation rather than stabilizing internal identity, leading to volatile self-worth.

Toxic Tribalism (Wall Distortion): The formation of rigid, antagonistic online groups. Here, the Rational Self is weaponized to construct logical-sounding arguments that defend an Emotionally rigid identity. The Wall becomes a fortress not for protecting a healthy self, but for attacking the "other," demonstrating a collapse of the Mirror function.

3. Stage 3 in the Wild: The Landscape of Authenticity and Role

The modern pressure to "be authentic" while navigating complex professional and social roles makes Stage 3 a central battlefield of contemporary life.

The Flame (Authenticity Orientation): The Psychological Heartbeat. The resolved Flame is the artist, the activist, the visionary leader. Their Emotional Self demands direct, passionate expression of inner truth. This authenticity is given sustainable form and impact through the discipline and focus of the Rational Self, which channels passion into coherent works, strategies, or messages.

The Mask (Role Orientation): The Psychological Scaffolding. The resolved Mask is not a sign of inauthenticity but of sophisticated psychological architecture. It is the functional identity—the "professional self," the "parent self," the "citizen self." The Rational Self constructs these roles as containers that allow the Emotional Self to navigate complex social systems without being overwhelmed. A healthy Mask allows the self to enter different rooms without sacrificing the flame; it is the architecture that lets authenticity move through the world.

Distortions in Modern Work:

Burnout (Flame Distortion): This occurs when the Flame is extinguished by the demands of a role. The Emotional Self's passion and vitality are depleted, leaving only hollow execution. It is often the result of a Mask that has become a cage, suffocating the authentic self.

Narcissism (Mask Distortion): The individual becomes fused with their role or persona. The CEO who cannot separate self from title, the influencer who is only their brand. Here, the Rational construction of the Mask eclipses the Emotional core entirely; the scaffolding mistakes itself for the building.

4. Stage 4 in the Wild: Stewards of Legacy and Meaning

In an age of global crises and information overload, the confrontation with mortality and meaning has never been more pressing.

The Seer (Clarity Orientation): The Psychological Lighthouse Keeper. The resolved Seer is the visionary, the elder, the philosopher. Their Rational Self confronts the inevitability of death and limitation with clear-eyed acceptance. This acceptance, in turn, allows the Emotional Self to find profound meaning and serenity in the present moment, offering guidance to others.

The Wound (Continuity Orientation): The Psychological Root System. The resolved Wound is the historian, the tradition-keeper, the mentor. Their Emotional Self feels the "scar" of mortality as a deep connection to what endures. This emotional need for continuity is preserved through the Rational Self's acts—writing history, teaching skills, building institutions, and raising the next generation.

Distortions in Public Discourse:

Despair and Nihilism (Wound Distortion): The collapse into meaninglessness in the face of climate change or political instability. This is a Wound that cannot find continuity; the Emotional Self is overwhelmed by futility, and the Rational Self can only articulate reasons for hopelessness.

Fundamentalism (Seer Distortion): The retreat into rigid, absolute belief systems. This is a pseudo-Seer orientation, where the Rational Self adopts a dogmatic "clarity" to escape the terrifying ambiguity of mortality. It is a false transcendence that avoids the genuine emotional confrontation with finitude.

Part II:

The Final Synthesis – The Ecology of a Conscious Life

1. The Interdependent Ecosystem

Society is not a collection of isolated individuals but a vast, interdependent psychic ecosystem. The stability of our institutions, the creativity of our culture, and the health of our civic life are direct reflections of the collective resolution of developmental confrontations. The start-up's innovation (Stage 1 Igniter) depends on the regulatory frameworks of government (Stage 1 Adaptor). Social justice movements (Stage 3 Flame) require the legal and political structures (Stage 2 Wall) to enact lasting change. This ecosystem is powered by the internal dance of millions of Rational and Emotional meta-functions, constantly translating experience into action.

2. The Final Confrontation: The Choice of Consciousness

Across the four stages, one theme remains constant: development is not passive. *DCΨ* reveals that the ultimate confrontation is not with the world, others, emotion, or death, but with the inescapable responsibility of choice in every moment. We are perpetually choosing, consciously or not, how to orient ourselves within these existential fields. Will we lean into Ignition or Adaptation? Will we build a Wall or seek a Mirror? Will we tend our Flame or adjust our Mask? Will we seek the clarity of the Seer or the continuity of the Wound? The unifying insight of *DCΨ* is that we are the architects of our own being, using the tools of Rationality and Emotion. The final, and most profound, confrontation is the choice to become conscious of this process.

3. The Unifying Vision: From the Womb to the World

The architecture of *DCΨ* is now complete. It begins with the Unborn Familiar, the primordial template of containment in the womb. It unfolds through the four staged confrontations—Self vs. World, Self vs. Other, Emotional Identity, and Mortality & Wisdom—each with its pathways of resolution and distortion. It leaves behind a record of these engagements in the Familiar Fossils of our collective history. And it culminates in the Living Familiar of our modern world, where these patterns are actively shaping our future. This is the coherent vision of *DCΨ*: human existence as a continuous, choice-driven process of confronting existential realities, the quality of which determines everything from individual pathology to the health of civilizations.

Coda: Paths Forward – Research and Insights

The DCΨ framework opens fertile ground for future exploration:

Research 1:

The Ethnography of the Living Familiar. Qualitative and quantitative studies mapping the distribution of stage orientations and meta-function balances within specific modern environments (e.g., tech startups, healthcare systems, online communities).

Research 2:

Digital Fossils: The New Cave Wall. Instagram is the new Lascaux. Twitter threads are the new totems. Our digital footprints are not merely content; they are the psychological fossil record of our unresolved stages. Computational analysis of social media data could serve as a powerful, real-time diagnostic tool for assessing collective developmental distortions on a mass scale.

Research 3:

Educational Interventions. Developing curricula for schools and organizations focused on "developmental intelligence"—teaching individuals to recognize their dominant orientations and balance their meta-functions to navigate life's confrontations more consciously.

Final Insight:

Developmental Confrontation Psychology provides more than a model of the mind; it offers a blueprint for conscious living. By understanding the architecture of our being—from the echo of the womb to the choices of the present moment—we gain the capacity to become conscious co-architects of our selves and our shared reality. The confrontation is inevitable; consciousness is the choice that defines our development.

The Architect Within

Afterword

What began in the womb does not end in the book, it begins again, in you.

This work was never meant to sit quietly on a shelf. It is a mirror, a rupture, a scar etched with language, inviting you to become its living continuation. *Developmental Confrontation Psychology (DCΨ)* was not written to be admired; it was built to be entered, confronted, and ultimately transformed by.

You are now standing at the threshold of the architecture: Igniter or Adaptor? Mirror or Wall? Flame or Mask? Seer or Wound?

These are no longer theoretical terms. They are your patterns. Your relationships. Your resistance. Your memory. Your future.

To read *DCΨ* is to awaken a confrontation inside yourself. But this confrontation is not violence, it is design. You are the builder now. The architect of your emotional structure, your psychological form, your symbolic legacy.

There is no final page. Only the return to the first breath, with knowledge in hand.

Becoming a Mirror of the Theory

Invitation to Application

This book has laid the foundation. But the work of *Developmental Confrontation Psychology (DCΨ)* is just beginning. The pages you've read are tools — waiting for minds, hands, and hearts to carry them forward into practice.

If you are a psychologist, a researcher, a teacher, a parent, or simply a seeker of truth, you are invited to reflect *DCΨ* in your domain. The theory lives through application, in the clinic, the classroom, the family, the institution, the mirror.

A professional toolkit is being developed for certified practitioners and research collaborators. This includes:

- The Stage Resolution Index (SRI) — a diagnostic lens for mapping distortions
- The DCPTT — a symbolic personality typology rooted in the four confrontational stages
- The DRT Toolkit — for therapeutic immersion through art, behavior, and existential insight

These tools will not be released publicly, but will be made available selectively to those committed to the theory's depth and precision.

This is not an invitation to use *DCΨ* lightly. It is a call to become it; in practice, presence, and principle.

Echo of the Unborn

Symbolic Coda

We return again to the *womb*.

But now, we carry *memory*.

The mirror is *cracked*; but we **recognize** ourselves.

The scar still *breathes*; but we **know** its name.

The flame *dances*; but we **no longer fear** its heat.

The vanishing *comes*; but we **choose** what remains.

You are not alone in this *echo*.

You are the echo.

And the **architect** of what it **becomes**.

DCΨ

Glossary

A

- **Adaptor:** The regulatory orientation in Stage 1 (Self vs. World), Focused on establishing safety and internal consistency through withdrawal and routine.

B

- **Burnout:** A distortion of Stage 3, specifically of the Flame orientation. It occurs when the demands of a role (the Mask) deplete the Emotional Self's passion and vitality, leading to exhaustion and a loss of authenticity.

C

- **Confrontation (*DCΨ*):** The central engine of human development; a necessary encounter with a reality that the self cannot assimilate without transformation of identity. Distinct from conflict or challenge.

- **Consciousness (The Choice of):** The ultimate confrontation identified by *DCΨ*. It is the active choice to become aware of one's dominant orientations and meta-functions, thereby becoming a conscious architect of one's own being.

- **Constitutional guarantees:** The protective principles (Law-7) that ensure the *DCΨ* framework resists bias, reductionism, and misuse.

D

- **Developmental Confrontation Psychology (*DCΨ*):** The psychological framework that maps human development as a series of staged confrontations with existential realities, navigated via dual orientations and the meta-functions of the Rational and Emotional Selves.

- **Despair/Nihilism:** A distortion of Stage 4, specifically of the Wound orientation. It is the collapse into meaninglessness, where the Emotional Self is overwhelmed by futility and the Rational Self can only articulate hopelessness.

- **Developmental Confrontational Theory (*DCT*):** The structural spine of *DCΨ*, outlining the four stages, their dual orientations, and the laws of development.

- **Distortion:** The pathological outcome that arises when a developmental confrontation is avoided or bypassed, leading to defensive, rigid personality structures.

E

- **Echoes Forward:** The constitutional principle (Law-3) that an unresolved confrontation in an earlier developmental stage will destabilize later stages, producing symptoms that are rooted in earlier fractures.

- **Emotional Self (Meta-Function):** One of the two primary meta-functions of the psyche. It is the source of passion, authenticity, empathy, vulnerability, and the drive for connection and meaning. It requires the structure of the Rational Self for sustainable expression in the world.

F

- **Familiar, The:** The core concept in *Developmental Confrontation Psychology (DCΨ)*, denoting the psyche's template for psychological safety, containment, and predictable order. It is the foundational state the self seeks to establish and maintain throughout development. The concept manifests in three primary dimensions:

- **Familiar Fossils:** The tangible remnants of past developmental confrontations and their resolutions or distortions, embedded in cultural artifacts, institutions, and historical records.

- **False Resolution:** A defensive adaptation that mimics stability but is built on the avoidance of a core confrontation; it collapses under stress.

- **Flame:** The authenticity orientation in Stage 3 (Emotional Identity), focused on establishing self through raw, passionate expression.

- **Fundamentalism:** A distortion of Stage 4, specifically a pseudo-Seer orientation. It is a retreat into rigid, absolute belief systems, where the Rational Self adopts dogmatic "clarity" to avoid the genuine emotional confrontation with mortality and ambiguity.

H

- **Healing Backward:** The constitutional principle (Law 3) that successfully resolving a confrontation in a later stage can retroactively reorganize and stabilize identity, repairing distortions from an earlier stage.

I

- **Igniter:** The exploratory orientation in Stage 1 (Self vs. World), focused on engaging the external world with curiosity and expansion.

- **Interdependent Ecosystem**: A *DCΨ* concept describing society as a vast network where the collective resolution of individual developmental confrontations determines the health and direction of culture, institutions, and civic life.

L

- **Living Familiar (The Modern Familiar):** The observable, real-time expression of developmental stages and meta-functions within contemporary society (e.g., in modern work, technology, and social life).

M

- **Mask:** The role orientation in Stage 3 (Emotional Identity), Focused on stabilizing identity through structured functions and social performance.

- **Mirror:** The Reflective orientation in Stage 2 (Self vs. Other), focused on building identity through recognition and resonance with others.

N

- **Narcissism:** A distortion of Stage 3, specifically of the Mask orientation. It occurs when an individual becomes fused with their role or persona, eclipsing the authentic Flame. The scaffolding mistakes itself for the building.

P

- **Psychological Fingerprint:** The unique, dynamic configuration of how an individual navigates the four developmental confrontations across their lifespan; the lived expression of *DCT.*

R

- **Rational Self (Meta-Function):** One of the two primary meta-functions of the psyche. It is the capacity for logic, structure, boundary-setting, planning, and role-construction. It translates the impulses of the Emotional Self into sustained action in the world.

- **Reckless Disregard:** A distortion of Stage 1, specifically of the Igniter orientation. It is the pursuit of novelty and disruption without sufficient Rational containment or consideration of consequences, as seen in "move fast and break things" cultures.

S

- **Seer:** The Clarity orientation in Stage 4 (Mortality & Wisdom), focused on confronting finitude with insight, truth, and acceptance.

- **Stage (Developmental):** In *DCΨ*, one of four sequential but overlapping life stages, each defined by a core confrontation: 1. Self vs. World, 2. Self vs. Other, 3. Emotional Identity, 4. Mortality & Wisdom.

- **Symbolic Authority:** A form of leadership that emerges not from role or power, but from having embodied the resolution of a developmental confrontation, thereby guiding others through the same threshold.

T

- **Toxic Tribalism:** A distortion of Stage 2, specifically of the Wall orientation. It is the formation of rigid, antagonistic in-groups, where the Rational Self weaponizes logic to defend an Emotionally rigid identity and attack the "other."

U

- **Unborn Familiar:** The primordial psychological template of containment and connection established in the womb, preceding all staged confrontations.

V

- **Validation-Seeking:** A distortion of Stage 2, specifically of the Mirror orientation. It is the outsourcing of self-worth to external sources (e.g., social media likes), where the Rational Self optimizes for approval rather than stabilizing internal identity.

W

- **Wall:** The Boundary orientation in Stage 2 (Self vs. Other), focused on stabilizing identity through clear self-other distinction and separation.

- **Wound:** The Continuity orientation in Stage 4 (Mortality & Wisdom), focused on transforming mortality into symbolic survival through legacy, children, or culture.

DCΨ

This book marks the foundation of Developmental Confrontational Psychology (DCΨ)

a new school of psychology and an original school of thought.

It presents the full theoretical framework, but does not include psychological tests,

therapeutic methods, or diagnostic tools.

For inquiries, collaborations, or access to future materials, contact the author at:

omar.ej.psy@gmail.com.

www.ingramcontent.com/pod-product-compliance
Lightning Source LLC
LaVergne TN
LVHW071203210926
848482LV00015B/713